**Investing in hospitals of the future**

The European Observatory on Health Systems and Policies supports and promotes evidence-based health policy-making through comprehensive and rigorous analysis of health systems in Europe. It brings together a wide range of policy-makers, academics and practitioners to analyse trends in health reform, drawing on experience from across Europe to illuminate policy issues.

The European Observatory on Health Systems and Policies is a partnership between the World Health Organization Regional Office for Europe, the Governments of Belgium, Finland, Norway, Slovenia, Spain and Sweden, the Veneto Region of Italy, the European Investment Bank, the World Bank, the London School of Economics and Political Science and the London School of Hygiene & Tropical Medicine.

# Investing in hospitals of the future

Bernd Rechel, Stephen Wright, Nigel Edwards,
Barrie Dowdeswell, Martin McKee

**Keywords:**
HOSPITALS – organization and administration – trends
CAPITAL FINANCING
INVESTMENTS
FINANCIAL MANAGEMENT, HOSPITALS – manpower
EFFICIENCY, ORGANIZATIONAL – economics
DELIVERY OF HEALTH CARE – economics – trends
EUROPE

Address requests about publications to: Publications, WHO Regional Office for Europe, Scherfigsvej 8, DK-2100 Copenhagen Ø, Denmark

Alternatively, complete an online request form for documentation, health information, or for permission to quote or translate, on the Regional Office web site (http://www.euro.who.int/pubrequest).

The designations employed and the presentation of the material in this publication do not imply the expression of any opinion whatsoever on the part of the European Observatory on Health Systems and Policies concerning the legal status of any country, territory, city or area or of its authorities, or concerning the delimitation of its frontiers or boundaries. Dotted lines on maps represent approximate border lines for which there may not yet be full agreement.

The mention of specific companies or of certain manufacturers' products does not imply that they are endorsed or recommended by the European Observatory on Health Systems and Policies in preference to others of a similar nature that are not mentioned. Errors and omissions excepted, the names of proprietary products are distinguished by initial capital letters.

All reasonable precautions have been taken by the European Observatory on Health Systems and Policies to verify the information contained in this publication. However, the published material is being distributed without warranty of any kind, either express or implied. The responsibility for the interpretation and use of the material lies with the reader. In no event shall the European Observatory on Health Systems and Policies be liable for damages arising from its use. The views expressed by authors, editors, or expert groups do not necessarily represent the decisions or the stated policy of the European Observatory on Health Systems and Policies.

**ISBN 978 92 890 4304 5**

Printed in the United Kingdom

# Contents

# About the authors

**Simona Agger** is member of the Evaluation of Investments Group, Ministry of Health, Italy.

**Svein Bjørberg** is Professor at the Norwegian University of Science and Technology, Trondheim, and member of Multiconsult, Norway.

**James Buchan** is Professor in the Faculty of Health Sciences, Queen Margaret University, Edinburgh, United Kingdom.

**Pieter Degeling** is Professor Emeritus, Durham University, Visiting Professor of Health Management at the University of Southampton, United Kingdom and Director of Health Management Solutions, United States.

**Geert Dewulf** is Professor of Planning and Development, and Head of the Department of Construction Management and Engineering at Twente University, the Netherlands.

**Barrie Dowdeswell** is Director of Research at the European Centre for Health Assets and Architecture (ECHAA) and former Executive Director of the European Health Property Network (EuHPN).

**Nigel Edwards** is Director of policy for the NHS Confederation, and Honorary Visiting Professor at the London School of Hygiene & Tropical Medicine, United Kingdom.

**Jonathan Erskine** is Research Associate at the University of Durham, United Kingdom, and administrator at the European Health Property Network (EuHPN).

**Stefanie Ettelt** is Research Fellow at the London School of Hygiene & Tropical Medicine, United Kingdom.

**Rosemary Glanville** is Head of the Medical Architecture Research Unit at London South Bank University, United Kingdom.

**Kunibert Lennerts** is Professor at the Institute for Technology and Management in Construction, University of Karlsruhe, Germany.

**Hans Maarse** is Professor of Health Care Policy and Administration in the Faculty of Health, Medicine and Life Sciences, University of Maastricht, the Netherlands.

**Nicholas Mays** is Professor of Health Policy in the Health Services Research Unit at the London School of Hygiene & Tropical Medicine, United Kingdom.

**Martin McKee** is Professor of European Public Health at the London School of Hygiene & Tropical Medicine, United Kingdom, and Research Director at the European Observatory on Health Systems and Policies.

**Phil Nedin** is Director of Arup and Global Healthcare Business Leader, United Kingdom.

**Ellen Nolte** is Senior Lecturer at the London School of Hygiene & Tropical Medicine, United Kingdom.

**Charles Normand** is Edward Kennedy Professor of Health Policy and Management at Trinity College Dublin, Ireland.

**Bernd Rechel** is Lecturer at the London School of Hygiene & Tropical Medicine, United Kingdom, and Research Officer at the European Observatory on Health Systems and Policies.

**Knut Samset** is Professor at the Norwegian University of Science and Technology, Norway and Programme Director of the Concept Research Programme on front-end management of major investment projects.

**Sarah Thomson** is Research Fellow in Health Policy at LSE Health and Social Care, United Kingdom, and Research Officer at the European Observatory on Health Systems and Policies.

**Marinus Verweij** is on the Board of Directors, Netherlands Board for Health Care Institutions, and Director of the Dutch Centre for Health Assets, part of TNO Rescarch, Utrecht, the Netherlands.

**Jonathan Watson** is Special Professor in Health and Public Policy at the University of Nottingham, United Kingdom, and Executive Director of Health ClusterNET.

**Stephen Wright** is Associate Director Human Capital in the Projects Directorate, European Investment Bank, currently seconded to be Executive Director of the European Centre for Health Assets and Architecture (ECHAA).

# Foreword

The hospital as a concept and a building had its European beginnings centuries ago. As a result, technologies and staff training of the time appear primitive through today's eyes. Over the years, the hospital has evolved into the institution and buildings that we know and trust, through the advance of scientific medicine. There have been revolutions in surgery (anaesthesia and asepsis), imaging (X-rays and magnetic resonance imaging (MRI)) and laboratory medicine (bacteriology and haematology), among many other fields. The locus of all these developments was the hospital, leading to its enormous significance today, although some activities are increasingly able to be carried out in other settings.

Hospitals are not only sites to provide health care: they carry out extensive programmes relating to research and development, education and training, and in their own right they are critical components of the urban fabric. Thus, although there are sure to be major evolutions in the nature and role of hospitals, the institutions themselves are unlikely to be displaced soon.

If only as a result of its importance as the place where scientific health care is focused, the hospital sector typically absorbs up to 50% of national expenditure on the health care system. This highlights the critical nature of the decision to invest capital in the construction of a hospital, given that this action commits society to a stream of future running costs which dwarf the original – already considerable – capital cost.

The European institution that I represent, the European Investment Bank (EIB), in appraising its projects for financing, has had to confront the issue of understanding these various dilemmas. We finance large-scale health care capital expenditures, often for hospitals, in the European Union (EU) and also partner countries, yet must continue to be aware of the wider context. Interestingly, that context increasingly involves a European dimension and related policy issues, including the growing availability of structural funds grant money. These capital resources, sometimes alongside EIB loans, will be enormously important in allowing the countries of central and eastern Europe, for example, to modernize their health sectors and adapt to a different approach to medicine.

This book is one of the first to offer a systematic treatment of the decision to invest in the health care estate (wider than hospitals alone, but this is a useful abbreviation). It is in some senses an interim report, attempting to understand the current state of evidence of what works, and to bring that evidence to bear for decision-makers. A sister volume, to be published in the Observatory Studies Series, reviews some topical case studies. This evidence – and more – has been subject to a searching examination. There are some cross-cutting themes: the importance of systematic planning; the increasing role of markets as a factor contributing to action but, even without that, an awareness of the financial and other resource flows entrained in the hospital; the human capital aspects of the workforce, which spends its whole working life – rather than just the few days of a typical patient – within the hospital walls; along with sustainability. It should not be neglected that hospitals are often the biggest single energy consumers, and therefore emitters of carbon, in a city.

Running through this book is the leitmotif of the critical nature of the model of care, explicit or perhaps even implicit, as a structure for the role of the hospital. "Form follows function", and thus the shape and size of the hospital are determined by the services it tries to deliver. In planning a hospital, it is naturally the future demands that are most important, futures that are always uncertain because of unpredictable trends and technological developments. Decision-makers should be aware that capacity is not usefully indexed simply by the number of beds, and space should be as "loose-fit" and flexible as can be designed and built. We can surmise that the more the underlying care processes can be systematized, the more efficiently and effectively flows of patients can be managed.

Perhaps inevitably, this volume raises more questions than it answers, and thus indicates a research agenda to come. In any event, the book should make a major contribution to a lively debate about the nature of the decision to invest in future hospitals.

*Philippe Maystadt*
*President*
*European Investment Bank*

# Acknowledgements

This volume is the result of a collaboration between the European Observatory on Health Systems and Policies and the European Health Property Network (EuHPN) (the research functions of which are now being taken forward by the European Centre for Health Assets and Architecture (ECHAA)). We are especially grateful to all the authors for their hard work and enthusiasm in this project.

In addition to the work of the authors (see list of contributors), this work draws on a series of case studies from across Europe, again the results of the joint collaboration, that will be published in a companion volume. The project benefited from two workshops that were held in Brussels and London. We appreciate the contributions of those who participated in these workshops. In addition to the authors of this volume, these were: Tit Albrecht, Juan Copovi-Mena, Enrico Davoli, Christiaan Decoster, Jani Dernic, Stephen Dunn, Josep Figueras, David Hastie, David Helms, Andras Javor, Lenka Medin, Asmund Myrborstad, Miklos Szocksa, Carlos Serrano Trescoli and Pontus Werlinder. We would also like to express our gratitude to Sue Gammerman and Caroline White for their help in organizing the workshops.

We are particularly grateful to the reviewers of this volume, James Barlow and Robin Guenther, for their helpful comments and suggestions, and to Andrew Lloyd-Kendall for his helpful comments on one of the chapters.

Finally, this book would not have appeared without the hard work of the production team led by Jonathan North, with the able assistance of Sue Gammerman, Caroline White and Nicole Satterley.

*Bernd Rechel*
*Stephen Wright*
*Nigel Edwards*
*Barrie Dowdeswell*
*Martin McKee*

# Glossary

| | |
|---|---|
| capacity planning | the process of organizing decisions and actions relating to the deliverability and distribution of health care |
| capital investment | spending money up front on new or modernized buildings, machinery and equipment |
| competitive dialogue | a procedure introduced by the European Commission for use in the procurement of "particularly complex projects", in which the contracting authority conducts a dialogue with the candidates admitted to that procedure |
| competitiveness and employment regions | European Union (EU) regions defined for purposes of Structural Funds other than those defined on grounds of low per capita income (convergence regions, see below) |
| contingency adaptability | ability to deal with unanticipated contingencies in a contractual framework |
| contract completeness | a complete contract is a contractual agreement between economic agents that specifies the responsibilities of each party in every possible situation or contingency |
| contract completion | contracts based on well-defined and fully comprehensive output specifications |
| convergence regions | EU regions with a gross domestic product (GDP) per capita below 75% of the EU average |
| descoping | the strategic abandonment and/or weakening of objectives within a public–private partnership contract |
| discount rate | a rate used to convert future costs or benefits to their present value |
| Foundation Trust | a new type of National Health Service (NHS) organization in England, established as independent, non-profit-making corporations with accountability to their local communities rather than central Government |
| life-cycle costing | a tool to model the effects through life of operational parameters on ownership |
| life-cycle costs | the total cost of ownership of machinery and equipment, including its cost of acquisition, operation, maintenance, conversion, and/or decommissioning |
| life-cycle economics | take into account the entire life-cycle cost of a facility, from the early design phase to planning, construction, use and demolition |

| | |
|---|---|
| life-cycle value | life-cycle value includes life-cycle economics and issues such as the environmental and social impact |
| limited recourse finance | financing arrangement where the lender can require the borrower to repay only in special conditions that are spelled out in the loan agreement itself, but otherwise – generally – must look to the cash flow generated directly by the asset as a source of repayment; borrowers may have to pay more for limited recourse financing |
| model of care | a multidimensional concept that defines the way in which health care services are delivered |
| monoline insurance | insurance involved in a single type of business (in context, insuring the repayment of limited recourse debt) |
| patient pathways | the route that a patient takes from their first contact with the health care system, through referral, to the completion of their treatment |
| phasing-in regions | EU regions that no longer qualify for full convergence funding, and would no longer qualify even if enlargement had not taken place |
| phasing-out regions | EU regions that no longer qualify for full convergence funding, but would have done so without enlargement |
| Private Finance Initiative (PFI) | a method, developed initially by the United Kingdom Government, to tap private funding for public–private partnerships |
| private sector equity | a form of financing which gives rise to ownership rights in the entity being financed and bears the risk of loss of capital |
| probity | unimpeachable honesty and virtue, shown especially by the performance of those obligations, called imperfect, which the laws of the State do not reach and cannot enforce |
| procurement | the process of obtaining goods or services |
| project finance | financing of long-term infrastructure and industrial projects based on a complex financial structure, where hypothecated debt and equity are used to finance the project |
| public sector comparator | a costing of a conventionally financed project delivering the same outputs as those of a PFI deal under examination |
| risk transfer | shifting risk from one party to another, such as from the public sector to the private sector in a PFI project |
| senior debt | debt that has priority for repayment in a liquidation situation |
| service life period | period between each change and refurbishment |
| special purpose vehicle | a company that is created solely for a particular financial transaction or series of transactions; a normal practice in public–private partnerships |
| spot purchase price | price for immediate payment and delivery |
| term specificity | describes how specific and detailed contract terms are |
| transaction costs | costs incurred in making an economic exchange |

# List of abbreviations

| | |
|---|---|
| AIDS | Acquired immunodeficiency syndrome |
| ASPECT | A Staff and Patient Environment Calibration Tool |
| BOT | Build, operate and transfer |
| CEE | Central and eastern Europe |
| CIS | Commonwealth of Independent States |
| COPD | Chronic obstructive pulmonary disease |
| CTQ | Critical to Quality |
| CT | Computerized tomography (scanning) |
| DBFM | Design, build, finance and maintain |
| DBFO | Design, build, finance and operate |
| DBO | Design, build and operate |
| DRG | Diagnosis-related group(s) |
| DTC | Diagnosis Treatment Combination(s) (Netherlands) |
| ECHAA | European Centre for Health Assets and Architecture |
| EIB | European Investment Bank |
| ERDF | European Regional Development Fund |
| EU | European Union |
| EU12 | Countries joining the EU in May 2004 and January 2007 |
| EU27 | All EU countries up to and including the January 2007 round of accession |
| EuHPN | European Health Property Network |
| FKT | Professional Association of Hospital Engineering (Germany) |
| GDP | Gross domestic product |
| GP | General Practitioner |
| HES | Health Episode Statistics |
| HIQA | Health Information and Quality Authority (Ireland) |
| HIV | Human immunodeficiency virus |
| HRG | Health care resource group |
| ICATS | Integrated Clinical Assessment and Treatment Services (Northern Ireland) |
| ICT | Information and communication technology |
| INO | Centre for Intensive Care, Emergencies and Surgery (Bern, Switzerland) |
| ISTC | Independent Sector Treatment Centre(s) (United Kingdom) |
| IT | Information technology |
| LIFT | Local Improvement Finance Trust (England and Wales) |
| MARU | Medical Architecture Research Unit (London South Bank University) |

| | |
|---|---|
| MI | Myocardial infarction |
| MOM | Management, operation and maintenance |
| MPs | Members of the Parliament |
| MRI | Magnetic resonance imaging |
| MRSA | Methicillin Resistant Staphylococcus Aureus |
| NHS | National Health Service |
| NSRF | National Strategic Reference Frameworks |
| NTPF | National Treatment Purchase Fund (Ireland) |
| NUTS | Nomenclature of Territorial Units for Statistics |
| OECD | Organisation for Economic Co-operation and Development |
| OPIK | Optimization of processes in hospitals (research project, Germany) |
| PbR | Payment by Results |
| PBT | Persistent bioaccumulative toxicant |
| PCI | Percutaneous coronary intervention |
| PCT | Primary Care Trust |
| PET | Positron emission tomography |
| PFI | Private Finance Initiative |
| PPP | Purchasing Power Parity |
| SARS | Severe Acute Respiratory Syndrome |
| SERI | Sustainable Europe Research Institute |
| SHA | Strategic Health Authority |
| SROS | Regional health plans (France) |
| SSDP | Strategic Service Delivery Partnership |
| TB | Tuberculosis |
| USAID | United States Agency for International Development |
| WHO | World Health Organization |

# List of figures, tables and boxes

*Figures*

*Tables*

*Boxes*

# Part one:
# The changing context of capital investment

# Chapter 1

# Introduction: hospitals within a changing context

*Bernd Rechel, Stephen Wright, Nigel Edwards, Barrie Dowdeswell,*
*Martin McKee*

## A book on improving capital investment

This book asks how to get the optimal results from capital investments in the health sector. Each year, across Europe billions of euros are invested in new and refurbished health care facilities. In Germany alone, capital investment in the health sector amounted to purchasing power parity (PPP) US$ 10.3 billion in 2005 (WHO Regional Office for Europe 2008). This scale of investment offers a remarkable opportunity to maximize health gain and to ensure that services are responsive to the legitimate expectations of users. Yet too often these opportunities are missed. Those making decisions about capital investment in the health sector are faced with a high level of uncertainty. There is little evidence that can inform them on the best way to configure hospital services or change the way hospitals operate (Edwards & Harrison 1999; Healy & McKee 2002b; Smith 1999). The lack of research on hospitals in general is even more pronounced when it comes to the question of capital investment. As the contributions to this volume highlight, there are a number of key dimensions of capital investment about which there is only sparse evidence. Which financing mechanisms are most appropriate for capital investments in hospitals? How can the entire life-cycle of health facilities be taken into account at the initial design stage? How can hospitals be made more sustainable and adaptable to future changes? What is the impact of systematized models of care on hospital functioning? How should the hospital be structured conceptually (as an entity responding to service needs) and as an actual building? These are questions for which there are often no ready-made answers.

This lack of research is surprising, given the importance of hospitals for health systems and the amount of health expenditure devoted to them. In the World Health Organization (WHO) European Region, the hospital sector typically absorbs 35–70% of national expenditure on health care (WHO Regional Office for Europe 2008). In the coming decades, Europe is likely to see even greater investment in health care facilities. In western Europe, many countries have failed to invest in health care facilities throughout the 1990s, resulting in a backlog of maintenance and refurbishment that must soon be remedied. In central and eastern Europe (CEE), many countries have not had significant capital investments in the health sector since the 1970s and 1980s (McKee & Healy 2002c), something they now have an opportunity to address with European Union (EU) Structural Funds. Any mistakes will be expensive, as decisions on capital investment will have important consequences for how health care is provided in the following 30–50 years (Black & Gruen 2005). Capital investment in the health sector typically only accounts for 2–6% of total health care expenditure in the countries of the WHO European Region (WHO Regional Office for Europe 2008), but development of a hospital predestines a large stream of operational and medical costs for decades to come – roughly the equivalent of the original capital costs every two years.

This book brings together the existing knowledge about key dimensions of capital investment in the health sector. While recognizing the limitations of the evidence, it is possible to identify critical lessons that increase the chances that capital projects will be successful. These include a variety of approaches for ensuring future flexibility of buildings, taking a whole systems perspective, building on systematized care, considering the life-cycle of health facilities, and ensuring the environmental and other sustainability of new buildings. Although there are often no easy answers to the specific requirements of capital projects, this book provides pointers on how to make investment more effective and sustainable. It will be of value to those interested in the planning, financing, construction and management of new health facilities. They include politicians, planners, managers, health professionals, architects, designers and researchers in both the public and private sectors.

A terminological clarification is necessary at the outset. While the book focuses on hospitals, it is important to keep in mind that the role of hospitals is shifting. Services that were formerly provided in hospitals are now often moved to community settings, and there is also a clearer recognition that hospitals are not closed systems, but need to take into account processes outside of hospitals. Although hospitals continue to consume by far the largest share of capital investment in the health sector, many of the same principles of successful capital investment also apply to other health facilities. In this sense, the term hospital can, in many cases, be considered as a proxy for all health facilities.

## The changing context of hospitals

This chapter examines the changing context of hospitals in Europe, one of the major factors that makes efficient capital investment in the health sector challenging. Hospitals are often remarkably resistant to change, both structurally and culturally (McKee & Healy 2002e). The long time it typically takes to design and build hospitals means that many are outdated by the time the building is opened (Guenther & Vittori 2008). Thus, the contemporary configuration of hospitals often reflects patterns of care and population of bygone eras (McKee & Healy 2002e).

To recognize the potential scale of future changes, it is helpful to consider how modern hospitals evolved. Until the late 19th century, hospitals were places where people went to die (Healy & McKee 2002a). Florence Nightingale reported how, as late as the 1860s, hospitals in London were recording mortality rates in excess of 90% (Komesaroff 1999). The modern hospital has its origins around the beginning of the 20th century, following developments in anaesthesia, infection control, medical science and technology (Black & Gruen 2005; Komesaroff 1999). Until the 1950s, however, hospitals were mainly places for bed rest and convalescence and the range of true medical interventions was limited (Hillman 1999). This changed in the years thereafter and, in the 1950s and 1960s, the scale of capital investment in the health sector increased tremendously, with a boom in hospital building in western Europe and the United States.

Today's hospitals in Europe face particular challenges. They have to adapt to many shifting but coalescing factors, including ageing populations, changing patterns of disease, a mobile health care workforce, the introduction of new medical technologies and pharmaceuticals, increasing public and political expectations, and new financing mechanisms.

There are some recent trends that seem destined to continue, such as a further compression of the length of stay, the use of market or quasi-market mechanisms, efforts to improve the quality of care, and greater use of ambulatory care and home care (Braithwaite & Hindle 1999). While it is possible to predict with some degree of certainty future trends in population and disease, it is much more difficult to predict technological changes or changes in the health system (McKee & Healy 2002d). What can be expected is that the pace of change in the 21st century will be faster than ever (Black & Gruen 2005; McKee &Healy 2002d). A key challenge for hospitals will be to incorporate a high degree of flexibility, so they can quickly adapt to changing needs and expectations.

They will need to deliver high-quality medicine, while ensuring high levels of access and close collaboration with primary care and other services located outside hospitals (Black & Gruen 2005).

It is also important to recognize the wide diversity that exists throughout Europe, a diversity which results from different histories, cultures and political trajectories. Not only do health systems differ in terms of funding, organization and governance, but the term "hospital" covers many different types of institution, stretching from "super-sized" university hospitals comprising several thousand staff to health facilities barely recognizable as "hospitals". Throughout Europe, there are different definitions and understandings of what "hospitals" are, and this makes comparisons difficult (McKee & Healy 2002b; McKee & Healy 2002e).

## Changes in population

The demographic composition of populations determines to a large degree which health services are required. One of the most important demographic trends in almost all European societies is population ageing (Fig. 1.1).

What are the implications of these demographic trends for hospitals? Older people typically account for approximately half the hospital workload, when measured in terms of bed-days (McKee & Healy 2002d), so that it is often assumed that an ageing population will increase the demand for hospital care. It has, for example, been estimated that demographic changes in the United States, such as population ageing and an increase in life expectancy, could result in a 46% increase in hospital bed demand by 2027 (Chaudhury, Mahmood & Valente 2006). However, even more important than age may be how long

**Fig. 1.1** *Percentage of population aged 65 years and over, 1970–2006*

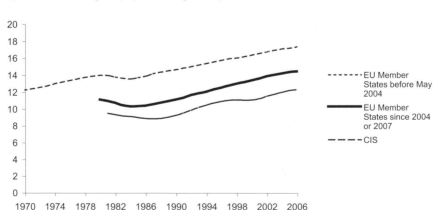

*Source*: WHO Regional Office for Europe 2008.

*Note*: CIS: Commonwealth of Independent States.

one takes to die (McKee & Healy 2002d), with lifestyle changes and greater use of new, safe and effective pharmaceuticals leading to what has been termed compression of morbidity (Fries 1980), where individuals not only live longer, but also remain longer in better health, with a potentially declining demand for hospital services.

What is certain, however, is that ageing populations will have different health care needs, with more cases of cancer, fractured hips, strokes and dementia, for example. More importantly, the complexity of health problems will increase as populations age, with more people suffering from multiple co-morbidities and chronic diseases, receiving a wide range of treatments that potentially interact with each other (Dubois, McKee & Nolte 2006; Hillman 1999; Saltman & Figueras 1997). On the other hand, if birth rates continue to fall, then the demand for obstetric and neonatal paediatric services will decrease (McKee & Healy 2002d).

## Patterns of disease

Hospitals need to provide services appropriate to the health needs of the population(s) they are serving. Existing health service structures are, however, often based on a historical pattern of disease that no longer exists (Saltman & Figueras 1997), while assumptions about future changes in morbidity are often not stated explicitly or supported by evidence (Edwards & Harrison 1999).

It is also important to recognize the huge diversity in patterns of disease across Europe, with a dramatic deterioration of health in the countries of the former Soviet Union after 1991. There are also huge cultural differences that affect how medical services are provided in different countries. German doctors, for example, prescribe 6–7 times as many cardiovascular pharmaceuticals as their colleagues in England and France, although they do prescribe fewer antibiotics (Black & Gruen 2005).

Patterns of disease have changed throughout human history, with old diseases disappearing and new ones emerging. As the cases of AIDS, Severe Acute Respiratory Syndrome (SARS) or Avian Influenza (bird flu) illustrate, new infectious threats may suddenly appear and are almost impossible to predict. There is also the re-emergence of old infectious diseases, partly related to emerging resistances (Gaydos & Veney 2002). One example is the resurgence of tuberculosis (TB) in many countries in CEE, with a growing incidence of multidrug-resistant TB. Another major problem is the rise of hospital-acquired infections, such as Methicillin Resistant Staphylococcus Aureus (MRSA).

With the ageing of the population, health services will need to be restructured from focusing on episodic care for single conditions to encompass the needs of older people, many of whom will have multi-pathologies. This will require multidisciplinary stroke units, and packages of care that involve orthopaedic surgery, geriatric medicine and rehabilitation for patients with fractured hips (Saltman & Figueras 1997). According to WHO projections of the burden of disease for 2030, the proportion of people dying from noncommunicable diseases will increase, while HIV/AIDS deaths will continue to increase in middle- and lower-income countries (Mathers & Loncar 2006).

Changing lifestyles will also result in changing patterns of ill health. The spread of unhealthy diets and fast food in many European countries is likely to increase levels of heart disease and other diet-related diseases. Progression of the tobacco epidemic in many countries in CEE can be expected to lead to an increase in tobacco-related morbidity and mortality.

Climate change, with its wide-ranging impact on the environment and on human societies, will also have a huge impact on population health, although it is much more difficult to estimate. What is certain is that the health effects of climate change will be tremendous and include cold- and heat-related deaths, skin cancer, malnutrition, vector-borne and waterborne diseases, and effects of air pollutants and ozone. There will also be health effects related to increasingly common extreme weather events, such as heat waves and hurricanes (Frumkin et al. 2008).

## Medical technologies

Technological developments are a key force driving change in hospitals and the wider health system – and have been shown as the predominant driver of health care system costs over recent decades. They can have a wide-ranging impact on the type and location of health services, with strong implications for the future use of hospitals and community health services. Recent developments in medical technologies allow, for example, selected services, such as community-based surveillance of chronic diseases, previously only provided in hospitals, to be provided in community clinics, mobile health units and in patients' homes (Rosen 2002).

Major technological developments achieved in recent years in screening, diagnosis, treatment and palliation draw on developments in pharmaceuticals, tests, equipment and surgical techniques (Rosen 2002). Tremendous advances in surgery and anaesthetics have transformed hospital services. The development of aseptic and antiseptic techniques and more effective anaesthesia gave rise to the modern hospital in the late 19th century. With new medical technologies in the 1950s, what had previously been prohibitively complex surgery became common (Hillman 1999). In the 1970s, advances in laboratory diagnostics, the expansion in pharmaceuticals and the diffusion of technologies out of teaching hospitals allowed for new areas of surgery to become commonplace, such as coronary artery bypasses, kidney and other organ transplantations, and microsurgery (McKee & Healy 2002a). Major advances in surgery in the 1990s include minimally invasive surgery, the better targeting of therapeutic agents, and radiosurgery, which is now used routinely to manage many intracerebral problems. Hip replacements have been joined by other joint replacements and there have been major advances in organ transplantations. New anaesthetic technologies and minimally invasive or keyhole surgery, making use of a video camera at the tip of endoscopes, have resulted in an increase in day procedures, a reduction of inpatient length of stay, and shorter recovery times, decreasing the risks of operating on elderly patients. Many procedures that were once provided in hospitals have now been dispersed towards stand-alone units and community settings.

There have also been huge advances in diagnosis, screening and monitoring. New methods allow greater use of imaging, as equipment such as ultrasound and magnetic resonance imaging (MRI) use no ionizing radiation. Interventional radiology, in which procedures can be undertaken using diagnostic equipment, has emerged as another specialization (Glanville & Francis 1996). These technological developments have important implications for future hospitals. Sophisticated monitoring techniques, for example, will allow many patients to be managed at home or in smaller regional centres (Komesaroff 1999). The increasing miniaturization of equipment will also have a profound impact on hospital design, with more equipment being taken to the patient than vice versa, a potentially important consideration when tackling hospital-acquired infection. It will reduce patient movement, obviate the need for some treatment rooms and affect the way health care workers work.

The development of new pharmaceuticals and pharmaceutical delivery technologies has transformed the treatment of many diseases, with some decreasing hospitalization and others offering new opportunities for hospital intervention. Through the development of ulcer-healing pharmaceuticals, for example, a previously complex surgical procedure for peptic ulcer has largely been replaced by a blood or breath test and, if necessary, minimally invasive diagnostic endoscopy often conducted in day-case centres or physicians' offices, before embarking on long-term treatment with pharmaceuticals. Targeting pharmaceuticals to an organ or specific cell may also replace surgery for some interventions (Glanville & Francis 1996).

In many European countries, AIDS has been transformed from a death sentence to a chronic disease (Matic, Lazarus & Donoghoe 2006), although in many countries in the former Soviet Union access to antiretroviral treatment is still unavailable for the majority of patients with AIDS (Bernitz & Rechel 2006). The development of new vaccines for diseases such as HIV, TB and hepatitis could dramatically change future patterns of disease. With the advent of effective pharmaceuticals, much mental illness can now be treated in the community (Black & Gruen 2005).

Advances in the field of genomics and computing technology offer the possibility of gene therapy, that is the artificial introduction of genetic material to replace deleted or defective genes to correct the processes leading to previously intractable diseases. However, in common with many other medical innovations, it is easy to overstate its impact, while failing to appreciate the power of innovations that at the moment appear to be insignificant.

Developments in information and communication technologies (ICTs) may also have a huge impact on health services in the future. These include the integration of all information systems through one network, the increasing use of electronic patient records and the increased use of telemedicine. The real-time clinical consultations made possible by telemedicine allow the provision of services closer to the patient, with small units linked to specialist centres when necessary (Dubois, McKee & Nolte 2006). Automation and the development of robotics could herald other major changes in hospital care. However, again, it is essential to ground the more optimistic predictions in reality, as information systems often fail to deliver what they promise and forecasters tend to underestimate the importance of human involvement in some transactions and procedures.

## Changes in the workforce

Health care is labour intensive and health care workers are at the heart of health systems, and thus of the changes taking place in hospitals. However, most health systems struggle to achieve the right numbers, skill mix, and distribution of the health care workforce (Rechel, McKee & Dubois 2006; WHO 2006). So far there is little evidence of capital replacing labour or enhancing staff effectiveness, a principle that has transformed industrial and commercial processes.

While the pool from which health care workers can be recruited will be shrinking, increasing numbers may be required, particularly on the interface between health and social care, where there will be greater demands for home-care workers, nurses, community health workers and physiotherapists (Dubois, McKee & Nolte 2006). As increasing numbers of patients suffer from more than one disease, the importance of multidisciplinary teamwork will increase, as will the challenge of coordination at key interfaces in the health system, such as between primary and secondary care (Boerma 2006; McKee & Healy 2002d).

Many western European countries already depend on health care workers from abroad. Within the EU, enlargement has opened borders to health care workers from the countries of CEE, leading to shortages and rising labour costs there. The consequences are even more alarming for many countries outside the EU, which are losing health workers at a faster pace than they can be trained.

An important trend is the increasing feminization of the workforce, which is expected to continue. This has implications for the organization of clinical work, as women are more likely to take career breaks or to work part-time. At the same time, in many countries men take a more active role in child care and increasingly reject the traditional culture of long and often antisocial hours. In many countries, an increase in part-time work can be observed and there is also a trend towards early retirement, triggering attempts to retain older workers within the workforce (Dubois, McKee & Nolte 2006).

Another incentive for change comes from the European Working Time Directive of 1993, which limits working time to 48 hours for each 7-day period, including overtime. Judgments of the European Court of Justice in 2000 and 2003 established that on-call duties count as regular working hours where presence at the health facility is required, while an amendment to the Directive was adopted in 2000 that clarified its extension to, inter alia, trainee doctors. Although several countries have yet to implement the Directive fully, it is almost certain to lead to a reconfiguration of hospital provision and of patterns of work within hospitals, with many small hospitals and specialist areas ceasing to be viable, while traditional professional task demarcations break down.

Traditional professional roles are continuously being revised or expanded. Health care workers are increasingly required to acquire new competences in order to perform their tasks. They also have to keep up to date with new developments in information technology (IT), as patient records are increasingly computerized (Dubois, McKee & Nolte 2006). One of the most powerful factors shaping change in hospitals has been increasing medical specialization (Edwards & Harrison 1999). In the future, technological advances will require an even more specialized workforce (WHO 2006). Greater specialization can particularly be expected in areas such as surgery, imaging, invasive cardiology, transplantation, oncology and genetics (Dubois, McKee & Nolte 2006). At the same time, a specialist may not always be the patient's best choice. In some countries, such as the United States, the new specialty of "hospitalist" has emerged, with a wide range of expertise, but is mainly focused on acute hospital medicine (Hillman 1999). In a similar vein, the new specialty of acute medicine has been promoted in the United Kingdom (Royal College of Physicians 2004). These developments are a response to the challenge of managing patients who are acutely ill, but where it is not yet clear which body systems are involved. There is also a trend towards strengthening nursing as an independent health profession, and some European countries have introduced various types of nurse practitioner (Dubois, McKee & Nolte 2006). A study of patient outcomes in relation to organizational characteristics found that better patient outcomes were achieved in hospitals with a culture that valued professional nursing expertise and allowed for greater nurse autonomy and better relationships between physicians and nurses (Aiken & Sloane 2002). Overall, the role of multidisciplinary teamwork is increasing, which will require new skills, attitudes to collaboration and mechanisms to ensure continuity of care (WHO 2006).

## Public and political expectations

The configuration of hospital services is not simply a technical or managerial issue, but to a large degree a political decision. Hospitals are often symbols of the welfare state and of civic pride and, in many European countries, hospital closures tend to encounter fierce local opposition.

There is also an increasing recognition of patients' rights, in particular in many countries in western Europe. The growth of "consumerism" – a social movement promoting and representing user interests in health services – has resulted in increasing protection of patients' rights through charters or laws (Black & Gruen 2005). Hospitals are also faced with popular expectations to reduce waiting times, introduce more convenient times for medical interventions, and make diagnostic and therapeutic services more widely available. The explosion of information available on the Internet is leading to greater health knowledge among users, who may be better informed about their condition(s) than their physicians. An international network of the WHO Regional Office for Europe on Health Promoting Hospitals was established in 1990, calling for the reorientation of hospitals towards the well-being of patients, relatives and staff, facilitating the healing process and contributing to the empowerment of patients (Pelikan, Krajic & Dietscher 2001; WHO 1997). In several new hospital projects, great emphasis is placed on early involvement of patients and staff.

Increasing patient orientation of hospitals has far-reaching implications for their configuration. Many patients now prefer single rooms, a demand that in many countries greatly exceeds supply (Jolley 2005; Kirk 2002). Single rooms have already become the industry standard in the construction of new acute care facilities in the United States (Chaudhury, Mahmood & Valente 2006) and in several European countries, such as Spain or the Nordic countries. They increase privacy and may reduce stress and hospital infections, enable nurses and health care workers to do a better job, and provide space for family members (Brown & Taquino 2001; Chaudhury, Mahmood & Valente 2006; Douglas & Douglas 2005; Lawson & Phiri 2000; Nightingale 2006). Single rooms may also result in cost savings, due to a reduction in transfer cost, a lower probability of dietary and medication mix-ups, higher bed occupancy rates and a reduction in labour costs (Chaudhury, Mahmood & Valente 2006).

More generally, patients are looking for ease of access, good signage and directions, and access to external areas and recreation and leisure facilities. They also value environments that support their normal lifestyle, provide accommodation for relatives and visitors, and allow for controllable lighting, reduced noise levels and temperature control (Douglas et al. 2002; Douglas & Douglas 2004; Douglas & Douglas 2005). There is also an increasing demand for television, radio and Internet access at every bedside (Nightingale 2006).

## Changes in the health system

Hospitals do not operate in isolation, and are only one element of the wider health care system. The role of hospitals has changed significantly in recent decades and this trend can be expected to continue. Since the 1980s many countries in western Europe have tried to reduce their hospital capacity and to shift care to alternative settings, while in CEE the overprovision of hospital beds that was a hallmark of the Semashko system has been significantly reduced. These trends are shown in Fig. 1.2 in terms of hospital bed numbers, which can be used as a first proxy for hospital capacity.

In western Europe, there have been three major developments that have influenced hospital care in recent decades: the transfer of long-stay psychiatric patients to community settings, the increasing provision of nursing care for the elderly outside hospitals and the restructuring of acute care, with more ambulatory treatment and rehabilitation outside hospital (McKee & Healy 2002a). In England, the decrease in hospital beds between 1984 and 1998 was almost exactly equivalent to the increase in nursing and residential home beds in the same period. Most of the increase in nursing home places was taken up by people who paid for themselves or used a feature of the benefits systems to receive a subsidy; these places allowed a significant reduction in the number of long-stay beds operated by the National Health Service (NHS) (Hensher & Edwards 2002). The move towards community settings has largely been driven by financial considerations (Glanville & Francis 1996), but is also due

**Fig. 1.2** *Acute care hospital beds per 100 000 population*

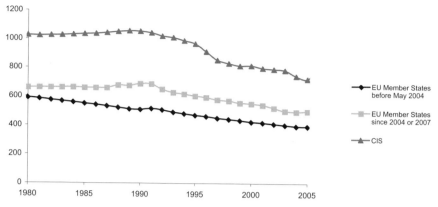

Source: WHO Regional Office for Europe 2008.
Notes: EU: European Union; CIS: Commonwealth of Independent States.

to the diffusion of technology into primary health care, largely in the form of pharmaceuticals, although new technologies may also lead to centralization due to the need for high-cost equipment (Saltman & Figueras 1997). Rehabilitation and palliative care are also increasingly provided nearer to the patient (Hillman 1999). A range of nurse-led primary care clinics have reduced the need for hospital outpatient facilities, while community-based services have been established for patients requiring palliative care (Nightingale 2006; Rosen 2002).

These changes have resulted in a decrease in the number of acute hospital beds and a decreasing average length of stay (Fig. 1.3). Admissions have risen, resulting in an increasing number of patients per bed and per hospital site (Hensher, Edwards & Stokes 1999; McKee & Healy 2002a). Reflecting the more efficient management of patients, new technologies and financial incentives to reduce length of stay, many more patients are passing through hospitals in much shorter periods of time (Hensher, Edwards & Stokes 1999). A higher turnover is often associated with greater peaks and troughs, so expanded capacity may be needed to retain sufficient flexibility (Edwards & Harrison 1999). With the growth of chronic disease and the tendency for many frail elderly people to be managed outside hospitals rather than in long-term hospital care, an increasing number of these admissions are patients who have many repeated admissions during the course of the year. While it is possible to identify these patients retrospectively, the potential to take preventative action is limited. There has also been a dramatic rise in day-case procedures, although these have often been in addition to inpatient care rather than substituting for it (Saltman & Figueras 1997).

**Fig. 1.3** *Average length of stay (acute care hospitals only)*

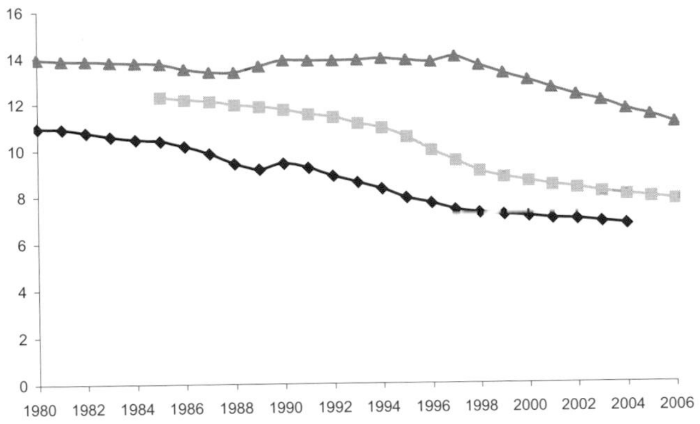

*Source*: WHO Regional Office for Europe 2008.
*Notes*: EU: European Union; CIS: Commonwealth of Independent States.

As hospital stays have become shorter and more intense, remaining inpatients tend to be more seriously ill, requiring more intensive care and high-dependency beds (Glanville & Francis 1996; Hillman 1999). Although the reduction of the average length of stay is a trend which is set to continue, it remains difficult to forecast future developments because of the law of diminishing returns (Edwards & Harrison 1999).

Primary care has developed dramatically since the 1970s, establishing itself as a legitimate partner of secondary and tertiary care (Saltman 2006). The Nordic initiative on primary health care in the early 1970s was followed in 1978 by the WHO Alma Ata Declaration, which emphasized that primary care should form an integral part of comprehensive health systems (WHO 1978) – a declaration that was often perceived as being directed against hospitals. The increasing importance of primary care continued throughout the 1990s. In CEE, state-run polyclinics were dismantled and replaced by independent general practitioners (GPs). Western Europe has seen different organizational changes, such as various experiments with networks of GPs and purchaser–provider splits, and a wide range of new activities in such areas as coordinated care for chronically ill and elderly people. In addition, community-level providers increasingly take on financial responsibilities for care delivered elsewhere, such as where GPs individually or general practice as a discipline take on budget-holding responsibilities, including for the purchase of specialist care from acute hospitals (Saltman 2006).

The spectrum of services provided for a designated population is gaining more attention than details of where they are delivered. Hospitals increasingly recognize the importance of patients' lives before and after their hospital stay and exhibit an increasing awareness of other parts of the health sector (WHO 1997). There is a growing trend towards planning on a system-wide basis (Douglas & Douglas 2005; Edwards & Harrison 1999; Smith 1999). New networks are emerging, for example, for the care for diabetes, asthma, heart disease or cancer that are based on integrated clinical pathways that cut across primary, secondary and social care (Saltman 2006).

## Redesign and re-engineering

Many European countries have been the setting for major internal hospital restructuring, often also known as process re-engineering. When crudely applied, this has generally involved redesigning job responsibilities with the object of reducing personnel. Reductions in nursing staff and a changing skill mix have been common targets, although there is little evidence that structural reforms have achieved their goals of greater efficiency (Aiken & Sloane 2002; Elkhuizen et al. 2006).

While some of this has not been well executed and has been carried out to result in short-term savings rather than as part of a strategic redesign of the way care is delivered, there are some lessons from the experiences that provide pointers to how services may develop in the future. A more careful application of this approach may have the potential to make significant and sustainable improvements to the efficiency of health systems. Such redesign starts from the insight that every system is perfectly designed to achieve the result it gets. In other words, to achieve changes in outcomes and the experience of care, it is necessary to make changes to the system and not simply make small improvements to individual component processes that are fundamentally flawed. A series of key assumptions, or rules, underpin the current system and, to arrive at a system that functions better, it is necessary to replace the current rules with ones more likely to produce the types of outcome(s) that the system requires. Proposed new rules highlight some of the thinking that the planners of hospitals will need to incorporate into new buildings and the systems in which they are embedded. Some examples, as well as the corresponding implications for the design of services, are provided in Table 1.1.

The implications of these new rules are that hospitals might develop more one-stop services, provide more services in community settings, reduce their bed numbers, split facilities between active areas and "hotel" ones, and reduce the enormous amount of space dedicated to waiting areas. The concern about climate change is also of significance here. One of the main products of most hospitals is carbon dioxide, particularly through the large number of journeys

**Table 1.1** *Potential changes in the way that patients use services*

| Old approach | New (idealized) approach |
|---|---|
| Patients use the system in a series of unconnected episodes | Need is anticipated and hospitals and health systems develop methods to manage the whole pathway of disease, support patients in their own home and have electronic records that help to ensure continuity of care |
| Patients are passive recipients of care | Patients are involved in the management of their own care |
| Patients are dealt with in batches and spend most of their time within the system waiting – this is because it is important to keep expensive staff and assets busy | Patients flow through the system with minimal waits. Sweating the assets and having staff busy is less important than achieving a smooth flow through the system |
| Patients are treated as though their time is free and are required to undertake significant amounts of unpaid work and movements for the convenience of the providers | Consumerism and the increasing time poverty of many people mean that a premium will be placed on convenience and speed |
| | The pressure for efficiency and the need to eliminate unnecessary steps in the process will also mean that moving information and staff – rather than patients – becomes a more accepted principle |
| Services are designed around the historic way providers are structured | Services are designed to meet the requirements of patients |
| Patients go to hospital for routine monitoring | Home-based technology and diagnostic equipment outside the hospital reduce the use of hospitals |
| Interaction is face to face and on a one-to-one basis | E-mail and telephone can be used and group visits seem to work for some issues |
| Providers determine follow-up and re-referral | Patients can initiate follow-up and have a right of return or direct access to specialist help if they think they need it – even if they have been discharged |
| Patients often die in hospital when they would have preferred to die at home | Patients have plans for end-of-life care |

they generate. The NHS in the United Kingdom currently produces emissions equivalent to approximately a million tonnes of carbon dioxide each year, accounting for 5% of all road transport emissions in the country (Mayor 2008). Many of these journeys could be rendered unnecessary through the better use of disseminated services and communication.

There is another set of new rules for the way that staff might work in response to shortages and the pressure for improvement (Table 1.2).

**Table 1.2** *Potential changes to the way staff work*

| Old approach | New (idealized) approach |
|---|---|
| See a junior member of staff who escalates | See a senior member who makes decisions and delegates – this should reduce the number of patients admitted to hospital and reduce the length of stay of those that are admitted |
| See a doctor | See the most appropriate professional |
| Reduce the skill mix to save money | Increase the skill mix to improve efficiency and outcomes |
| Staff develop "work-arounds" for problems | Staff undertake root cause analysis to create sustainable solutions |
| Large amounts of time are wasted by poor work process design – safety may also be compromised | Unnecessary staff movement can be reduced by the proper design of work processes and the work environment as well as the use of IT systems |
| Many services stop at weekends and in the evenings | Specialist consultation, diagnostics and other support services are available for much longer than the traditional working week |
| Beds are a mark of prestige and a source of income | Beds are a cost centre and emergency non-surgical admissions are seen as a sign of system failure |

There are a number of important insights stemming from this approach to thinking about the hospital. First, many traditional approaches to improvement are futile. Improving the efficiency of a part of the system may not improve overall efficiency. For example, attempting to improve the speed of patient care by purchasing an additional MRI scanner without changing other aspects of the care process may simply transfer the delay to the period after the scan, where the patient will wait for a decision. The key insight here is that, in common with most complex organizations, the ratio of work that actually creates value for patients (or gives them what they need) to work that creates no value is at best 1:10. This means that even a 50% improvement in the aspects that add value only translates into a 5% improvement in the overall process, and less if the time saved by the improvement is swallowed up by waiting and delays elsewhere (Fillingham 2008).

Second, the lack of a whole system perspective means that unexpected and often adverse consequences are much more likely to arise because a key interaction has not been understood properly or has been missed. Third, the application of systematic and deliberately designed approaches to care delivery will become increasingly important as a means of improving cost, improving outcomes and reducing harm from the particularly large number of avoidable adverse incidents in many hospitals.

There has been a general belief that improving quality in health care increases cost. There appears to be growing evidence that the opposite is true. One issue, however, is that some quality improvements reduce cost for the whole system, but increase cost for individual parts of it. For example, using percutaneous coronary intervention (PCI) as the treatment of choice for myocardial infarction (MI) may be more expensive for the hospital, but the cost for the whole system may be reduced. This means that the design of payment systems and incentives needs to reflect quality and best clinical practice.

The lessons from the poor application of redesign and re-engineering approaches are that the project must use appropriate methodology adapted to a clinical setting, it needs to be clinically led, to define its outcomes in terms of clinical quality and effectiveness as well as costs, and be regarded as a long-term project that is central to the organization's goals, not an add-on executed by management consultants or special teams. The potential for reducing activities that add little or no value and for releasing space, staff time and resources is particularly significant.

## Changes in financing

In many countries of Europe there is increasing concern over the growing costs of health care. The ageing of the population, higher levels of chronic disease and disability, developments in medical technologies and rising public expectations have exerted an upward pressure on health-related expenditure in most western European countries (Mossialos & Le Grand 1999). As most hospitals in Europe lie within the broadly defined public sector and remain dependent primarily on government for funds for investment, and as hospitals typically consume the largest share of the health budget, they have become main targets of efforts to contain spending (McKee & Healy 2002c). Recent years have seen a vast array of measures to contain health spending, improve technical efficiency and raise the quality of care (McKee & Healy 2002d), and these efforts can be expected to intensify in the future.

One of the ways which has been used to finance hospitals involves greater use of public–private partnerships. In this model, the private sector is contracted by the public sector to build, manage and maintain a health facility and certain services within it for a certain period of time. This is a key feature of the Private Finance Initiative (PFI) in the United Kingdom, the country at the forefront of this kind of procurement (McKee, Edwards & Atun 2006).

Other countries have introduced market incentives in the revenue streams flowing to hospitals. In the Netherlands, for example, the introduction of competitive diagnosis-related groups (DRGs) has been an important driver of change in hospitals, moving on to a privatization of insurance and freeing the system from much regulatory control.

EU Structural Funds will have an important impact on the hospital infrastructure in the new Member States. More than a third of the budget of the EU is devoted to regional development and economic and social cohesion. Most important for the health sector is the European Regional Development Fund (ERDF), which finances infrastructure, job-creating investment, local development projects and aid for small firms. Structural Funds were used in the early 1990s to support hospital investments in Portugal and Greece (Figueras et al. 1991), and have now become available to new Member States, where they can help to renew the outdated health infrastructure.

## Problems with planning

Despite a comparatively good evidence base regarding the mega-trends in health care, capital investment strategy (planning, design and procurement) continues to lag behind service delivery in terms of innovation, responsiveness to changing circumstances and measurable value. There are a number reasons for this asymmetry between service and capital.

First, there is a mismatch generated by the long lead time for planning and construction, and assumptions about the ability of the system to deliver new types of care are either over-optimistic or not linked to a realistic delivery plan. Second, hospitals are increasingly part of wider systems of health care and cannot be planned as though they are stand-alone entities. Hospitals emerged because there was logic for bringing functions together (such as operating theatres, laboratories and X-ray departments), generating some economies of scope and scale from grouping specialist services. Some of this logic is being challenged by changes in medicine and technology (such as minimally invasive surgery, near-patient testing and ultrasound) and consequent opportunities to unpack the hospital into components that can be located in new settings, operate in novel ways, and have quite different relationships with other parts of the system.

On the one hand, the growing complexity of health care and the trend towards increasing specialization seem to support the development of a small number of specialist centres for relatively rare and complex conditions. At the same time, there is an increased capability in primary care and community-based services, a movement of a great deal of imaging and other diagnostic services out of the hospital setting, and the fact that in many countries specialists already offer services outside the hospital. This means that rather than a self-contained provider of end-to-end care, the hospital is only responsible for part of the whole care pathway. Even large specialist centres are increasingly part of wider systems, because of the need to support smaller hospitals and for large populations to support specialist teams and clinical research. The staff and resources from large centres will increasingly form part of a network, with smaller hospitals, services in the community and enhanced primary care providing elements of the care pathway. The specialist centres may retain the work that requires high levels of expertise or multidisciplinary teamwork and responsibility for overseeing education and clinical elements, but they nevertheless will be part of a network and dependent on it. This makes the planning of hospitals a much more difficult task. Planners have to identify the various streams of activity, determine the different options for how these services can be provided and what the most appropriate and cost-effective solution might be, and then project how demand, technology and a range of other uncertain environmental factors are likely to change this. The situation is complicated further by the diverse needs of those using health care systems. There is particular uncertainty about how best to configure services for children. Much of the historical hospital workload (dominated by infectious diseases) has decreased markedly. On the one hand, there is growing need for community services addressing issues such as psychological disorders, while at the same time, the care provided in hospitals – now dominated by cancers, chronic diseases and genetic disorders – has become vastly more complex.

The planning process is further complicated by the involvement of politicians, both national and local, and the fact that the technology of medicine changes at a much faster pace than the lifespan of many of the investments that often prove to be particularly inflexible. This process is even further complicated by the problem of disruptive innovations and other changes that are difficult to predict and can change significant aspects of how care is delivered.

## Conclusions on the context for improving capital investment

As this chapter has argued, hospitals have to respond to changing circumstances, many of which are difficult to predict. There are some trends which are likely to continue, such as the ageing of European societies or future trends of certain diseases, but their impact on hospital services is far from clear. One conclusion that can be drawn is that the future is particularly uncertain. Future hospitals will need to anticipate the unexpected and incorporate a high degree of functional flexibility.

Another conclusion is that, given the complexity of hospitals and the varying needs they have to accommodate, there will be no easy answer that fits all contexts. The countries of Europe face different challenges in the future, including different patterns of disease and different popular expectations. These will obviously need to be taken into account when planning hospitals.

A major factor that has inhibited progress in improving capital investment is the difficulty of quantifying the resulting benefits. In most commercial settings, capital investment is an investment which needs to be justified by measurable, economically viable and predictive returns. In the health sector, however, it is particularly difficult to make reliable, evidence-based connections between investment in capital and health gain achieved. Ideally, in the health sector, capital investment should deliver measurable contributions in the following areas:

- contributing to health gains and improved health status of the local population
- contributing to improved clinical outcomes
- improving cost-efficiency
- helping to achieve performance management targets, such as reduced waiting times
- contributing to the local economy.

Often, planners only take account of cost-efficiency and performance management, so that nonclinical performance characteristics still dominate the decision-making process. A stronger focus on the health gains achieved through capital investment could result in more efficient and sustainable investments. Moreover, five overall success factors have to be fulfilled: efficiency, effectiveness, relevance, impact and sustainability. These imply that projects should have no major negative effects; their objectives should be consistent with societal needs and priorities; and they should produce not only short-term efficiency, but also long-term benefits. These are requirements that go far beyond the issues that are usually covered by health planners and decision-makers.

## Structure of the book

This chapter has provided an overview of the many challenges current and future hospitals and other health facilities face. It provides the background for the more detailed examination of key issues relevant to capital investment in the remaining chapters of this book. Chapter 2 concludes the first part of the book and examines new models of long-term care, particularly for chronic conditions, and the implications these have for the redesign of health services.

Part two of the book examines ways in which capital investment can be influenced so as to meet current and future needs. Chapter 3 explores the issue of capital planning, which aims to establish what facilities are needed and where they should be. Chapter 4 explores the seeming difficulty governments have in developing long-range capital concepts that effectively cross-match operational service effectiveness with the long lifespan of buildings. Chapter 5 reviews the impact of capital investment on the health care workforce and makes the case for involving health care workers in the design of new facilities.

The chapters that follow in Part three are concerned with economic aspects of capital investment. Chapter 6 reflects on the impact of markets and competition on capital investment, while Chapter 7 examines systems used for procurement and financing and draws conclusions on the process of making decisions to invest. Chapter 8 argues that the whole life-cycle of health facilities needs to be taken into account when deciding on capital investments. Chapter 9 explores facility management and its implications for hospital design and Chapter 10 addresses the wider impact of capital investment on the local community and economy.

Part four goes on to explore the design issues arising in building the hospital of the future. Chapter 11 tackles the question of how care models can be translated into capital asset solutions and Chapter 12 explores the issues of therapeutic and sustainable design.

The final chapter, Chapter 13, draws together the key lessons of this study. It seeks to identify the critical success factors that increase the chances of successful outcomes in the increasingly complex area of capital investment planning and practice.

## References

Aiken L, Sloane D (2002). Hospital organization and culture. In: McKee M, Healy J. *Hospitals in a changing Europe*. Buckingham, Open University Press:265–278.

Bernitz BL, Rechel B (2006). HIV data in central and eastern Europe: fact or fiction? In: Matic S, Lazarus JV, Donoghoe MC, eds. *HIV/AIDS in Europe. Moving from death sentence to chronic disease management*. Copenhagen, WHO Regional Office for Europe:232–242.

Black N, Gruen R (2005). *Understanding health services*. Maidenhead, Open University Press.

Boerma W (2006). Coordination and integration in European primary care. In: Saltman RB, Rico A, Boerma W. *Primary care in the driver's seat? Organizational reform in European primary care*. Maidenhead, Open University Press:3–21.

Braithwaite J, Hindle D (1999). Research and the acute-care hospital of the future. *Medical Journal of Australia*, 170:292–293.

Brown P, Taquino LT (2001). Designing and delivering neonatal care in single rooms. *Journal for Perinatal and Neonatal Nursing*, 15:68–83.

Chaudhury H, Mahmood A, Valente M (2006). Nurses' perceptions of single-occupancy versus multioccupancy rooms in acute care environments: an exploratory assessment. *Applied Nursing Research*, 19:118–125.

Douglas C et al. (2002). Primary care trusts. A room with a view. *Health Services Journal*, 112:28–29.

Douglas CH, Douglas MR (2004). Patient-friendly hospital environments: exploring the patients' perspective. *Health Expectations*, 7:61–73.

Douglas CH, Douglas MR (2005). Patient-centred improvements in health-care built environments: perspectives and design indicators. *Health Expectations*, 8:264–276.

Dubois C-A, McKee M, Nolte E (2006). Analysing trends, opportunities and challenges. In: Dubois C-A, McKee M, Nolte E. *Human resources for health in Europe*. Maidenhead, Open University Press:15–40.

Edwards N, Harrison A (1999). The hospital of the future. Planning hospitals with limited evidence: a research and policy problem. *British Medical Journal*, 319:1361–1363.

Elkhuizen SG et al. (2006). Evidence-based re-engineering: re-engineering the evidence – a systematic review of the literature on business process redesign (BPR) in hospital care. *International Journal of Health Care Quality Assurance Incorporating Leadership in Health Services*, 19:477–499.

Figueras J et al. (1991). *Health care infrastructure: needs in the lagging regions*. Brussels, European Commission.

Fillingham D (2008). *Lean health care: Improving the patient's experience*. Chichester, AKD Press.

Fries JF (1980). Ageing, natural death, and the compression of morbidity. *The New England Journal of Medicine*, 303:130–135.

Frumkin H et al. (2008). *Climate change: the public health response. American Journal of Public Health*, 98:435–445.

Gaydos LMD, Veney JE (2002). The nature and etiology of disease. In: Fried BJ, Gaydos LMD, eds. *World health systems: challenges and perspectives*. Chicago, Health Administration Press:3–24.

Glanville R, Francis S (1996). *Scanning the spectrum of health care from hospital to home in the UK*. MARU Viewpoints Seminar Programme 1996. London, South Bank University Medical Architecture Research Unit.

Guenther R, Vittori G (2008). *Sustainable healthcare architecture*. Hoboken, John Wiley & Sons.

Healy J, McKee M (2002a). Improving performance within the hospital. In: McKee M, Healy J. *Hospitals in a changing Europe*. Buckingham, Open University Press:206–225.

Healy J, McKee M (2002b). The role and function of hospitals. In: McKee M, Healy J. *Hospitals in a changing Europe*. Buckingham, Open University Press:59–80.

Hensher M, Edwards N (2002). The hospital and the external environment: experience in the United Kingdom. In: McKee M, Healy J. *Hospitals in a changing Europe*. Buckingham, Open University Press:83–99.

Hensher M, Edwards N, Stokes R (1999). The hospital of the future: international trends in the provision and utilisation of hospital care. *British Medical Journal*, 319:845–848.

Hillman, K (1999). The changing role of acute-care hospitals. *Medical Journal of Australia*, 170:325–328.

Jolley S (2005). Single rooms and patient choice. *Nursing Standard*, 20:41–48.

Kirk S (2002). Patient preferences for a single or shared room in a hospice. *Nursing Times*, 98:39–41.

Komesaroff PA (1999). Is the hospital obsolete? *Medical Journal of Australia*, 170:17–19.

Lawson B, Phiri M (2000). Hospital design. Room for improvement. *Health Services Journal*, 110:24–26.

Mathers CD, Loncar D (2006). Projections of global mortality and burden of disease from 2002 to 2030. *Public Library of Science Medicine*, 3:2011–2030.

Matic S, Lazarus JV, Donoghoe MC (eds.) (2006). *HIV/AIDS in Europe. Moving from death sentence to chronic disease management*. Copenhagen, WHO Regional Office for Europe.

Mayor S (2008). NHS should bring in measures to reduce its carbon footprint, BMA says. *British Medical Journal*, 336(7647):740.

McKee M, Edwards N, Atun R (2006). Public–private partnerships for hospitals. *Bulletin of the World Health Organization*, 84:890–896.

McKee M, Healy J (2002a). The evolution of hospital systems. In: McKee M, Healy J. *Hospitals in a changing Europe*. Buckingham, Open University Press:14–35.

McKee M, Healy J (2002b). Future hospitals. In: McKee M, Healy J. *Hospitals in a changing Europe*. Buckingham, Open University Press:281–284.

McKee M, Healy J (2002c). Investing in hospitals. In: McKee M, Healy J. *Hospitals in a changing Europe*. Buckingham, Open University Press:119–149.

McKee M, Healy J (2002d). Pressures for change. In: McKee M, Healy J. *Hospitals in a changing Europe*. Buckingham, Open University Press:36–58.

McKee M, Healy J (2002e). The significance of hospitals: an introduction. In: McKee M, Healy J. *Hospitals in a changing Europe*. Buckingham, Open University Press:3–13.

Mossialos E, Le Grand J (eds) (1999). *Health care and cost containment in the European Union*. Aldershot, Ashgate.

Nightingale N (2006). University Hospital in Coventry: light and space. *Hospital Development*, 14 November (www.hd.magazine.co.uk/hybrid.asp?typeCode=525&putCode=10, accessed 14 October 2008).

Pelikan JM, Krajic K, Dietscher C (2001). The health promoting hospital (HPH): concept and development. *Patient Education and Counselling*, 45:239–243.

Rechel B, McKee M, Dubois C-A (eds.) (2006). *The health care workforce in Europe. Learning from experience*. Copenhagen, WHO Regional Office for Europe.

Rosen R (2002). Introducing new technologies. In: McKee M, Healy J. *Hospitals in a changing Europe*. Buckingham, Open University Press:240–251.

Royal College of Physicians (2004). *Acute medicine: making it work for patients*. London, Royal College of Physicians.

Saltman RB (2006). Drawing the strands together: primary care in perspective. In: Saltman RB, Rico A, Boerma W. *Primary care in the driver's seat? Organizational reform in European primary care*. Maidenhead, Open University Press:68–82.

Saltman RB, Figueras J (1997). *European health care reform. Analysis of current strategies*. Copenhagen, WHO Regional Office for Europe.

Smith R (1999). Reconfiguring acute hospital services. *British Medical Journal*, 319:797–798.

WHO (1978). *Alma-Ata 1978. Primary health care*. Report of the International Conference on Primary Health Care, Alma-Ata, USSR, 6–12 September 1978. Geneva, World Health Organization.

WHO (1997). *The Vienna Recommendations on Health Promoting Hospitals*. Adopted at the 3rd Workshop of National/Regional Health Promoting Hospitals Network Coordinators, Vienna, 16 April 1997.

WHO (2006). *The world health report 2006*. Geneva, World Health Organization.

WHO Regional Office for Europe (2008). Health for All database (HFA-DB) [offline database]. Copenhagen, WHO Regional Office for Europe (July 2008 update).

# Chapter 2

# New models of long-term care and implications for service redesign

*Pieter Degeling, Jonathan Erskine*

## Introduction

The location and arrangement of the physical space of health facilities have an important impact on the quality, appropriateness, effectiveness and efficiency of service delivery. Capital development, informed by service planning, should be a catalyst for engendering changes in the delivery of care. This chapter argues that these linkages between service and capital planning may not work out in practice, in large part because of cultural factors, and offers some guidance on how to do it better. The chapter is organized in three parts.

The first section opens with a brief overview of the social, economic and political factors that, since the 1970s, have thrown into question significant aspects of existing approaches to organizing and managing health service delivery in most countries in western Europe. In doing this, we outline factors that are stimulating searches for new models of care, particularly for people with long-term conditions. These new models imply changes to the range of settings in which care might be provided, the nature of interventions undertaken, the duration of care processes and how care models differ in their understanding of the patient.

The second section examines the redistributive effects of service redesign, as well as some context-specific factors (structural and cultural) that limit the scope of service redesign and affect its implementation. Gaps between promise and performance in service and capital planning are explained by the limitations of existing approaches to these processes. They underestimate the paradigm shifts that are required to bring about substantive service redesign and overestimate the leverage for change that the prospect of significant capital investment will provide. Against this background, we show how the impact of capital investment plans that are oriented towards service improvement depends on the extent to which new service models (such as those outlined below for long-term conditions) are part of a broad range of interventions and are supported by contextual factors.

The concluding section considers the implications of these findings for capital investment that is oriented towards service reform. It argues that, to be successful, increases in capital investment for primary and community care settings will need to be accompanied by cultural and structural changes that transcend the fragmentation between hospital care, primary care, community care and social care.

## New models of long-term care

Until the mid-1970s, the bulk of health service delivery in most countries in western Europe was structured around two poles. At one end of the continuum were doctors working in general practice; at the other were medical specialists located in district hospitals which were expected to provide the full spectrum of acute care for the populations within their catchment areas.

Since the 1980s, many aspects of this medically centred and hospital-focused model of service delivery have been questioned. Within policy circles, for example, medicine's traditionally privileged position is increasingly being judged in terms of its capacity to influence service demand and cost and to regulate itself. Equally, within clinical settings, medicine's increasing dependence on other occupations has eroded its position as the sole reservoir of knowledge and expertise about disease, illness and cure. Finally, at a societal level, rapidly increasing access to IT has enabled patients to be better informed about their condition(s) and the efficacy of available treatment options. This development, together with the campaigning proclivities of the media and the emergence of more consumerist orientations in the population at large, has markedly recast relations between doctors and patients. What previously was construed as deference-based gift exchange is now increasingly seen as a transaction between a skilled service provider and a consumer.

There has also been growing concern about the efficiency of hospitals and their ever increasing impact on health care costs and the economy as a whole. Equally, there are concerns about the system's overriding dependence on hospital-based service delivery and its capacity to cope with expansions in demand that will result from developments in medical technology and the growing prevalence of chronic disease (see Chapter 1). Broadly speaking, the policy and funding response to these challenges has taken two forms. First, in the interest of inserting "a logic of productivity and service improvement", policy and funding authorities have promoted the introduction of management structures and practices capable of supporting systematization of clinical work within and between service settings. Second, in attempts to move beyond the confines of the traditional hospital-focused medical treatment model, efforts have been directed at developing new models of care reflecting the range of settings in which care is provided, the nature of interventions undertaken and the duration of care processes, as well as practices that will empower patients in co-producing their own health.

Central to this have been efforts to shift from a focus on hospital beds – a stock concept not well suited to describing potential output flows – to a focus on the services required. These either do not involve hospitals or do so only as repositories of technology, knowledge and skills, but which the patient attends for the briefest time possible. Significant components of service provision occur either in multipurpose community care settings or at home. Such models of care erode boundaries between acute and social care, and/or constitute patients as co-producers of their own health. Some descriptors for distinguishing between care models are set out in Table 2.1.

**Table 2.1** *Models of care*

---

Care setting

*From:* Hospital-based care (accident and emergency, inpatient wards, day-case surgery, outpatient clinics) and general practice

*To:* A community-based outpatient clinic which operates openly as a multi-agency one-stop shop

---

Nature of intervention

*From:* Specialized clinical treatment

*To:* Remote IT monitoring, secondary prevention and psychosocial support

---

Duration of care

*From:* Extended inpatient admission

*To:* Health provision from multiple service settings, including health and social care and the voluntary sector

---

Social construction of the patient

*From:* Passive and dependent

*To:* An engaged co-producer with rights and responsibilities

---

What may be involved here becomes clear when we consider the service implications of moving from one model of care to another for a patient with a long-term condition.

In Model A, the main service setting is a hospital ward where a passive and dependent patient is rendered available for specialized clinical procedures over an extended inpatient admission period and then discharged until the next time they experience a major exacerbation of their underlying long-term condition. In Model B, the patient constitutes a co-producer of her/his health, and the main service setting is a community-based multi-agency "one-stop shop". The content of the intervention is registered in a personalized care plan that, in the interest of slowing down disease progression and preventing a major exacerbation, specifies not only the clinical dimensions of care, but also what will be done by the co-producing patient, as well as the support that they will be able to call on from community-based health services, social services and voluntary agencies.

The differences between the models are found in the way that they construe the role of the patient, and in the range of care settings on which each depends. Model A involves coordination between just two sectors within health care: primary and secondary care. In contrast, Model B calls for coordinated action by players in general practice, community-based health services, acute care settings, social services and, potentially, multiple voluntary organizations.

The key issues in the shift from Model A to Model B become apparent when we consider the service design issues raised by people with long-term conditions. WHO defines long-term conditions as "health problems that require ongoing management over a period of years or decades" (WHO 2004). Long-term conditions[1] have significant deleterious effects on the lives of patients and their carers (Callery 1997; Olsson, Lexell & Soderberg 2005), the health care system (Wilson, Buck & Ham 2005) and society at large (United Kingdom DoWaP 2003; McIntyre et al. 2006; Wagner et al. 2001). The full scope of this impact becomes clear when we consider the size of the population affected. In England in 2001, for example, this was estimated to be 17.5 million people out of a population of 50 million (United Kingdom DoH 2004a).

Judged against the backdrop of a rapidly ageing population, these data point to the size and complexity of the service design issues that need to be addressed (United Kingdom DoH 2004a). Singh (2005) estimates that up to 80% of primary care consultations involve people with long-term conditions. Equally, as noted by Wilson, Buck and Ham (2005), 66% of emergency hospital admissions in England involve people with long-term conditions (see also

---

[1] Classic examples would be diabetes and asthma; but cancers and psychiatric diseases, along with many other conditions, share the same features, as does HIV.

United Kingdom DoH 2004a). The NHS Improvement Plan (England) notes that 5% of hospital admissions account for 42% of acute hospital bed-days and that a large proportion of these have two or more co-morbidities (United Kingdom DoH 2004b). A recent analysis of Health Episode Statistics (HES) data for England suggests that 15 of the top 40 health care resource groups (HRGs), accounting for 47% of emergency admissions, are related to long-term conditions (CCMD et al. 2005).

Much depends on how people with long-term conditions are "managed" in primary care (Wilson, Buck & Ham 2005). Noteworthy here are findings, illustrated in Fig. 2.1, which show how the rate of repeat emergency admissions for patients with chronic obstructive pulmonary disease (COPD) varies by general practice. These variations cannot be accounted for by factors, such as deprivation, list size or the demographics of individual practices (CCMD et al. 2005). In somewhat more circumspect terms, the National Public Health Service in Wales noted that "poor management of chronic conditions can lead to avoidable emergency admissions to hospitals ... (that) ... could be prevented if patients ... are well managed in primary, community and intermediate care" (National Public Health Service for Wales 2005).

"Avoidable admissions" are important because of the way that their occurrence impacts on the lives of people and carers, as well as on the wider health system. For a person with a long-term condition, an admission to hospital marks not merely an inconvenient disruption to their daily lives (as well as the lives of their carers), but may also represent a further decline in their general well-being (Chu et al. 2004; United Kingdom DoH 2004a). It is likely that their admission to hospital will have been occasioned by an acute exacerbation of their underlying condition. The repeated occurrence of such exacerbations can contribute to accelerating the deterioration of the condition (Chu et al. 2004).

Table 2.2 provides some indications of how "avoidable admissions" impact on the health system. It shows the estimated bed-day savings in seven NHS trusts in the United Kingdom, if readmission rates were reduced to the average for acute trusts in England.

Table 2.2 also indicates how current medical approaches to managing specific long-term conditions fall short of the ideal. The sources of this failure, at least in part, are found in conceptual, clinical and practical shortcomings that are inherent in the hospital based models that, until recently, have informed clinical service provision to people with long-term conditions. These models, which were oriented towards the treatment of clinical symptoms, have also, to a large extent, determined how service provision to people with long-term conditions was funded, organized and managed (WHO 2004).

**Fig. 2.1** *Repeat admission rates for chronic obstructive pulmonary disease, by GP practice in four English regional health economies*

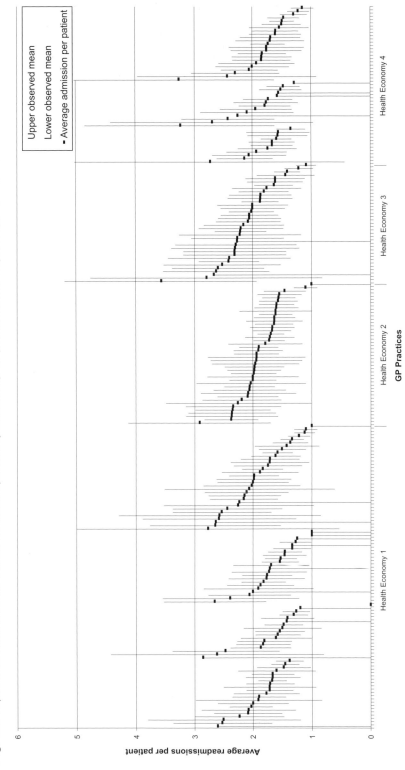

*Source:* NHS Health & Social Care Information Centre 2005.

*Notes:* The diagram shows repeat admission rates for individual GP practices in four health economies. The larger the confidence interval, the higher the variability of repeat admissions within the individual GP practice.

**Table 2.2** *Estimated bed-day savings per day in seven NHS trusts*

| | | % of emergency admissions that have higher-than-expected readmission rate | Potential bed-day savings for all emergency admissions (£) | Bed-day savings per day (£) | Savings as a % of total trusts' beds per day |
|---|---|---|---|---|---|
| Strategic Health Authority 1 | Trust 1 | 20 | 49 956 | 137 | 12 |
| | Trust 2 | 25 | 134 789 | 369 | 12 |
| | Trust 3 | 17 | 34 957 | 95 | 11 |
| Strategic Health Authority 2 | Trust 4 | 19 | 27 560 | 75 | 10 |
| | Trust 5 | 20 | 18 787 | 51 | 11 |
| | Trust 6 | 21 | 45 972 | 125 | 10 |
| | Trust 7 | 23 | 67 807 | 185 | 14 |

*Source*: CCMD et al. 2005.

The service modalities available to many people with long-term conditions are characterized by their high dependency on acute care, their singularly clinical focus, their reactive character, their fragmented and sporadic nature, their lack of emphasis on personal experience, and the residual character of community services and secondary prevention (Wilson, Buck & Ham 2005). All too often, the work of primary care is limited to haphazard monitoring and, at the onset of a crisis, acting as a referral point into hospital-based medical expertise. In addition, service providers in both acute and primary care are either ignorant of or ignore the potential and functional centrality of their patient's contributions to managing and determining both short and long-term outcomes (Gravel, Legare & Graham 2006; Lorig 2002).

These findings, together with similar results from other studies (Cretin, Shortell & Keeler 2004; Wagner et al. 2001; Singh & Ham 2006) demonstrate the clinical, social and resource utilization benefits that would derive from redesigning existing models of service delivery to people with long-term conditions (WHO 2004). Accordingly, at the core of Model B is a personalized care plan, jointly designed with a person with a long-term condition. This care plan outlines what the person will do to maintain or extend their health, and specifies the support that will be provided from multiple service settings within health, social services and the voluntary sector.

## The redistributive effects of service redesign

The potential benefits that will flow from service redesign along the lines envisaged in Model B do not, however, guarantee its adoption or smooth implementation. Redesigned services may undermine the standing of the existing hospital, and service redesign may be impeded or facilitated by context-specific structural factors, such as the degree of integration between acute, primary and social care, the funding available for each sector, hospital governance characteristics and the employment status of medical staff.

The perceived clinical standing of a locality's hospital, for example, is adversely affected by service models that concentrate highly specialized care in another locality. Somewhat similar processes are likely to ensue when service plans reduce a hospital's bed count, following a shift to day surgery, reductions in lengths of stay for admitted patients, or shifts from hospital to community-based settings in the service provision for people with long-term conditions.

The impact of these changes, however, goes beyond what they imply for a capital investment plan. Apart from the location, size and configuration of a hospital's buildings, all those employed within a hospital, as well as those in the wider community, also think and talk about their hospital as:

- a primary reference point for clinical referral networks
- a venue for building professional careers
- a locale for pursuing teaching and research
- a significant component of the local economy
- a reflector of community values and expectations
- a vehicle for demonstrating community spirit and private beneficence.

The availability of these "identities" and the way that they are mobilized indicate not only the range of players who can claim to have an interest in the future of their hospital, but also the institutionalized agendas and mobilizations of bias that underpin the centrality of the hospital in existing approaches to service delivery.

In addition to a hospital's contribution to the economy of its locality, its importance lies in the way that it symbolizes a community's solidarity, shared identity and history. It is not surprising that service models that threatened bed closures (and hence a hospital's perceived standing) will be judged in terms of their negative impact on wider local society. The referral patterns into a local hospital, based on existing service models, are the outcomes of long-established patterns of communication and influence. They also maintain existing patterns of resource allocation, not only between acute and primary care, but also between health and social care. As discussed earlier, with regard to existing approaches to managing long-term conditions, hospital-based doctors, by naming and framing the world in their terms, produce acute care-oriented assessments, diagnoses and solutions.

Not only are these accounts likely to be different from those put forward by people working in community medicine, social work and district nursing, in all likelihood they will also be to the benefit of acute care interests and concerns. Moreover, because preservation of existing service models of care is likely to be central to the career aspirations of hospital-based specialists, as for example represented by their involvement in teaching and research, it follows that new service models will be assessed not only in terms of improvements to access, appropriateness, quality and efficiency, but also in the way that their implementation will threaten significant aspects of what is already in place. Similar assessment criteria will be in play in general practice, community health care and social care, which – even if they stand to "benefit" from a change in service model – will nevertheless have to accept changes in behaviour and responsibilities.

Accordingly, successful implementation of community-based service models for long-term conditions will be determined by the changes that are implied for existing specialist service settings and by the number of organizational boundaries that will need to be traversed. The more individual settings are constituted as separate and distinct organizations (with their own history, accountability structure, distinct profession-based career structures and streams of funding), the more understandings will differ with regard to problem definition, possible interventions and role distribution (Birrell 2006; Currie & Suhomlinova 2006).

## The limitations of locality-based networks

Calls for locality-based partnerships and networks are a stock response to this fragmentation. More often than not, however, such calls ignore the underlying fragility of networks and the complexities of network formation and maintenance (Ansell 2000; Barringer & Harrison 2000; Kirkpatrick 1999). Efforts to establish and maintain networks are often purely rhetorical. While in some places much attention and energy is spent in meetings extolling the importance of partnership and collaboration and in devising and refining new structures and processes, all too often tangible achievements on the ground are minimal (Elston & Fulop 2002; Rodriguez et al. 2007).

The literature on how to address these gaps between promise and performance swings between two poles: one emphasizes the behavioural dimensions of effective networks and the second their structural preconditions. On the first issue, some studies have highlighted the pivotal role of managers of inter-organizational networks and the skills and competences they require in fulfilling their "boundary-spanning" roles (McGuire 2006; Noble & Jones

2006; Williams 2002). Other studies have identified the importance of factors such as trust and open communication, consensus about goals and the scope of the network, shared awareness of issues and strategies, and a willingness to establish and maintain relationships across organizational boundaries (Hudson 1987; Webb 1991).

This begs questions of why these common sense attributes are difficult to achieve. Much of the explanatory literature is limited by a tendency to treat surface symptoms as if they are root causes. For example, while uncertainty about the capability and reliability of other network partners is often cited as undermining trust, the range of factors that may be the source of this uncertainty remains unexamined (Shipilov, Rowley & Aharonson 2006; Tomlinson 2005). The cause of this shortfall lies in the inherently contingent character of network membership and the limited extent to which it will be a primary factor in how network partners structure and conduct their relations with others. Despite their membership in a network, for most network partners their employing organization remains their primary affiliation. They therefore remain part of the "mobilization of bias" that constitutes the substance and form of its day-to-day operations and is fundamental for its long-term survival (Birrell 2006; Currie & Suhomlinova 2006).

This means that neither network members nor the specialist organizations from which they are drawn are disposed to become what they are not, that is, to erase the frameworks, agendas and specialized regimens that differentiate them from others. They will rather do whatever is necessary to protect their organization's existing agendas, themes and patterns of resource allocation from threats that would arise if the concerns of other specialist organizations or the network were taken seriously. While this may include compliance with the requirement that they participate in a network, the outcomes produced will be limited to what is marginal to the core of their existing agendas (Degeling 1995; Stern & Green 2005).

In addition, the management styles of network partners' "home" organizations may affect their room for manoeuvre. In situations where the performance and the priorities of local operatives are subjected to tight hierarchical controls, their capacity to contribute creatively to joined-up working at a local level is constrained (Cowell & Martin 2003; Krott & Hasanagas 2006). The literature also shows how policy disjunctions at the centre reduce the functionality of locality-based networks. Put simply, effective joined-up "local-to-local" collaboration requires equivalent joined-up governance at the centre (Downe & Martin 2006; Exworthy & Powell 2004). Finally, there is evidence of how change in members' home organizations increases the fragility of local network arrangements and with it the level of trust between network partners. As field operatives become concerned about the career implications of changes in their home organizations, they understandably look inward and network partners wonder about who will be around to make good on commitments (McMurray 2007).

On a more hopeful note, other studies illustrate how trust between network partners and hence a network's stability depend on the network's past and continuing success in acquiring strategic resources. These might range from raising funds to gaining the attention and authoritative support of key players located within the organizational settings on which the network depends (De Wever, Martens & Vandenbempt 2005). On a different tack, there is evidence showing how trust and network stability depend on the extent to which network partners (by way of contracts) have formalized what they can expect of each other and have established robust governance arrangements through which partners can be held to account (Bryson, Crosby & Stone 2006; Marchington & Vincent 2004; Thomson & Perry 2006). These findings suggest that a network's effectiveness depends to a large extent on the degree to which its membership has been able to institutionalize both its internal operations and its independent existence from its sponsoring organizations.

## Contextual factors for service redesign

The implications of these considerations become clear when we compare how acute, primary and social care services are organized and funded in certain regions of England, Italy, the Netherlands, Northern Ireland and Spain (Table 2.3). This section draws to a large extent from the relevant analysis in chapters of the accompanying case studies volume.

As illustrated in Table 2.3, health and social care are separate in England. The fragmentation that this creates will increase, as hospitals are reconstituted as self-standing public interest companies and then funded (albeit out of the public purse) according to service ("Foundation Trust" status and "Payment by Results" (PbR)).

In Northern Ireland, community health and social care are part of single area-based administrative structures, to which local hospitals also belong. The potential for integration afforded by these arrangements is reinforced by the way that each element is funded from the public purse. While general practices within Northern Ireland may see themselves as standing outside of these arrangements, the fact that they are paid from the public purse, via a capitation system, affords policy and funding authorities some levers to influence their behaviour. Finally, signalling a shift in the underlying paradigm of service delivery, Northern Ireland has committed itself to building 35 community-

**Table 2.3** *System descriptors*

| Dimension | Characteristics | Northern Ireland | Netherlands | England | Spain (Valencia – Alzira Model) | Italy (Tuscany) |
|---|---|---|---|---|---|---|
| **Across systems integration** | Acute, primary and social care each operate as stand-alone systems | | X | X | | |
| | Acute and primary care run as parts of an integrated area-based system, with social care as a separate system | | | | X | X |
| | Acute, primary care and social care operate as parts of an integrated area-based system | X | | | | |
| **Hospital governance** | Private profit-making | | | | X[1] | |
| | Self-standing, non-profit-making, charity | | X | | | |
| | Public interest company (Foundation Trust) | | | X | | X |
| | Publicly owned and managed as part of an area-based service structure | X | | | | |
| **Hospital funding (recurrent expenditure)** | Activity-adjusted allocation from public funds via an area-based administrative structure | X | | | | |
| | Payment by occasion of service from public funds | | | X | | X |
| | Payment by occasion of service from insurance funds | | X | | | |
| | Direct payment from patient | | | | | |
| | (Fee-based) capitation | | | | X | |
| **General practice funding** | Capitation-based system from public funds | X | | X | X | X |
| | Payment by occasion of service from public funds | | | | | |
| | Payment by occasion of service from insurance funds | | X | | | |
| | Direct payment from patient | | | | | |

*Note*: [1] The private company running the primary and secondary care services in Valencia's "Alzira Model" does so on the basis of a capitation fee on behalf of the local authority: that is, private health care is provided under the umbrella of a public service administration.

based facilities, each serving a population of between 60 000 and 100 000. In addition to housing community health and social service staff, these new facilities also contain general practices, consulting rooms for use by hospital-based specialists, and dedicated spaces for local community services that might range from a Citizens' Advice Bureau to a local library.

In contrast, in the Netherlands, primary and social care operate as distinct systems, each with their own agendas, accountability arrangements, profession-based career structures and dedicated streams of funding. Similar sources of organizational differentiation will be found in the self-standing non-profit-making charities that are at the core of hospital care provision. Moreover, the service impact of these organizational separations will increase, as new market-based funding arrangements offer incentives to provider organizations either to shift costs or to compete with other service settings. The Maasland hospital in Sittard, the Netherlands, exemplifies the tensions involved in brokering the foregoing interests. The owners, Orbis Concern, have undertaken a replacement of the existing hospital on the basis of a business plan based on total systematization of care processes within the hospital environment and a shift towards providing only the core "clinical products" within the hospital per se. Departments such as diagnostics, imaging and rehabilitation are now seen as separate business units, constituted to service not only the Maasland hospital, but also a range of potential customers in the surrounding district. Orbis Concern recognizes the need for integration between acute and primary care and has developed an IT programme to link Dutch family doctor practices with the hospital's electronic patient records. However, the current organizational and financial environment stands in the way of this aim.

We see the same, partially realized drive towards an integrated service structure in the case of the "Alzira Model", as implemented by the autonomous community in Valencia, Spain. Here, a long-standing political commitment to provide a new development of approximately 220 000 people with a local acute care hospital, coupled with a shortfall in public capital investment funds, led to the local authority offering a ready-made hospital area for private tender. The winning organization (UTE-Ribera) committed to build and operate a new hospital, employing salaried clinical staff, on the basis of a capitation fee funding system. Some years into the first concession period, it became apparent that UTE-Ribera would not remain financially viable, while the boundaries between (public) primary care and (private) hospital services remained in place. A period of renegotiation saw the creation instead of an area-wide health care organization that spans both the primary care and acute sectors. In order to manage the flow of patients into the Hospital de la Ribera, and in line with a commitment to a care pathway-based service model, UTE-Ribera has since moved in the direction of enhanced primary care centres, and has (like Orbis Concern) made the electronic patient record a key integrating factor between the primary and secondary care sectors. However, social care remains outside the remit of UTE-Ribera, and it remains to be seen whether the current financial model will continue to be viable in the future.

Service redesign in Italy's Tuscany region provides an interesting contrast with Northern Ireland. The Italian NHS has been subject to successive waves of reform – administrative, financial and legislative – since the early 1990s. The result is that, while regulatory frameworks and standards are still set by central Government, regional governments across the country have a considerable element of autonomy in organizing social, primary and hospital care. In many regions, however, this overarching, cross-boundary responsibility has not resulted in an integrated service structure. This is due to many reasons, chief amongst them being the quasi-independent trust status afforded to many public hospitals; the mix of public, social fund and private payments for primary, secondary and tertiary care; and some degree of administrative and political inertia. Tuscany has tackled these barriers to redesign through adoption of a patient-centred, region-wide master plan for primary and hospital care. The region was faced with large numbers of small, outmoded district hospitals that were struggling to cope with increasing numbers of patients presenting with long-term conditions, and finding it increasingly difficult to recruit high-quality clinicians. In response, the Tuscan authorities drew up a radical plan for concentration of hospital resources in a smaller number of centres, a reduction in bed numbers, and an expansion of primary care and public health services. A large measure of public control of capital and recurrent expenditure has aided Tuscany in implementing this vision, but perhaps more important has been the evidence of political will and the determined engagement of senior clinicians. Ultimately, however, the long-term success of reform of health service provision here is dependent on a political determination that may not live long enough to embed the new, care pathway-oriented service settings. Furthermore, the complex mix of social care providers still acts as a barrier to a truly integrated health service capable of tacking the clinical and financial load related to chronic illness.

These experiences from across Europe suggest that efforts to implement the model of care for long-term conditions outlined in the early sections of this chapter are more likely to be successful in Northern Ireland than in England, Italy, the Netherlands or Spain. As noted earlier, the more that service settings (as between primary, acute, community and social services) are constituted as separate and distinct organizations, the more beliefs will differ about what should be done and who is best placed and equipped to do it. The "service gaps" that then result are unlikely to be resolved by, for example, "better networking". Because the new service models proposed for long-term conditions of necessity challenge the biases of existing approaches to service delivery in acute, community and social care settings, mere administrative solutions (such as the establishment of a network) are rarely able to produce what is required. Rather, policy and funding authorities are likely to find that success will depend on the extent to which they have set in place new institutional arrangements and patterns of resource allocation (including pre-eminently commitments of capital) that will support the required forms of service integration between different service settings. The extent to which policy and funding authorities are frustrated in this regard by system-wide factors will also be important, some of which (such as the recent adoption of market-based funding systems in England and the Netherlands) may be the consequence of their own policy decisions.

## Conclusions: implications for capital investment oriented towards service reform

Many of the case studies in the accompanying case studies volume, as well as other chapters of this volume, reflect broad similarities in the challenges facing health care in Europe with respect to pressures to improve the technical and allocative efficiency of service delivery, as well as service quality and appropriateness. The material also indicates growing recognition of how the physical characteristics of existing health facilities may have contributed to shaping the prevailing approaches to service delivery that are the focus of current programmes of reform.

As demonstrated earlier, recognition of these linkages does not mean, however, that past capital investment strategies are the unique source of the problems that policy and funding authorities are seeking to address, nor will any new strategies be sufficient to correct the problems.

As demonstrated by this chapter, how clinical work has been performed, organized and accounted for in health care settings was a direct by-product of the privileged standing that was, until recently, accorded to medicine as a whole and the hospital setting in particular. The community-based modalities of service provision that characterize new service models for long-term conditions are not something that can be bolted on to what is already in place. As demonstrated earlier, successful implementation requires not merely displacing existing medically centred and hospital-dominated approaches to service delivery, but also acceptance of the desirability of this move by hospital-based clinicians and managers. Also important will be the development of alternative structures and processes, which, by blurring boundaries between primary, community and social care, promotes levels of service integration between these settings that hitherto are far too fragmentary. Moreover, the success of these efforts will likely depend on the extent to which policies on other fronts either provide incentives for transcending existing tendencies towards service fragmentation or exacerbate these. Accordingly, while increasing the priority and amount of capital devoted to primary and community care settings will help support the community-based models of service provision envisaged for long-term conditions, this of itself will not be sufficient.

# References

Ansell C (2000). The networked polity: regional development in Western Europe. *Governance – An International Journal of Policy and Administration*, 13(3):303–333.

Barringer BR, Harrison JS (2000). Walking a tightrope: creating value through interorganizational relationships. *Journal of Management*, 26(3):367–403.

Birrell D (2006). The disintegration of local authority social services departments. *Local Government Studies*, 32(2):139–151.

Bryson JM, Crosby BC, Stone MM (2006). The design and implementation of cross-sector collaborations: propositions from the literature. *Public Administration Review*, 66:44–55.

Callery P (1997). Paying to participate: financial, social and personal costs to parents of involvement in their children's care in hospital. *Journal of Advanced Nursing*, 25(4):746–752.

CCMD et al. (2005). *Improving clinical management: the role of the ICP-based clinical management systems*. A report of the Clinical Management Development Project. Durham, University of Durham Centre for Clinical Management Development.

Chu CM et al. (2004). Re-admission rates and life-threatening events in COPD survivors treated with non-invasive ventilation for acute hypercapnic respiratory failure. *Thorax*, 59:1002–1025.

Cowell R, Martin S (2003). The joy of joining up: modes of integrating the local government modernisation agenda. *Environment and Planning C: Government and Policy*, 21(2):159–179.

Cretin S, Shortell SM, Keeler EB (2004). An evaluation of collaborative interventions to improve chronic illness care. *Evaluation Review*, 28(1):28–51.

Currie G, Suhomlinova O (2006). The impact of institutional forces upon knowledge sharing in the UK NHS: the triumph of professional power and the inconsistency of policy. *Public Administration*, 84(1):1–30.

De Wever S, Martens R, Vandenbempt K (2005). The impact of trust on strategic resource acquisition through interorganizational networks: towards a conceptual model. *Human Relations*, 58(12):1523–1543.

Degeling P (1995). The significance of sectors in calls for urban public health intersectoralism: an Australian perspective. *Policy and Politics*, 23(4):289–301.

Downe J, Martin S (2006). Joined up policy in practice? The coherence and impacts of the local government modernization agenda. *Local Government Studies*, 32(4):465–488.

Elston J, Fulop N (2002). Perceptions of partnership. A documentary analysis of health improvement programmes. *Public Health*, 116(4):207–213.

Exworthy M, Powell M (2004). Big windows and little windows: implementation in the 'congested state'. *Public Administration*, 82(2):263–281.

Gravel K, Legare F, Graham ID (2006). Barriers and facilitators to implementing shared decision-making in clinical practice: a systematic review of health professionals' perceptions. *Implementation Science*, 1(16):1–15.

Hudson B (1987). Collaboration in social welfare: a framework for analysis. *Policy and Politics*, 15(3):175–182.

Kirkpatrick I (1999). The worst of both worlds? Public services without markets or bureaucracy. *Public Money and Management*, 19(4):7–14.

Krott M, Hasanagas ND (2006). Measuring bridges between sectors: causative evaluation of cross-sectorality. *Forest Policy and Economics*, 8(5):555–563.

Lorig K (2002). Partnerships between expert patients and physicians. *Lancet*, 359(9309):814–815.

Marchington M, Vincent S (2004). Analysing the influence of institutional, organizational and interpersonal forces in shaping inter-organizational relations. *Journal of Management Studies*, 41(6):1029–1056.

McGuire M (2006). Collaborative public management: assessing what we know and how we know it. *Public Administration Review*, 66:33–43.

McIntyre D et al. (2006). What are the economic consequences for households of illness and of paying for health care in developing country contexts? *Social Science and Medicine*, 62:858–865.

McMurray R (2007). Our reforms, our partnerships, same problems: the chronic case of the English NHS. *Public Money and Management*, 27(1):77–82.

National Public Health Service for Wales (2005). *A profile of long-term and chronic conditions in Wales*. Cardiff, National Public Health Service for Wales.

NHS Health & Social Care Information Centre (2005). *Hospital episode statistics*. Durham, University of Durham Centre for Clinical Management Development.

Noble G, Jones R (2006). The role of boundary-spanning managers in the establishment of public–private partnerships. *Public Administration*, 84(4):891–917.

Olsson M, Lexell J, Soderberg S (2005). The meaning of fatigue for women with multiple sclerosis. *Journal of Advanced Nursing*, 49(1):7–15.

Rodriguez C et al. (2007). Governance, power, and mandated collaboration in an interorganizational network. *Administration & Society*, 39(2):150–193.

Shipilov AV, Rowley TJ, Aharonson BS (2006). When do networks matter? A study of tie formation and decay. *Ecology and Strategy*, 23:481–519.

Singh D (2005). *Transforming chronic care: evidence about improving care for people with long-term conditions*. Birmingham, University of Birmingham and Surrey and Sussex PCT Alliance.

Singh D, Ham C (2006). *Improving care for people with long term conditions: a review of UK and international frameworks*. Birmingham, University of Birmingham Health Services Management Centre & NHS Institute for Innovation and Improvement.

Stern R, Green J (2005). Boundary workers and the management of frustration: a case study of two Healthy City partnerships. *Health Promotion International*, 20(3):269–276.

Thomson AM, Perry JL (2006). Collaboration processes: inside the black box. *Public Administration Review*, 66:20–32.

Tomlinson F (2005). Idealistic and pragmatic versions of the discourse of partnership. *Organization Studies*, 26(8):1169–1188.

United Kingdom DoH (2004a). *Improving chronic disease management. A note for PCT, NHS Trust and SHA management teams*. London, United Kingdom Department of Health.

United Kingdom DoH (2004b). *The NHS improvement plan: putting people at the heart of public services*. London, Her Majesty's Stationery Office.

United Kingdom DoWaP (2003). *Incapacity benefit and severe disablement allowance: quarterly summary statistics*. London, United Kingdom Department of Work and Pensions.

Wagner EH et al. (2001). Quality improvement in chronic illness care: a collaborative approach. *Joint Commission Journal on Quality Improvement*, 27(2):63–80.

Webb A (1991). Coordination: a problem in public-sector management. *Policy and Politics*, 19(4):229–241.

WHO (2004). *Chronic conditions: the global burden*. Geneva, World Health Organization.

Williams P (2002). The competent boundary spanner. *Public Administration*, 80(1):103–124.

Wilson T, Buck D, Ham C (2005). Rising to the challenge: will the NHS support people with long term conditions? [Review]. *British Medical Journal*, 330(7492):657–661.

# Part two:
# Influencing capital investment

# Chapter 3

# Planning health care capacity: whose responsibility?

*Stefanie Ettelt, Martin McKee, Ellen Nolte, Nicholas Mays, Sarah Thomson*

## Introduction

Most industrialized countries share the vision that publicly funded health care should provide a comprehensive range of clinically effective services, cover the entire population, and strive for continued improvements in standards of quality, equity and responsiveness of care. They differ in how and by whom these goals are to be achieved. However, while the details vary, there is a widespread acceptance of the need for a mechanism to plan how health facilities should be configured to achieve these goals.

This chapter describes the arrangements for planning health care capacity that are in place in nine industrialized countries, seven of which are in Europe and two (Canada and New Zealand) beyond. They include countries that are constitutionally federal (such as Germany) and unitary (such as England), and ones that plan health services at different levels or none. While not claiming to be comprehensive, the chapter offers a broad cross-section of the approaches taken in western Europe and North America. It also draws, where relevant, on evidence from other countries and especially those in CEE.

The chapter is, of necessity, essentially descriptive. A key message that emerges is the need for research on whether some approaches are better than others. The absence of such research is symptomatic of a general failure to learn lessons from the diversity of health care provision in Europe.

## Is planning really necessary?

While, as noted earlier, almost all industrialized countries have some mechanism for planning health care capacity, support for planning is not universally shared among commentators on health policy. The critics of planning largely base their argument on a belief that planners, who may be remote from the delivery of care, are unable to detect and respond to the signals emerging from the health care market. As a consequence, their plans, which may cover many years, may be insufficiently adaptable to emerging needs. At its purest, this view would leave the organization of health care facilities to the market, with those that are responding to need thriving, while those that do not would disappear.

The opposing argument relies on four main considerations. The first is that asymmetry of information pervades health care. A patient may know that they are ill, but may not know why. The physician may know why that patient is ill, but may know nothing about those individuals with similar complaints who did not consult their physician. That physician may also know what s/he can do for the patient, but not how to configure the complex network of services that they may require from others, including, potentially, a range of different specialists and therapists. This is especially so for rare conditions that an individual physician may see only a few times in a professional career, but which, collectively, may place substantial and often highly specific demands upon health systems.

The challenges arising from asymmetry of information are compounded by the increasing complexity of modern health care. The modern hospital is expected to manage patients with a wide range of problems and the services required to do so are often intimately interconnected. Obviously, a neonatal intensive care unit would be of little value in the absence of an obstetrics unit. However, some interrelationships are less obvious. This can be illustrated by the example of major trauma, where, for example, a family injured in a traffic accident may require the skills of orthopaedic, plastic, abdominal and ophthalmological surgeons, anaesthetists, microbiologists and haematologists, as well as a range of specialist nurses and paramedical staff. The combination of information asymmetry and the need for complex responses involving many different actors means that market signals will be attenuated severely and will be most unlikely to yield the optimal result in the absence of a planning mechanism.

From this perspective, the benefits of a planning approach can be seen in France, where regional hospital agencies, operating in a system where there is extensive private provision alongside public facilities, created new centres specializing in the management of two complex conditions, HIV/AIDS and cancer (McKee & Healy 2002b). They are also apparent from a comparison of neonatal intensive care in the Trent region of England, where services were provided in a number of small hospitals, and in the state of Victoria, in Australia, where planning of provision had concentrated services into a single unit. Mortality among infants admitted to an intensive care unit in Trent was twice as high as in Victoria (odds ratio 2.09, 95% confidence intervals 1.37–3.19) (Pearson et al. 1997).

A second consideration is that, in the absence of intervention, there will be cream-skimming. Left to their own devices, individual providers will seek to maximize revenue and minimize uncertainty by treating the least complex conditions. This is apparent when contrasting the willingness of private providers in some countries to enter the market to offer non-urgent surgery to low-risk patients or disease management programmes for patients with a single disorder with their reluctance to offer services for managing patients with complex and unpredictable needs, such as major genetic disorders or multiple co-morbidities. In the absence of intervention, it may be difficult to provide any services, and especially appropriately integrated ones, for the latter groups of patients (Nolte & McKee 2008). Cream-skimming may also exclude patients who are considered "difficult" in other ways. Thus, for several centuries, and long before states established comprehensive health care systems, authorities (often at town or city level) planned and implemented services for those with mental disorders, whose needs the market would not have met. Today, similar considerations might apply to migrants, especially where linguistic and cultural differences make the delivery of care more difficult (McKee 2008). Even in countries that have universal health coverage, a failure to plan for migrants' needs has meant that they depend on services provided by groups such as Médecins sans Frontières.

A third consideration is the presence of supplier-induced demand. In many middle-income countries, where planning mechanisms are rudimentary or exclude major elements of the health care sector, investment in facilities is often driven by the scope for maximizing financial return on investment, regardless of the appropriateness of care. Such systems are characterized by a high density of sophisticated diagnostic equipment such as MRI scanners, while basic needs are unmet (Hutubessy, Hanvoravongchai & Edejer 2002). Overprovision of such equipment creates a powerful incentive for inappropriate usage. Thus, in the unplanned cervical screening activity that takes place in Germany, where screening is opportunistic and there are no call and recall systems, a typical German woman may have up to 50 cervical smears over the course of a lifetime, compared with only seven in Finland (Zatonski, personal communication). Yet the death rate from cervical cancer in Finland is half that in Germany (WHO Regional Office for Europe 2008).

This has led, in some countries, to controls on the purchase of advanced technology, sometimes referred to as Certificate of Need schemes. In American states that have such schemes, cancer care is concentrated in fewer hospitals (Short, Aloia & Ho 2008). This assumes importance in the light of evidence that hospitals with higher volumes achieve better outcomes for many common cancers. Similarly, survival following coronary artery bypass grafting has been shown to be higher in American states with such schemes (Vaughan-Sarrazin et al. 2002), although more recent data, following implementation of a range of other measures that has reduced the number of low-volume providers, suggest that the gap has now closed (DiSesa et al. 2006).

Finally, the provision of health care involves long lag periods. A decision today to increase the number of health professionals being trained will not show results for many years. It may take a decade or more from the decision to build a new hospital to actually opening it to patients. Waiting for signals from the market to become apparent may be too late.

Together, these factors explain why all industrialized countries have established some form of planning for health care facilities, although its extent and nature vary considerably.

## Where should planning take place and who should do it?

Health services must respond to the needs of people with many different conditions, some of which are common, while others are extremely rare. Self-evidently, planning services for common conditions can be undertaken within territories with small populations. Thus, it would not be unreasonable for the distribution of primary care facilities to be planned for a population of perhaps 300 000, while services for genetic disorders may more appropriately be planned for a population of 10 million or more. From a purely theoretical perspective, it would be possible to construct a graph plotting frequency of a disorder against the optimal population aggregation for planning.

This would, however, ignore geographical and political realities. Small countries still have to plan services for rare conditions, even though their population may produce only a few cases each year (and in this case, planning may lead to a decision to obtain care abroad, in centres where the case load is sufficient to ensure sufficient experience and hence quality). The loci for health care decision-making often reflect administrative boundaries that were created for very different reasons.

Although it is conventional to divide administrations into three tiers – national, regional and municipal – European comparisons are problematic because of the particularly diverse nature of the territories involved. Again, using the example of Germany, *Länder* vary in size from 1 million population (Saarland) to 18 million (North-Rhine Westphalia). Comparisons among countries are further complicated by the different levels of decision-making power, with power in some states being centralized, whereas others are federations or even (as in Switzerland) a confederation. The situation is even more complicated in the United Kingdom, where the Scottish Government and the Northern Ireland Assembly have greater powers than the Welsh Assembly and where legislation on health care in England is decided by Scottish, Welsh and Northern Irish Members of the Parliament (MPs) at Westminster, as well as by English MPs.

Given this complexity, some simplification is essential to even begin to describe the systems in place. For the purpose of this chapter, "regional authorities" comprise regional or provincial governments within federal states, as well as regional or district health authorities (that is, arm's length bodies with mainly appointed members). "Regions" refer to geographical areas as diverse as Canadian provinces, German *Länder*, Danish counties and New Zealand's health districts. "Local authorities" refer to bodies responsible for organizing health care at a lower level, again representing diverse entities responsible for populations of varying sizes. Table 3.1 provides an overview of tiers of health care governance at the regional and local level in nine countries.

**Table 3.1** *Tiers of health care capacity planning in nine countries*

| Country | Regional authorities | Local authorities |
|---|---|---|
| Canada | Provincial/territorial governments | Regional health authorities (where applicable) |
| Denmark | Regional councils | Municipal councils |
| England | Strategic health authorities | Primary care trusts |
| Finland | Hospital district councils and executive boards | Municipal councils |
| France | Regional hospital agencies | Not applicable |
| Germany | *Länder* governments | District, town and city councils (if involved in planning) |
| Italy | Regional governments | Local health units |
| Netherlands | Devolved to regional hospital associations (acute sector) | Not applicable |
| New Zealand | District health boards | Primary health care organizations |

In the absence of empirical evidence about which level of planning is best, the most that can be done is to describe the arrangements that countries have put in place. Of those considered in this chapter (which excludes the smaller countries of Europe, many of which will, of necessity, engage in planning at national level), most locate health care capacity planning at the regional level, with local (municipality) authorities also playing an important role, in Denmark and Finland for example (Table 3.2).

Regional/local planning entities may or may not overlap with regional/local political structures; some countries have established regional/local (elected and/or appointed) bodies that are exclusively responsible for health care (such as hospital district councils in Finland, regional hospital agencies in France, SHAs and Primary Care Trusts (PCTs) in England and district health boards in New Zealand). In all cases, the precise arrangements derive from the nature of political decentralization within the country, which may involve devolution to elected bodies; deconcentration, with regional branches of central government; or delegation to para-state bodies such as insurers and provider associations.

The Netherlands provides an example of a country that has largely liberalized capacity planning in the health care sector. The central government is responsible for the overall health system; however, it is not directly involved in health care planning and neither are its relevant tiers at the provincial and local levels. Following the 2006 health care reform, planning of acute health care has been devolved to regional hospital associations (in collaboration with health insurers), subject to government approval. The gradual abolition of

**Table 3.2** *Lead responsibility for capacity planning*

| Country | Lead responsibility for capacity planning |
| --- | --- |
| Canada | Planning is the responsibility of the provinces/territories, guided in some cases by national frameworks with participation from local authorities |
| Denmark | Counties and municipalities plan different areas of health care autonomously with some central supervision |
| England | National and regional planning directed by the central Government with participation of local authorities |
| Finland | Planning is a responsibility of municipalities and hospital districts (formed by municipalities) |
| France | Regional hospital agencies plan hospital care within a centrally set framework in consultation with regional stakeholders |
| Germany | *Länder* governments plan hospital care based on national and regional legislation in consultation with regional stakeholders |
| Italy | Regional governments plan health care (mainly hospital care) guided by a national health plan |
| Netherlands | Regional provider organizations plan acute hospital care (but require approval from the central Government) |
| New Zealand | Responsibility for planning is shared by the central Government and district health boards |

governmental planning in the Netherlands since the 1980s reflects a political climate that favours regulated market forces over central control.

The extent to which non-state organizations are involved in planning also seems to reflect decisions made for other reasons. Active involvement of provider associations in the planning process is also characteristic of France and Germany, two countries with a strong corporatist tradition. Involvement, usually through consultation, of the general public and other stakeholders such as the health professions, forms an integral part of the planning process in England, Italy and New Zealand, although long-standing statutory bodies designed to give the public a voice in service configuration have recently been abolished in England. In Denmark and Finland, public involvement in planning is mainly through representation by elected members of county and municipality boards.

So where should planning take place and who should do it? The answer is clearly "it depends". A fundamental consideration is the nature of government in the country concerned and, especially, the extent to which health care is retained centrally or devolved to regions. This, in turn, is a function of the size of the country, although as experience in countries such as England and Denmark shows, this can change as a consequence of administrative reform. In general, most large countries have devolved responsibility to some form of regional entity. Where responsibility is devolved to smaller entities, as with the Finnish municipalities, there is a tendency to form regional groupings. However, such arrangements must have a degree of flexibility and, even in countries where there is a high degree of devolution, it will often be necessary for regional bodies to work together to plan the provision of the most specialized services, where only one or a few facilities are required nationally.

## Strategic and operational planning

Conceptually, planning is associated with two different functions: strategic and operational planning (Figueras 1993). *Strategic planning* involves framework setting and the definition of the principles of the health system and its general directions. Strategic planning is most frequently undertaken by authorities at the highest level of health system governance, such as the national Ministry of Health (England, France, Italy, New Zealand) or the respective regional or local tier in decentralized systems (provincial/territorial governments and regional health authorities in Canada; federal states in Germany (hospital care only)) (Table 3.3). In contrast, there is only limited central strategic planning in Denmark and Finland, where planning has been devolved to regional and local authorities. The degree of involvement of lower-level administrations in strategic planning will, to a large extent, be determined by their level of autonomy and decision-making power(s).

**Table 3.3** *Types of planning/functions of health plans*

| Country | National plan(s) | Regional plan(s) | Local plan(s) | Relationship between planning levels |
|---|---|---|---|---|
| Canada | not applicable | Strategic | Strategic and operational | Vertical integration |
| Denmark | not applicable | Operational | Operational | Coordinated but separate plans |
| England | Strategic | Strategic and operational | Operational with some local strategy | Vertical integration |
| Finland | not applicable | Operational | Operational | No integration |
| France | Strategic | Strategic and operational | not applicable | Vertical integration |
| Germany | not applicable | Strategic and operational | not applicable | No integration |
| Italy | Strategic | Strategic and operational | not applicable | Vertical integration |
| Netherlands | not applicable | not available | not applicable | not applicable |
| New Zealand | Strategic | Strategic and operational | not applicable | Vertical integration |

*Operational planning* aims to translate the strategic plan into activities, which may cover the whole range of operations involved in health care provision, including the allocation of budgets and resources, the organization of services, and the provision of staff, facilities and equipment. This function is most often carried out by regional authorities but may also involve local authorities (such as regional health authorities in Canada; municipalities in Denmark and Finland; PCTs in England).

A key consideration is the extent to which strategic and operational plans are integrated. A few countries have established explicit mechanisms for this to take place, while respecting the different political competences at each administrative or political tier. In some cases, national health plans require that regional authorities integrate, to varying degrees, their health plans with the national strategies (*vertical integration*). This is the case in England, France, Italy (Box 3.1) and New Zealand, as well as in Canada, where regional health authorities have to adopt and implement health plans developed by provincial/territorial governments.

In Denmark, different levels within the system are responsible for different sectors of health care, with regions planning most areas of health care, while municipalities are in charge of preventive medicine, health promotion and (non-hospital based) rehabilitation.

> **Box 3.1** *Vertical integration of planning in Italy*
>
> Responsibility for health care planning in Italy is shared between the central Government and the regions. The Ministry of Health sets the basic framework and develops a 3-year national health plan. The plan sets out the national health strategy, including a definition of health care objectives, targets and performance indicators. A benefits package which must be made available to all residents in the country (*Livelli Essenziali di Assistenza*) is defined nationally and updated regularly (France & Taroni 2005). Regional health departments are involved in the production of national strategies and plans. However, once finalized, the national health plan is binding for regional health authorities and its implementation is monitored by the Ministry of Health in Rome.
>
> Regional health departments then translate the national plan into regional health plans. Within the boundaries established by the national framework, the regions organize care according to their own needs and define their own objectives, provided they meet the targets set out in the national plan. Not all national objectives are binding; it has been suggested that regional health departments tend to adopt those targets that suit their regional needs and local political agendas (France & Taroni 2000), illustrating the challenge of central target-setting in a largely decentralized health system.

## What facilities should be included in the plan?

In most countries considered here, hospital capacity planning includes all hospitals that have an agreement or a contract with a (usually) regional authority. While the nature and scope of agreements and contracts differs, reflecting the plurality of approaches, they most commonly include some form of agreement on funding and on the conditions (and sometimes volume) for service provision, thereby establishing a link between public resource allocation and the implementation of regional health plans.

In all countries, planning is mainly focused on hospitals. Regional or national planning is only seen in the ambulatory care sector in Denmark, England, New Zealand and, to some extent, Finland (Table 3.4).

Countries vary in the extent to which planning includes both public and private (profit-making and non-profit-making) providers, mainly (although not always) reflecting whether private providers qualify for reimbursement under the public system. Thus, hospital and health plans in Canada, France, Germany and Italy incorporate both public and private hospitals, whereas planning in Denmark, England, Finland and New Zealand mainly applies to public facilities. In England the position is changing, as more private providers enter the market, and they will need to be included in capacity planning.

**Table 3.4** *Scope of planning and sectors covered*

| Country | Scope and sectors |
|---|---|
| Canada | Planning of hospital care (public and private providers); no planning in ambulatory care |
| Denmark | Planning of all areas of care, including ambulatory care provided by self-employed doctors and public hospital care |
| England | Planning of hospital and ambulatory care provided in the NHS |
| Finland | Planning of care provided in public hospitals and some planning of ambulatory care provided by self-employed doctors |
| France | Planning of hospital care only (public and private hospitals) |
| Germany | Planning of hospital care only (public and private hospitals) |
| Italy | Planning of hospital care only (public and private hospitals) |
| Netherlands | Limited planning of (acute) hospital care |
| New Zealand | Planning of hospital care provided in the public sector and ambulatory care provided by self-employed doctors |

*Note*: NHS: National Health Service.

Integrated plans must not only consider the public–private mix. In some countries, responsibility for health facilities is widely dispersed within the public sector (Gaál 2004). An example is Hungary, where county governments own large multi-specialty county hospitals that provide secondary and tertiary inpatient and outpatient care, while municipalities own polyclinics, single-specialty dispensaries and some multi-specialty hospitals. Several national ministries also own hospitals, including the ministries of health, defence, interior, and justice. Teaching hospitals are owned by the Ministry of Education. There is a widespread consensus that there is a need for major reconfiguration, although the plethora of actors involved in this has made it difficult to achieve; a situation complicated further by continuing controversy over changes to health care financing. A similar situation exists in other countries of central Europe (Rokosová et al. 2005). A review of hospital reconfiguration in western Europe concluded that this was most difficult where ownership of facilities was highly dispersed (Healy & McKee 2002).

Clearly, there is a strong argument for taking a whole system perspective when planning, although the extent to which this is possible will obviously depend on the regulatory norms in existence. There is a particularly strong argument for including the entire spectrum of care, from ambulatory to highly specialized care. The changing role of the hospital, with many traditionally hospital-based services now being provided in ambulatory care facilities, means that plans confined to hospitals will be increasingly limited in scope.

## What should be planned?

Hospital planning has several dimensions, including: planning of capital investment in existing facilities and new developments; investment in expensive equipment and technology (such as MRI scanners); service delivery; and allocation of human and financial resources.

Most countries plan the number of hospitals and the amount of capital made available for investment in these facilities, as well as investment in expensive equipment. However, there is considerable variation in the scope and detail of planning. Some health plans outline the number and location of facilities only, mostly based on existing structures. An example is the Bulgarian National Health Map, created at a time when funds for investment were limited and ad hoc in nature. This simply provided a basis for future plans (Georgieva et al. 2007). Others take planning much further, determining in detail the number and design of specialty departments and their geographical distribution within a defined area. Traditionally, bed capacity has been the preferred unit of planning. Finland, Italy and New Zealand, as well as most provinces/territories in Canada and most *Länder* in Germany, still use bed capacity as their preferred unit for planning hospital care on a specialty basis. England and France, in contrast, have recently departed from this approach by substituting bed capacity with service volumes and activity in certain health service sectors.

This makes sense given the decreasing relevance of hospital beds as a measure of health care capacity. It is also important, when engaging in international comparisons, to be aware that what is included in reported figures varies considerably (McKee 2004).

A notable feature of most existing approaches to planning is that they are based on structures (typically expressed in terms of inpatient bed numbers or items of equipment, such as scanners) rather than on clinical processes. A rare exception is in Northern Ireland, as described in the accompanying case studies volume. There, the Integrated Clinical Assessment and Treatment Services (ICATS) initiative has been used to redesign the way in which services are accessed, beginning with the patient journey. It seeks to ensure that patients are referred through the most appropriate step(s) in the care pathway, with services provided by integrated multidisciplinary teams of health service professionals working in a variety of primary, community and secondary care settings. Where possible, when patients must see a hospital specialist, all the necessary diagnostic tests will be completed first.

The approach (Fig. 3.1) takes account of the distribution of population in Northern Ireland, which is concentrated in the urban area surrounding Belfast, while the west of the province is sparsely populated. It envisages one regional

**Fig. 3.1** *Health service infrastructure in Northern Ireland*

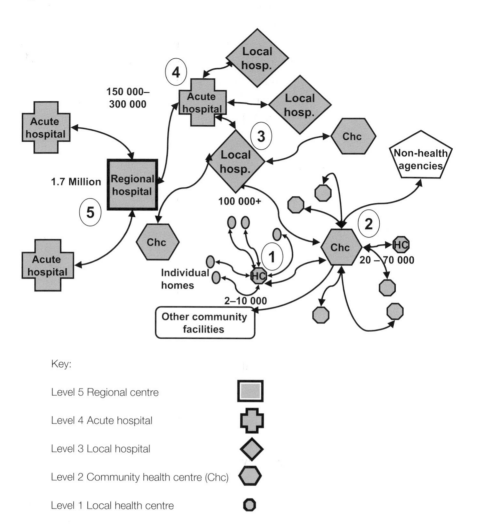

Key:

Level 5 Regional centre

Level 4 Acute hospital

Level 3 Local hospital

Level 2 Community health centre (Chc)

Level 1 Local health centre

*Source*: DHSSPS 2002.

acute hospital providing comprehensive specialist services for Northern Ireland's 1.7 million population. Acute hospitals will serve a population of 150 000– 300 000 and will provide emergency departments, acute medicine and surgery, paediatric care, and diagnostic facilities. Local hospitals, serving a population of approximately 100 000, will provide ambulatory surgery and diagnostics, urgent (but not emergency) care, and rehabilitation facilities. Health centres will include an enhanced range of treatment and diagnostic provision.

A similar approach has been taken in Estonia, although confined to hospitals. The newly independent Estonian Government inherited 120 hospitals in 1991, many of which were obsolete. A series of reconfigurations and mergers reduced the total to 50, a process that is continuing in the 2003 Hospital Network Development Plan. This envisages a hierarchy of hospitals of differing levels of complexity. Regional hospitals will be located in the capital, Tallinn, and the university city of Tartu, with other major settlements served by central hospitals, supported by general and local hospitals in smaller settlements. The country is divided into a number of catchment areas, and the location of hospitals has been chosen so that acute care is available to everyone at a distance of 70 km or 60 minutes' drive (Koppel et al. 2008).

## Planning of capital investments

Major capital investments in hospital infrastructure are usually regulated and planned separately from operational procedures and, where these apply, operational budgets. In Denmark, Finland, Germany and Italy new hospital developments and major restructuring projects are funded and planned at the regional level, that is, by county councils (to be transferred to regions), hospital districts, ministries of the *Länder* and regional health departments, respectively. In France (Box 3.2) and New Zealand (Box 3.3) hospital plans are developed at regional level but within a national framework. In most countries, regional and (sometimes) national authorities are also involved in financing major investments and thus are accountable to taxpayers and other stakeholders. An alternative approach is taken in the Netherlands, where hospital developments and investments are entirely privately financed, leaving the financial responsibility primarily with the provider. The growing importance of private funding sources is also apparent in other countries; in Canada, investments in hospitals are frequently supported by charitable funds linked to individual hospitals.

Procedures for capital and investment planning vary significantly between countries. Many apply different mechanisms for long-term and short-term investment planning. In Finland, for example, long-term investments covering a period of up to 10 years are planned and overseen by the hospital districts, whereas short-term (typically smaller) investments are usually proposed by sub-districts, although subject to approval by the hospital district.

## Health workforce planning

Although most countries regulate entry into the medical profession and control medical student numbers, there is an increasing awareness that this may not be sufficient to respond to future challenges facing the health care workforce. The need for workforce planning is driven by demand- and supply-side

---

**Box 3.2** *Planning of activity volumes in France*

In France, regional hospital authorities develop regional health plans (*Schéma régional d'organisation sanitaire,* SROS) in consultation with the Ministry of Health and with other regional actors, such as the regional representation of health professions, the public and private hospital federations, patient representatives and politicians (Republique Française 2005). The regional health plans are the key instrument for hospital planning. They specify the number of facilities in each region and subregion per area of care, such as in general medicine, surgery, maternity care, intensive and emergency care and many others. They also define the amount of expensive technical equipment such as MRI scanners. For certain types of services, the SROS also defines volumes of activities to be provided within a region. These volumes can refer to a variety of units, including the number of patients to be treated, the number of sites, days (length of stay), performed procedures and admissions (ARHIF 2006). By planning volumes of hospital capacity, France has amended its previous approach to planning bed capacity in an attempt to address perceived overcapacity of hospital services in some regions.

---

**Box 3.3** *Planning capital investments in New Zealand*

In New Zealand the planning function is shared by the central Government and 21 district health boards. Health care planning is embedded in a legislative framework that defines the accountability of the district health boards, requiring them, among other things, to produce a 5-year strategic health plan, annual statements of intent, annual operational plans and regular monthly and quarterly reports.

District health boards must also provide a strategic asset financing plan and a strategic asset management plan to ensure that investment decisions are well informed (Ministry of Health 2003). Asset management plans must be updated regularly and sent annually to the Ministry of Health in Wellington. A national capital plan, developed by the Ministry of Health, outlines the long-term investment needs of the public element of the health sector for a period of 10 years. Capital investments by the district health boards require the approval of the Ministry of Health and the Treasury, if investments exceed a threshold of NZD 10 million (approximately € 5.3 million) or 20% of total assets of the district health boards, if the investment requires Crown equity support, or if it potentially affects the performance of the district health boards.

---

developments, including ageing populations, rising demand for health care, an increasingly mobile and (at the same time) ageing workforce, as well as changes in skill mix and training requirements. However, despite some efforts to address the issue, only a few countries have as yet engaged in systematic planning of the health care workforce or at least subsections thereof (such as in Canada).

## The changing environment

As illustrated in previous sections, any approach to health care planning will reflect, to a considerable extent, the health system's institutional, legislative and regulatory framework as determined by the wider political, social, economical and cultural system. As a consequence, processes of and approaches to planning will often be influenced by changes that, in their intention, have little to do with the health sector. For example, the 2007 reform of the administrative system in Denmark merged counties to form larger regions and the redistribution of responsibility for health care between regions and municipalities. This had a significant impact on the approach to capacity planning.

Administrative decentralization in the health sector is another development affecting health care planning. Thus, in Italy regionalization has transferred major responsibility for planning from the centre to the regions (see Chapter 10 by Watson & Agger). Similarly, in France, responsibility for planning and organizing hospital care has been transferred from the central health ministry to regional authorities (Sandier, Paris & Polton 2004). However, the French Government has retained an overall steering role.

Conversely, some countries with a strong tradition of decentralization have experienced increased levels of central government involvement in regional and local matters. For example, in Denmark there are plans to increase the supervisory role of the central Government in planning and delivering health care through its subordinate body, the National Board of Health. In Finland the central Government increasingly influences local health care decision-making through earmarked budgets and the financing of particular projects to be implemented by municipalities. The trend towards increasing central involvement in these two countries reflects a heightened awareness of and reduced level of (political) acceptability of regional inequalities in health care (also promoted through the media, for example with regard to waiting times). There is also discussion in Finland about whether the role of the existing "Social Welfare and Health Care Target and Operational Plan" should be strengthened as a central steering tool.

Health care reforms, including organizational changes, may also affect planning. The introduction of DRGs to fund hospitals in Germany, for example, is expected to influence approaches to hospital planning by the *Länder* (Mueller & Offermann 2004). New forms of health care delivery, such as the involvement of private providers in a predominantly public primary care sector, through commissioning, may also lead to further developments in planning methodologies, as indicated by the case of Finland.

The 2006 health insurance reform in the Netherlands reshaped the provider landscape by introducing individual contracts between private health insurers and providers. If this dynamic is seen to affect access to care, it has been speculated that Dutch regulators may consider reintroducing planning as a means of ensuring availability of services. A return to planning following experiments with markets and competition is seen in New Zealand, where health plans and planning frameworks have been reintroduced following their abolition in the 1990s.

These examples demonstrate the challenge for governments to reconcile responsibility for providing equitable, affordable and accessible health care with concepts such as decentralization, market competition and pluralism aimed at improving responsiveness and efficiency. The diversity of approaches to planning (or not planning in some sectors or countries) illustrates the difficulty of balancing local, regional and central decision-making on the one hand and provider competition and regulation on the other.

## Planning in action

The major part of this chapter describes the institutional framework within which planning takes place, but does not describe what planning actually involves. Unfortunately, there is no simple approach to planning health care capacity. Health care planning, as with the planning of any activity involving the public, is an activity that requires both technical and political skills.

Technical skills include demographic and epidemiological expertise, to enable forecasting of the future size and composition of the population and expected health needs. They also include skills in health services research, to provide insights into changing patterns of care. Several countries, such as England, have been establishing horizon-scanning facilities, whose task it is to anticipate future developments that may impact on how health care is provided, although these tend to be confined to high-cost innovations only. In the Netherlands, a Steering Committee for future Health Scenarios was established as long ago as 1983 (Abel-Smith et al. 1995). Although often less formalized, this general approach has been used in several countries to respond to the specific challenge of cancer, developing mechanisms to link different providers into regional networks that ensure this disease is identified early and referred to the appropriate facility rapidly. Currently, researchers in several European countries are exploring a range of scenarios for the future provision of paediatric care, a specialty whose nature has changed markedly as the decline in common infectious diseases has emptied once busy wards in general hospitals, while services must now combine care for children with chronic disorders (including developmental difficulties) in the community with highly specialized care for children with complex genetic disorders and cancer. Poland provides an example of planning to restructure emergency care (Kuszewski & Gericke 2005).

Expertise in geography and modelling is also required (Trye et al. 2002). This is especially important in understanding how the reconfiguration of facilities will impact on patterns of travel, something that is of growing importance given the imperative to reduce the carbon footprint of the health sector. Unfortunately, in many countries, these skills are in short supply in the health sector, although there are examples available for others to draw on, not only from western Europe but also from some former Soviet countries (Ensor & Thompson 1999; Street & Haycock 1999). There is also a need for data, which, despite the enormous potential offered by modern information systems, often remain elusive.

The need for political skills is apparent from the evident popular concern that often accompanies reconfigurations of health care provision (McKee & Healy 2002a). As described elsewhere in this volume, a hospital is much more than simply a place for treating patients. It has a symbolic function and its presence or absence can impact considerably on the local economy. Changes inevitably involve a broad range of stakeholders, some of whom will be winners and others losers. The challenge is to maximize the former and minimize the latter, at the same time as taking steps to ensure that those involved understand why change is needed (assuming it really is). It will also be important to try and involve the public and other stakeholders in any planning activity as early as possible.

Yet, no matter how skilled a planning team is, a key message that emerges in many chapters of this volume is the importance of integrating flexibility into plans. There are simply too many parameters that are unknowable (McKee 2006). One recent example includes the migration to western Europe from the countries that joined the EU in 2004, which simultaneously depleted the stock of health workers in their countries of origin and partially solved shortages in their countries of destination. As many of those who moved were in their peak reproductive years, this development may also help to reverse long-term downward trends in birth rates in some western European countries, potentially safeguarding obstetric units from planned closures. A recurring theme throughout this volume is the importance of building flexibility into structures, identifying those parts of the hospital where change is most likely to impact, and ensuring that they can be changed as easily as possible. Another is the importance of monitoring the effects of changes. In the present context, there are many examples of planned reconfigurations of health care delivery that have not achieved what was intended (McKee 2004; Barrett et al. 2005).

Yet, there are many areas where the future can be anticipated with somewhat greater certainty. Everywhere there are long-term trends in smoking-related mortality, with implications for the provision of thoracic surgery and oncology. These reflect decisions by individuals to begin smoking, or not to, three or four decades previously (Shkolnikov et al. 1999). There is no reason to anticipate any sudden discontinuity. In other cases, the future can only be expressed in probabilities. A contemporary example is pandemic influenza. While it is virtually certain that this will occur sometime, it cannot be predicted when. Thus, given the massive implications that a pandemic would have for health systems, it is essential to have plans in place and to update them regularly (Mounier-Jack & Coker 2006).

## Conclusions

This chapter has described the arrangements for planning health care capacity that are in place in nine industrialized countries. One of the key messages emerging from this is that the approach to health care planning largely reflects the health system's institutional, legislative and regulatory framework, as determined by the wider political, social, economic and cultural system of the country in question. There are strong theoretical and, increasingly, empirical arguments for establishing mechanisms to plan the capacity and configuration of health facilities. These arguments are becoming stronger in the face of growing complexity of care. The nature of these mechanisms will depend on the administrative and geographical features of the country concerned, with the locus of health planning usually determined by the degree of political centralization or decentralization.

In an ideal world, the level at which planning would take place would be determined by the frequency of the conditions being considered. Clearly, it is possible to plan for delivery of care for common conditions in small territorial units, while particularly rare conditions may require planning at national (or even, for some disorders, European) level. As planning decisions are, instead, determined by administrative arrangements, the implication is that it is important to have good links between the different levels at which planning takes place.

Plans vary in scope, with some covering public and private provision, some hospital and ambulatory sectors, and others being far narrower. Again, this usually reflects historical arrangements. There is, however, a strong argument for taking a whole system approach, although how this is to be done will depend on the health system.

Existing plans often focus on structures, and especially those that can easily be counted, such as hospital beds. Yet such measures are increasingly obsolete indicators of capacity to deliver health care. There is an increasing tendency to plan around patient pathways, in many cases for specific complex disorders (typically cancer), but in a few cases, such as Northern Ireland, taking a system-wide approach. Furthermore, the planning of health care delivery should recognize that plans need to be continually reviewed and adapted in response to changing circumstances.

## References

Abel-Smith B et al. (1995). *Choices in health policy: an agenda for the European Union*. Aldershot, Dartmouth.

ARHIF (2006). *Schéma régional de l'organisation sanitaire de troisième génération 2006–2010*. Paris, ARHIF (http://www.parhtage.sante.fr/re7/idf/site.nsf/(WebPub)/SROS_3, accessed 17 October 2008).

Barrett B et al. (2005). Hospital utilization, efficiency and access to care during and shortly after restructuring acute care in Newfoundland and Labrador. *Journal of Health Services Research and Policy*, 10(2):31–37.

DHSSPS (2002). *Designing better services: modernising hospitals and reforming structures*. Belfast, Department of Health, Social Services and Public Safety.

DiSesa VJ et al. (2006). Contemporary impact of state certificate-of-need regulations for cardiac surgery: an analysis using the Society of Thoracic Surgeons' National Cardiac Surgery Database. *Circulation*, 114(20):2122–2129.

Ensor T, Thompson R (1999). Rationalizing rural hospital services in Kazakstan. *International Journal of Health Planning and Management*, 14(2):155–167.

Figueras J (1993). *Effective health care planning – the role of financial allocation mechanisms* [thesis]. London, University of London.

France G, Taroni F (2000). Starting down the road to targets in health. The case of Italy. *European Journal of Public Health*, 10(4 suppl.):25–29.

France G, Taroni F (2005). The evolution of health-policy making in Italy. *Journal of Health Politics, Policy and Law*, 30(1–2):169–187.

Gaál P (2004). *Health Care Systems in Transition: Hungary*, 6(4):1–152.

Georgieva LP et al. (2007). Bulgaria: Health system review. *Health Systems in Transition*, 9(1):1–156.

Healy J, McKee M (2002). The evolution of hospital systems. In: McKee M, Healy J. *Hospitals in a changing Europe*. Buckingham, Open University Press:14–35.

Hutubessy RC, Hanvoravongchai P, Edejer TT (2002). Diffusion and utilization of magnetic resonance imaging in Asia. *International Journal of Technology Assessment in Health Care*, 18(3):690–704.

Koppel A et al. (2008). Estonia: Health system review. *Health Systems in Transition*, 10(1):1–230.

Kuszewski K, Gericke C (2005). *Health Systems in Transition: Poland*, 7(5):1–106.

McKee M (2004). *Reducing hospital beds. What are the lessons to be learned?* Copenhagen, WHO Regional Office for Europe.

McKee M (2006). The future. In: Marinker M. *Constructive conversations about health: policy and values*. Oxford, Radcliffe Medical Press:215–229.

McKee M (2008). Solidarity in a unified Europe. *European Journal of Public Health*, 18(1):2–4.

McKee M, Healy J (2002a). *Hospitals in a changing Europe*. Buckingham, Open University Press.

McKee M, Healy J (2002b). Réorganisation des systèmes hospitaliers: leçons tirées de l'Europe de l'Ouest. *Revue Médicale de l'Assurance Maladie*, 33:31–36.

Ministry of Health (2003). *Guidelines for capital investment*. Wellington, Ministry of Health (http://www.moh.govt.nz/moh.nsf/49b6bf07a4b7346dcc256fb300005a51/e3c114507edccd8b cc256dda00132da2/$FILE/GlinesCapitalInvestment.pdf, accessed 28 July 2008).

Mounier-Jack S, Coker RJ (2006). How prepared is Europe for pandemic influenza? Analysis of national plans. *Lancet*, 367(9520):1405–1411.

Mueller U, Offermann M (2004). *Krankenhausplanung im DRG-System. Expertenbefragung des Deutschen Krankenhausinstituts*. Düsseldorf, Deutsches Krankenhausinstitut e.V.

Nolte E, McKee M (eds) (2008). *Caring for people with chronic conditions. A health system perspective*. Maidenhead, Open University Press.

Pearson G, et al. (1997). Should paediatric intensive care be centralized? Trent versus Victoria. *Lancet*, 349(9060):1213–1217.

République Française (2005). *Projet de loi de financement de la sécurité sociale (PLFSS)*. Paris, République Française (http://www.sante.gouv.fr/htm/dossiers/plfss/2005/annexe/annc.pdf, accessed 17 October 2008).

Rokosová M et al. (2005). *Health Care Systems in Transition: Czech Republic*, 7(1):1–100.

Sandier S, Paris V, Polton D (2004). *Health Care Systems in Transition: France*, 6(2):1–145.

Shkolnikov V et al. (1999). Why is the death rate from lung cancer falling in the Russian Federation? *European Journal of Epidemiology*, 15(3):203–206.

Short MN, Aloia TA, Ho V (2008). Certificate of need regulations and the availability and use of cancer resections. *Annals of Surgical Oncology*, 15(7):1837–1845.

Street A, Haycock J (1999). The economic consequences of reorganizing hospital services in Bishkek, Kyrgyzstan. *Health Economics*, 8(1):53–64.

Trye P et al. (2002). Health service capacity modelling. *Australian Health Review*, 25(4):159–168.

Vaughan-Sarrazin MS et al. (2002). Mortality in Medicare beneficiaries following coronary artery bypass graft surgery in states with and without certificate of need regulation. *Journal of the American Medical Association*, 288(15):1859–1866.

WHO Regional Office for Europe (2008). Health for All database (HFA-DB) [offline database]. Copenhagen, WHO Regional Office for Europe (July 2008 update).

Chapter 4

# Concept planning: getting capital investment right

*Knut Samset, Barrie Dowdeswell*

## Introduction

The point of departure in this chapter is the seeming difficulty governments have in developing long-range capital projects that enable the effective provision of services over the lifespan of health facilities. The chapter explores the strategic and tactical considerations and decisions that come into play throughout a project's life-cycle, and discusses how the strategic performance of capital projects can be improved through front-end governance regimes for public investment projects, based on examples in the United Kingdom and Norway.

News of unsuccessful hospital projects frequently hits the headlines. This happens in particular when costs exceed budgets or when projects are significantly delayed. However, these issues are particularly limited and premature measures of a project's success. If judged from a broader perspective, a successful project is one that significantly contributes to the fulfilment of its agreed objectives. Moreover, it should have at worst only minor negative unintended effects, its objectives should be consistent with societal needs and priorities, and it should produce the intended long-term benefits. These requirements were first formulated for United States-funded international development projects by the United States Agency for International Development (USAID) in the 1960s and subsequently endorsed by the United Nations, the Organisation for Economic Co-operation and Development (OECD), and the European Commission. They comprise five success factors that have to be fulfilled: the project's efficiency, effectiveness, relevance, impact and sustainability. These are tough requirements that go far beyond the issues that are usually covered by the media or indeed many health planners and decision-makers. Efficiency measures are only one aspect of whether a project is successful in achieving its goals. There are many examples of projects that score high on efficiency, but subsequently prove to be disastrous in terms of their effect and utility. There are also numerous projects that fail to pass the efficiency test but still prove to be tremendously successful both in the short and long term.

## Tactical and strategic performance

A crucial distinction when assessing the success of projects is their *tactical* and *strategic* performance. Tactical considerations typically are those based on criteria "of the moment", such as the presumed ability to meet short-term performance targets, politically inspired new building programmes, and trade-offs to keep stakeholders on board, all of which are likely to prove ephemeral when matched against the lifespan of most health buildings. This includes the often proclaimed success of a project simply because it has been "on cost and on time". Strategic performance is much more important, but strategic success will only emerge over time, when the building has sustainable impact and remains relevant and effective over its lifespan.

Projects that perform successfully, both in tactical and strategic terms, on all five criteria, are rare. The tactical performance of projects relates to how the project is managed during its restricted period of implementation, once it has been designed and construction agreed. It is essentially a project management issue. When judged in strategic terms, however, it is not clear that an entirely successful hospital project exists anywhere. There may be some consensus among politicians, researchers, health authorities and planners on what such an ideal project should entail, but there is still a huge discrepancy between some of these visions and what is actually being built.

While it "may seem unnecessary to define a hospital since everyone knows the nature of a hospital" (Frederick 2003), there is no common understanding of what the hospital of the future should look like. Diverse players in the health care arena may use different criteria, such as:

- more equitable patient access

- better cost-efficiency

- improved clinical outcomes

- enhanced health status of the local population.

In most business cases, the first two of these points are generally well described, but what is often ignored is how the proposed investment supports improved clinical outcomes and a better health status of the population. The potential of a new "iconic" building often blocks the view. A better perspective would be generated by projecting these different criteria over the planned life-cycle of the project, when functional adaptability and economic sustainability gain greater prominence.

Whilst there is no template for what the ideal hospital might look like, it is still useful to position hospitals with regard to their tactical and strategic performance (Fig. 4.1).

It is difficult to identify hospitals that are successful in both tactical and strategic terms, corresponding to Category 1 of Fig. 4.1. Projects that qualify for the remaining three categories are more common.

**Fig. 4.1** *Strategic and tactical performance*

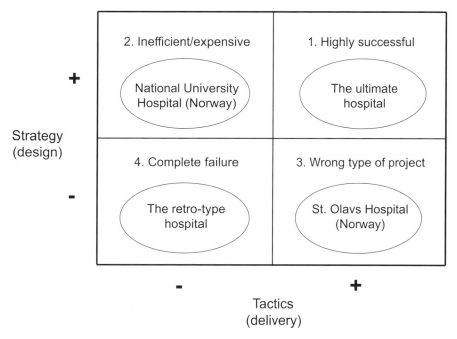

Category 2 projects are viable in strategic terms, but inefficient tactically. One example for this is the National University Hospital in Norway (*Rikshospitalet*), which was completed in 2000, one year behind schedule and with considerable cost overrun. Newspapers maintained comprehensive coverage of developments during the construction phase and a public inquiry was subsequently commissioned to establish the reasons for the problems. Clearly, cost overrun was considerable, although it was equivalent to only a few months of operational costs for the hospital and therefore was rather insignificant when seen in the context of a lifetime perspective (see Chapter 8). The inquiry established that a large share of the cost increase was due to necessary amendments and expansions that were needed to keep pace with changing circumstances, thus increasing the efficiency and utility of the hospital's operations. The designers failed to (or perhaps were unable to) foresee many of these needs when the project was planned. In strategic terms, the need for the project has proved unquestionable. Seen in retrospect, and when viewed in terms of clinical and societal benefit, the project is generally considered a great success. Furthermore, the adaptable design characteristics of the building (one of the causes of the initial cost overrun) have facilitated a number of functional changes since the hospital opened, illustrating success in meeting the moving target of service needs and public expectations.

Category 3 projects are not successful in strategic terms, but efficient tactically. An example from Norway that illustrates this category is one of the regional university hospitals (St Olavs Hospital), where a major expansion of the existing hospital is taking place, adding a number of large new buildings to the existing compound. In tactical terms, the project is progressing as planned and so far without major cost overrun, so it is considered to be cost-effective. In strategic terms, success may not be so evident. The project was conceived not in response to well-defined needs, but to seize an opportunity to gain public funds from the central Government for developments in the region. It was a case of tactical budgeting, where costs initially were underestimated and benefits overestimated, a common device to get projects "into the programme". The total budget is now largely expended although the project remains incomplete, and funding to secure the final stage of the project has not yet been secured. Major delays are expected, which are already adversely affecting the hospital's performance. Furthermore, the hospital seems to be oversized for a large geographical region with a relatively small population and low population density. It is not expected to operate efficiently, partly because available operational funding is insufficient for this scale of operations, with the result that facilities are left unused or are operated at high costs. The design, although generally regarded as a European exemplar for being patient friendly and society focused, may, at least in its present form, not deliver effective life-cycle service and economic sustainability.

Finally, the more conspicuous Category 4 projects – the total failures – can be left to the reader's imagination to visualize. They would have many of the features of the Category 3 project, described earlier. Generally speaking, they would be retro-type hospitals, over- or undersized, badly designed, inefficient, technologically outdated, largely restricted to curative treatment, and with high hospitalization rates. In addition, they would have a low tactical performance during implementation. Unfortunately, there are still many hospitals being built that fall into this category.

Projects bordering on Category 3 or 4, however, can be transformed. The La Ribera hospital in the Valencia region in Spain was designed to deliver modern interventions in a self-contained environment for a new population. It was therefore built as a tactical response to a new need. It quickly became evident that, whilst tactically the project looked good, strategically it would never cope with the dynamics of changing service demand, rapidly changing clinical technologies, and re-appraisal of health priorities by the contracting state authority. A decision was made to re-appraise the investment against more robust economic criteria informed by long-range strategic visioning. The hospital has now been transformed and has become a hub for the provision of fully integrated primary and secondary care services. It has moved away from a hospital-focused project towards a more balanced portfolio of capital assets (see the relevant case study in the accompanying volume). A key factor in these developments was the shift from tactical positioning to strategic sustainability.

In general, politicians, the media and the public seem to be preoccupied with underperformance in tactical terms (Category 2 and 4 projects), and disregard strategic potential or performance. This results in a focus on problems deriving from weaknesses in project management decisions. However, the obvious focus should rather be on addressing strategic underperformance (Category 3 and 4 projects). Even projects that prove to be complete failures strategically seem to escape public attention, as long as they perform acceptably in tactical terms.

This problem is widespread and not solely confined to the health sector. There are numerous examples of projects where the original purpose of the proposal has been overwhelmed by short-term tactical concerns that seem more seductive and appealing to politicians, professionals, the media and the public, rather than projects that are sustained or developed as a means of hoping to ward off inevitable change. An example is the construction of a regional air traffic control centre in Norway, which continued despite technological trends, apparent at the time, that made national (and now Nordic) centralization inevitable. Similarly, in the United Kingdom some new hospital developments are driven through, precisely to avoid service rationalization. It is difficult to "rationalize" a newly commissioned hospital.

The Channel Tunnel between the United Kingdom and France is an example in which technological brilliance, combined with the uniqueness of undersea travel, masked difficult decisions about long-term economic viability and business rationality. Partly due to the competitive response of ferry companies, utilization rates were lower than forecast, but political considerations outweighed a critical analysis of such contingencies.

By far the most demonstrable front-end problems are the attempts by public services to plan and implement IT projects. Research by the European Services Strategy Unit showed that of 105 outsourced public sector ICT contracts in the United Kingdom, 57% had cost overruns, 33% were delayed and 30% were terminated (Whitfield 2007) (Table 4.1 and Table 4.2).

**Table 4.1** *Contract summary of 105 outsourced public sector ICT projects*

| Sector | Total value of ICT contracts, £ million | Total cost overruns and write-offs, £ million |
|---|---|---|
| Central Government, NHS public bodies and agencies | 28 058 | 8 876 |
| Local government | 1 446 | 18 |
| Total | 29 504 | 8 994 |

*Source*: Whitfield 2007.

*Notes*: ICT: Information and communication technology; NHS: National Health Service.

**Table 4.2** *Summary of cost overruns, delays and terminations*

| | Number of contracts | % of contracts |
|---|---|---|
| Contracts with cost overruns | 60 | 57 |
| % average cost overrun per contract | – | 30.5 |
| Contracts with delays | 35 | 33 |
| Contracts terminated | 31 | 30 |
| SSDP contracts terminated or substantially reduced | 4 | 12.5 (% of SSDP contracts) |

*Source*: Whitfield 2007.

*Note*: SSDP: Strategic Service Delivery Partnership.

The National Audit Office reported on such failures in 2004, noting reasons such as the "lack of a clear link between the project and the organizations' key strategic priorities, including measures of agreed success, lack of stakeholder engagement and absence or failure of senior management and ministerial ownership and leadership" (National Audit Office 2004). The report of the European Services Strategy Unit further comments that "the private sector frequently believes its own hype and PR about 'world class' services and thus often overstates its ability to deliver. It can often underestimate the complexity of public service provision" (Whitfield 2007). The public sector should look beyond this smokescreen and exercise its responsibility to deliver value, but all too often it succumbs to the rhetoric of the private sector. The United Kingdom Treasury announced that the financing instrument PFI would no longer be used for ICT projects, because:

- it is difficult to codify long-term IT requirements into an effective contract, due to rapid technological changes and the fact that IT is closely linked to business operation needs;

- as IT is highly integrated into other business systems, it is hard to define areas of responsibility between the client and the supplier, and so transfer risk effectively;

- the costs of delivering IT projects are dominated by annual running costs rather than costs upfront.

However, the application of the PFI for hospital provision in the United Kingdom continues, despite the fact that the same criteria often apply to the rapidly changing provision of health care.

## Project life-cycle and stakeholders

Major public projects are typically conceived as the result of politically expressed needs emerging in dialogue between various stakeholders. This is followed by a lengthy process of developing the project and making the necessary decisions, typically involving government at various administrative levels, but also political institutions, the public, the media, and consultants and contractors in the private sector. Such processes are often complex and unpredictable, as described in a study of 60 major projects (Miller & Lessard 2000). The processes can also be deceptive and irresponsible, affected by hidden agendas, rather than openness and social responsibility (Flyvbjerg, Bruzelius & Rothengatter 2003; Miller & Hobbs 2005).

In projects that fail strategically, the problem can often be traced back to decisions in their earliest phases, when the initial idea was conceived and developed. What happens during the front-end phase is therefore critical to a project's success. A study by the World Bank, based on a review of 1125 projects, concluded that 80% of the projects with satisfactory "quality-at-entry" (an indicator used to characterize the identification, preparation and appraisal process that the projects had been subjected to up front) were successful, while only 35% of those with unsatisfactory quality-at-entry were successful (World Bank 1996). Tactical performance tends to be less dependent on the initial choice of concept and more on decisions made during planning and implementation. Most projects would probably benefit from a clearer distinction between tactical and strategic decisions, so that the strategic focus is not blurred by tactical project management concerns during the front-end phase.

Numerous decisions are made during the entire lifetime of a project, resulting from a decision-making process that runs in parallel with an analytic process, providing input to decision-makers, as illustrated in Fig. 4.2.

**Fig. 4.2** *Decision and analysis throughout a project's life-cycle*

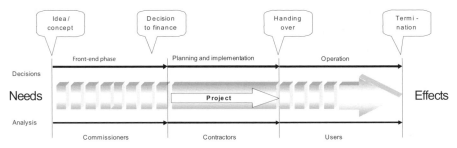

It is helpful to distinguish between the front-end, the implementation and the operational phases of projects. The front-end phase commences when the initial idea is conceived and proceeds as a complex and often unpredictable process, aiming to generate information, consolidate stakeholders' views and positions, and arrive at a final decision on whether or not to finance the project. In other words, the initial idea is transformed into the choice of a specific concept. This may take years or, in some large public investment projects, even decades. The key stakeholder during the front-end phase is the commissioning party, which is attempting to arrive at a choice of concept in dialogue with and, sometimes, in opposition to other stakeholders. Ideally, the five success criteria mentioned earlier (efficiency, effectiveness, relevance, impact and sustainability) will be applied. Such decisions clearly have implications for the planning and implementation of the project, but more so for its effect and utility. The management perspective is – or at least should be – secondary in this phase of the project, and the emphasis should be on the justification and potential benefits that arise from the anticipated project. Once the decision to proceed with a project has been made, subsequent decisions during the front-end phase tend to have less effect on the choice of concept as such, but instead focus increasingly on issues that have to do with budgeting, planning and implementation. This is bordering on and merging with project management issues.

The implementation phase commences once the decision to finance the project has been made, and includes detailed planning, mobilization of resources and implementation, resulting in the delivery of the project's outputs. The main stakeholders are the contractors, while the commissioning party's involvement largely depends on the contractual arrangement. The contractors have a restricted view of the project and their main aim is to deliver the agreed outputs according to specifications and to make a profit at the same time. For contractors, the initial choice of concept is of little significance; their responsibility is to implement whatever they are commissioned to.

The operational phase commences once the outputs have been delivered or are being used. The main stakeholders are therefore the users. Decision-makers at this stage are responsible for operational questions and will have to make do with what has been produced, with limited possibilities to make strategic changes. The users can be compared to passengers on a journey; they are generally detached from the foregoing decision processes with little possibility to make a difference.

In a typical case, the three groups of decision-makers have different interests in and perspectives on the project. They often operate in separate sequences, without much interaction. However, there is generally some sort of alignment of interests, and in many projects the contractors and users have, to a limited extent, opportunities to influence decisions during the front-end phase of a project.

## Decisions and performance

Challenges are abundant and complex. One particular issue is tactical budgeting, where agencies at various levels tend to underestimate costs in order to increase the chance of obtaining government funding for a project. Another challenge is to ensure a transparent process to avoid adverse effects of stakeholders' involvement and political bargaining. It is important that the process is predictable, since the front-end phase in large public projects commonly extends over at least one parliamentary election period. In this chapter, we distinguish decisions to improve both the project's tactical and strategic performance, and apply the five criteria of success mentioned at the outset. Many of the strategic performance problems facing major public investment projects can be interpreted in terms of deficiencies in the analytical or political processes preceding the final decision to go ahead, and in the interaction between analysts and decision-makers within this process.

## Decisions determining tactical performance

Decision-makers are charged with the responsibility to secure efficient delivery of project outputs in terms such as scope, quality, timing and budgetary compliance. The point of departure is the commissioner's specifications and requirements, as well as any contractual obligations. The main challenge is to translate the specifications into a project design and implementation plan that is realistically achievable, allowing for uncertainties that might affect the undertaking. These tasks are clearly described, for instance by the Project Management Institute in its "Body of Knowledge" (Project Management Institute 2005). It involves management of project integration, human resources, communication, procurement, design, planning, cost estimation and risk. Although deficiencies in project management might have serious economic implications, the problems might still be marginal when seen in a wider strategic perspective, as illustrated by the case of the National University Hospital in Norway, discussed earlier. What remains noteworthy in much public service investment is the continuing high-profile emphasis on tactical dimensions. In the United Kingdom, for example, the PFI is becoming synonymous with the government mantra "on time, on cost" as the dominant defining factor of success (although even this criterion is limited, as it measures the time from agreeing the contract to completion of construction, and not the period of contract negotiation which, if included, would mean that most PFI projects take longer in total than the earlier public sector model).

## Decisions determining strategic performance

In order to succeed strategically, four of the five success criteria mentioned earlier need to be satisfied (efficiency is less important in this respect, being primarily a tactical issue). The project's intended effect should be useful (relevance), the effect should be achieved in time (effectiveness), there should be no major negative effects (impact), and the positive effects should be sustained (sustainability).

Relevance is essentially a question of aligning objectives with needs and priorities, but this often does not take place. The case of the regional university hospital suggests a case of overinvestment, guided by the availability of public funds rather than by a scrutiny of local needs. This may have caused a "white elephant" type of hospital that is operated inefficiently, and which might prove to have adverse effects on other parts of the health system in the region.

The next challenge is to ensure that the project's objectives are realistically achievable and that the intended effect will be realized as planned (effectiveness). There are a number of formal requirements that have to be satisfied in the strategic design of a project. Objectives should be consistent in the sense that they are logically linked, both sequentially and in parallel. They should also be realistic and essential risks should be identified and considered. Clearly, a project with formally agreed objectives that are unrealistic is certain to fail when achievements are measured against these objectives. In the case of the regional university hospital, the project was guided by a number of unclear objectives pointing in different directions. In order to facilitate decisions, an architectural competition was organized at the outset that produced a physical model of the hospital. This was premature, as is often the case, since it provided the physical framework and restrictions for the project at a stage when there was no consensus regarding the project's justification, what it was meant to achieve and how.

Securing sustainability and avoiding adverse impacts is essentially a question of understanding the complexity of the context in which the project is implemented. This includes its institutional setting, market demands and restrictions, stakeholder needs and priorities, and technological and environmental opportunities and challenges. The task up front is one of carrying out comprehensive analyses, identifying stakeholders, and facilitating communication and involvement. Such activities may delay decision-making, but experience strongly suggests that this often is necessary to avoid some of the strategic pitfalls that lie ahead.

One huge paradox in the front-end management of major projects is that even the largest public investment projects often originate as a single idea, without systematic scrutiny or consultation. In addition, in too many cases, the initial idea will remain largely unchallenged and therefore end up as the preferred concept – even in cases in which it subsequently proved to be a strategic underperformer or failure. Improved front-end management is therefore likely to pay off if seen in terms of a wider life-cycle perspective (Miller & Lessard 2000). There is much to be gained from improving quality-at-entry at the earliest stage of the process. This can be achieved by challenging the initial ideas and applying simple analyses, extracting and making use of previous experience from similar undertakings, and consulting and involving stakeholders.

## Design of hospital projects

Effective strategic planning is necessary, but is not a sufficient condition in a stand-alone capacity for a project's success. Regardless of whether or not it has been conceived and designed with a particular strategic goal in mind, any project can be construed as an element that fits into a wider strategy. This overall strategy can be visualized as a hierarchy of objectives that need to be fulfilled in order to accomplish the ultimate goal. The project as such represents a smaller hierarchy of objectives within the larger strategic hierarchy. The project is implemented in order to help achieve certain parts of the objectives. The objectives that are formally agreed for that particular project may be incompatible with, or even in violation of the broader strategy. One reason could be that there are major flaws in the project's formal design so that the objectives are not logically consistent, or are misaligned with what the project is actually meant to achieve.

Up front, during the initial design phase, hospital projects, like any other capital development, must find their place in the wider strategic hierarchy. In the case of hospitals, the ultimate objective is health improvement. Taking health as a "state of physical, mental and social well-being and not merely the absence of disease or infirmity" (WHO 1946), the hierarchy would have to be correspondingly broad and include not only curative treatment of symptoms and disease, but also promotion of health and prevention of disease.

Experience suggests that most projects fail to meet these simple requirements in their initial conceptual stage. At the time of writing, the insight and visions to guide strategic planning are at hand, but they are still not well translated into viable conceptual solutions. More often than not projects are conceived and start their tour through the landscape of planners and decision-makers without clear objectives, often with a number of confounding or even conflicting objectives that leave the fate of the project entirely to the interpretation of various stakeholders as the process unfolds. The potential for improvement is therefore huge. If this is not done up front, it is certain that it will not happen during the subsequent, often politicized, decision process.

The case studies across Europe published in the accompanying volume illustrate many differences in the focus of projects. At one end of the spectrum are those projects generated in response to opportunistic and often ephemeral policy initiatives: short-term government drives to reduce waiting lists, replacing poorly maintained buildings without evidence of future need, or simply meeting pre-election manifesto pledges. Many in this category also benefit from capital financing models that are underwritten by governments to speed procurement, thus damping down local risk assessment, which in other circumstances, and almost universally in the commercial and private sector, would transfer attention to strategic dimensions such as sustainability, in order to assure life-cycle financial probity. Many of the current PFI projects in the United Kingdom NHS seem to fall into the tactical category.

Conversely, there are projects that have emphasized the longer-term strategic needs of health systems that are recognized as being in a state of continual transition. These tend to build the planning, design and capital financing models around core service processes and acknowledge that they will change and flex, as care models and service priorities evolve. Many of these obtain capital financing through the commercial banking sector. The rigour applied by commercial financiers in assessing the long-term viability of projects seems to strip out and discount short-term tactical factors in favour of long-term strategic effectiveness, which is the primary concern of lenders in assessing the viability of debt servicing. The link between sustainable service effectiveness and life-cycle financial probity may emerge as one of the most important levers for improving front-end quality.

## Devices to improve front-end governance of investment projects

There are various approaches to improving the front-end governance of projects. The first example is the Gateway process adopted for public sector capital investments in the United Kingdom. The process emanates from the Office of Government Commerce and examines programmes and projects at key decision points in their life-cycle. It looks ahead to provide assurance that they can progress successfully to the next stage. The various Gateway stages are:

- Gate 0 – strategic assessment

- Gate 1 – business justification

- Gate 2 – procurement strategy

- Gate 3 – investment decision

- Gate 4 – readiness for service

- Gate 5 – benefits evaluation.

The Gateway process is mandatory for central government procurement, IT and construction programmes and projects. In essence, it delivers a "peer review", in which independent practitioners from outside the programme or project examine the progress and likelihood of successful delivery. They are intended to highlight risks that, if not addressed, would threaten the successful delivery of the programme or project. The length of each review depends on the scope and risk involved and usually lasts between three and five days, including a preparatory planning day. The reviews are not part of the approval process, but usually coincide with the end of each project stage.

"The timing and short duration of the reviews, coupled with the use of existing project documentation, are designed to minimize demands on the project teams and ensure no, or minimal delay to the project" (Office of Government Commerce 2003).

While the process is logical and theoretically appealing, there are several problems. Large parts of the project are often completed before real-life testing of what has been proposed as a solution has taken place. Only on completion of the project will it become clear whether the solution works or not. There is also a danger that the Gateway exercise is simply seen as another hurdle and that tactical devices are applied to surmount these stages in order for the project to flow straight through to validation. Finally, a review process of three days is particularly short and may not allow time for a thorough review. Given that the outcomes of Gateway reviews are not available for public scrutiny, there is no means of knowing how well the review system functions in practice.

However, given the many well-publicized examples of failure in procurement of IT projects, it is apparent that they do not guarantee success.

Another example of front-end governance of investment projects comes from Norway, where, in the year 2000 the Ministry of Finance introduced a mandatory quality-at-entry regime. The emphasis was to improve budgetary compliance in public investment projects, thus avoiding major cost overruns. From 2005 onwards the regime has been expanded to include assessment of the quality of the initial choice of concept. The intention is to make sure that the right projects get started, and to dismiss unviable projects. For this to work, it is vital to enforce changes in existing processes early enough, when there are still alternative options available. In parallel, the Ministry of Finance initiated a research programme designed to study the effects of the regime, so as to help to improve it.[2]

The governance system was designed to improve analysis and decision-making in the front-end phase, and particularly the interaction between the two. It was based on the notion that the necessary binding rules for decision-making were already in place; however, there were no binding rules that could ensure quality and consistency of analysis and decisions.[3] In an ideal technocratic model of decision-making, this would not be necessary. Here, decision and analysis follow in a logical and chronological sequence that would eventually lead to the selection and initiation of the preferred project, without unforeseen interventions or conflicts (Fig. 4.3).

**Fig. 4.3** *A model of up-front technocratic decision-making*

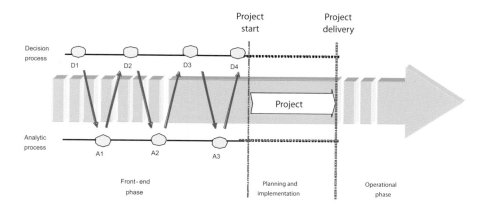

[2] See NTNU, Norwegian University of Science and Technology, www.concept.ntnu.no.
[3] A parallel here would be the private financial institutions, where investment projects are handled almost exclusively based on a review of the investors' credibility and collateral available, but with little regard to substantial issues or characteristics of the investment projects as such.

In reality, the process may often resemble an anarchic procedure buffeted by various stakeholders, resulting in a process which is complex, less structured and unpredictable. Analysis may be biased or inadequate, and decisions may be affected more by political priorities than by rational analysis. Political priorities and alliances, along with pressures from stakeholders, may change over time. In addition, the amount of information is often overwhelming and may be interpreted and used differently by different parties. The possibility for disinformation is therefore considerable.

A response to these challenges would obviously not be a strict and comprehensive regulatory regime. It would rather be:

- to establish a distinct set of milestones and decision "gates" that would apply to investment projects in all sectors, regardless of existing practices and procedures in the different ministries or agencies involved;

- to ensure political control with fundamental go-ahead/no-go decisions;

- to ensure an adequate basis for decisions; and

- to focus decisions on essential matters, not on the details.

The approach that was chosen in Norway was:

- to anchor the most critical decisions in the Cabinet;

- to introduce a system of quality assurance that was independent of the Government and sufficiently competent to overrule the analysts; and

- to make sure that the governance regime was compatible with procedures and practices of the ministries and agencies concerned.

The quality-at-entry regime in Norway is essentially a top-down regulatory scheme that was introduced to enforce a qualitative change in government procurement that would improve the quality-at-entry of major investments. During its first four years, it did not interfere with current procedures, but merely aimed to improve on existing documents that are an essential basis for the political decision-making process. Although the regime has been controversial, it has also been met with constructive responses from the ministries and agencies involved, which have adapted their practices to meet the new quality requirements, and in some cases also adopted the scheme as a self-regulatory procedure.

This is possibly due to three factors. First, the regime does not interfere with existing procedures for analysis or political decision-making, but merely aims to raise the professional standard of underlying documents. Second, it does not require changes in procedures in the involved institutions. Third, the introduction of the scheme has been supported by the creation of a forum for exchange of experience, through meetings at regular intervals headed by the Ministry of Finance, with representatives of involved ministries, agencies, consultants and researchers. This has facilitated openness and cooperation among the parties to discuss standards and practices and to develop the scheme further.

There has, however, been some resistance to the scheme. This seems to be primarily rooted in the fact that it challenges the professional judgement of the agencies involved, but also that it has focused increased media attention on budgetary control of public investment projects.

The extended quality-at-entry regime, introduced in 2005, adds another dimension, in that it anchors the decision regarding the choice of concept within the Prime Minister's office. The reason for this is that the choice of concept is considered the single most important decision that will determine the viability and utility of a project, and hence the extent to which public funds are used effectively. Lifting the decision from the administrative to the political level seeks to create distance from narrow perspectives and professional biases. This might be expected to be controversial. The response, however, seems to be rather coloured by an understanding that this is a sensible and logical step in the right direction and in agreement with fundamental democratic principles.

The United Kingdom model, on the other hand, tends towards "checking for success", with no clear mandate about quality-at-entry. It is therefore questionable whether this seeks to generate a systemic change in front-end evaluation and quality, as opposed to improving tactical delivery of a project.

## Conclusions

Project governance has only recently attracted interest in the project management community. In order to move forward in this field, there are numerous questions to be answered. What procedures are currently applied in different countries and what are their effects? What would it take to develop more effective governance regimes at international, government or corporate level(s) to ensure maximum utility and return on investment for society and investors? What would be the optimal mix of regulations, economic means and information in improved governance regimes for major investment projects?

Overall, the greatest challenge is to lift the perspective of those implementing projects above the horizon defined by the delivery of the project to look at the broader strategic vision within which the project is situated. Increased understanding and sensitivity in this area could be of mutual benefit to both the financing and the implementing parties.

# References

Flyvbjerg B, Bruzelius N, Rothengatter W (2003). *Megaprojects and risk. An anatomy of ambition.* Cambridge, Cambridge University Press.

Frederick M (ed.) (2003). *Webster's New World Medical Dictionary, 2nd Edition.* New York, Wiley Publishing.

Miller R, Hobbs B (2005). *Governance regimes for large complex projects.* Paper for the European Academy of Management (EURAM) 2005 Annual Conference. Montreal, University of Montreal.

Miller R, Lessard DR (2000). *The strategic management of large engineering projects: shaping institutions, risk and governance.* Cambridge, MA, MIT Press.

National Audit Office (2004). *Improving IT procurement. The impact of the Office of Government Commerce's initiatives on departments and suppliers in the delivery of major IT-enabled projects.* London, The Stationery Office.

Office of Government Commerce (2003). *Managing successful programs.* Norwich, The Stationery Office.

Project Management Institute (2005). *A guide to the Project Management Body of Knowledge PMBOK® Guide.* Washington, DC, Project Management Institute.

Whitfield D (2007). *Cost overruns, delays and terminations: 105 outsourced public sector ICT projects.* Duagh, European Services Strategy Unit (Report No. 3).

WHO (2007). Constitution of the World Health Organization. In: *Basic documents, Forty-sixth edition.* Geneva, World Health Organization.

World Bank (1996). *Evaluation results 1994.* Washington, DC, The International Bank of Reconstruction and Development.

# Chapter 5

# Capital investment and the health care workforce

*Bernd Rechel, James Buchan, Martin McKee*

## Introduction

Health care workers, as the largest input into health care, are critical to the success of capital investments. In order to provide high-quality medical care, hospitals and other health facilities require appropriate numbers of well-trained and motivated health care workers (Dieleman & Hammeijer 2006). Health capital planning needs therefore to place sufficient weight on future human resource availability and competences (Dechter 2004).

This is particularly the case in view of the shortage of nurses and some other occupations that many health systems in Europe and elsewhere face (International Council of Nurses 2007b; Milisen et al. 2006; WHO 2006). One of the major reasons for problems in recruiting and retaining nurses is their poor working environments (International Council of Nurses 2007b). Improving these environments can be an important investment in terms of improving recruitment, retention and motivation of staff (Markus 2006).

This chapter explores how capital investment and the design of health facilities impact on the health care workforce. This is an issue much less researched than the impact of design on patients (see Chapter 12 by Glanville & Nedin) and, consequently, many conclusions drawn in this chapter are to some degree tentative. However, it is safe to say that many traditionally designed hospitals impact negatively on staff recruitment, retention and performance. Improved design, on the other hand, can lead to better working conditions and staff safety, and enables staff to do their jobs more effectively.

## Healthy working environments

In recent years, the impact of the working environment on health care workers has come increasingly into focus, as it is realized that they are the people who spend most of their time in health care facilities – relative to the 8.9 days that constitutes the average length of stay of patients in acute hospitals in the WHO European Region in 2005 (WHO Regional Office for Europe 2008). Nurses, the largest group of health care professionals, are the health care workers that have received most attention. The International Council of Nurses declared "positive practice environment" the theme of the International Nurses Day in 2007 and in many countries there is a growing awareness about the poor professional practice environments of nurses. This growing interest in healthy working environments is partly stimulated by increased competition between health care providers, but also by the alleged adverse effects of restructuring operations involving re-engineering (Gunnarsdóttir & Rafferty 2006). Working environments that support excellence and attract and retain nurses have come to be called "positive practice environments" (International Council of Nurses 2007b). The beneficial effects of positive practice environments on health service delivery, health worker performance, patient outcomes and innovation are well documented (International Council of Nurses 2007a). "Providing safe and healthy working conditions for employees is one of the best investments a business can make" (Registered Nurses' Association of Ontario 2008), with potential improvements in productivity, absenteeism and employee morale.

Despite a growing awareness, physicians, nurses and other health workers often continue to face unhealthy environments and poor employment conditions, characterized by heavy workloads, long working hours, unfavourable work–life balances, poor administrative support, insufficient remuneration, low professional status, difficult relations in the workplace, violence by patients, problems carrying out professional roles and a variety of workplace hazards (Baumann et al. 2001; Gunnarsdóttir & Rafferty 2006; International Council of Nurses 2007a; International Council of Nurses 2007b).

These unhealthy environments can affect the physical and psychological health of workers. For example, the working environments of nurses often contain biological, chemical, physical and psychological hazards, which put nurses at risk from job burnout, stress, work-related illnesses and injuries, infectious disease and musculoskeletal disorders (Registered Nurses' Association of Ontario 2008). In the United States, health care workers account for more than 40% of occupationally related adult-onset asthma, tied to exposure to cleaning products (Rosenman, Reilly & Schill 2003). Furthermore, nurses have one of the highest rates of work-related musculoskeletal injury of any professional group (Gunnarsdóttir & Rafferty 2006; International Council of

Nurses 2007b; Nelson et al. 2006). They have a higher absentee and disability rate than almost any other profession, which results in significant costs to the health system and wider society (Baumann et al. 2001).

## The role of capital investment

Some of the poor employment conditions, such as occupational hazards or unreasonable workloads, can very likely be attributed to inadequate consideration within capital investment appraisal. There is a crucial distinction here between the design of new facilities and how these facilities are equipped. While items of equipment have been identified by relevant international organizations as impacting the health of staff, no such recognition has yet been extended to the built environment. For example, in the Information and Action Tool Kit on positive practice environments developed by the International Council of Nurses (International Council of Nurses 2007b), the importance of appropriate equipment and supplies are recognized, but the built environment is not considered. Similarly, considerations of the built environment are missing from the best practice guidelines on healthy work environments from the Registered Nurses' Association of Ontario (Registered Nurses' Association of Ontario 2008).

A different development, however, can be discerned in the growing number of "green" building tools that are being developed, which have paid attention to the needs of health care workers. In the United Kingdom, one of these tools is ASPECT (A Staff and Patient Environment Calibration Tool). This tool supports the evaluation of health care environments based on eight major performance areas, including views for patients and staff; the comfort level of staff and patients; their ability to control their environment, such as lighting levels; and the ability of staff to lead personal lives and perform professional duties, such as through resting and relaxing in places segregated from patient and visitor areas (Guenther & Vittori 2008). Similarly, the Green Guide for Health Care that has been developed in the United States includes credits related to places of respite for staff and the acoustic environment, and prioritizes daylight and views for staff in nursing units. It seems that "green" building tools, with a focus on overall environmental quality, have significant crossover with workplace issues.

## Impact of equipment

The importance of proper equipment and supplies is well recognized. In *The world health report 2006*, WHO noted, for example, that "[n]o matter how motivated and skilled health workers are, they cannot do their jobs properly in facilities that lack clean water, adequate lighting, heating, vehicles, drugs, working equipment and other supplies" (WHO 2006). For example, in many countries of the former Soviet Union, these basic preconditions of providing medical care are still not met. Furthermore, in many cases, there has been hardly any capital investment in recent decades and the fabric of many facilities has deteriorated (Afford & Lessof 2006). However, even in western Europe, workplace ergonomics and the provision of adequate and appropriate supplies often leaves much to be desired. The ergonomics of the work environment of health care workers has received far less attention from major furniture manufacturers than the commercial office environment, despite the greater level of workplace injury and the high-stress nature of the hospital environment. So far, overall assessments of health care workplaces are still rare; these should include both mental and physical exposure to workplace hazards and health outcomes (Baumann et al. 2001).

Better equipment can reduce the risk of injuries and minimize the hazards to which health care workers are exposed. One obvious example is equipment used for handling patients. Such equipment, coupled with injury prevention programmes, can yield significant benefits. A musculoskeletal injury prevention programme in six nursing homes in the United States consisting of mechanical lifts and repositioning aids, a zero lift policy, and employee training on lift usage, resulted in a significant reduction of staff injuries, compensation costs and lost work days (Collins et al. 2004). A programme to prevent injuries associated with patient handling tasks in 23 high-risk units in the United States found that the new equipment was found by nursing staff to be most effective in improving patient handling. The initial capital investment for patient handling equipment was repaid after only 3.75 years, due to savings in occupational compensation and lost work days, while job satisfaction increased (Nelson et al. 2006).

Nurses in particular face a high risk of accidental injuries caused when using needles, which account for the highest share of occupationally transmitted infectious diseases. An obvious example of how equipment can improve the working conditions of health workers is the availability of sterilized needles and the safe disposal of syringes and needles. There are now safer disposal devices available, which have in-built safety features that remove or destroy the needle after use. The provision of suitable protective equipment, including powder-free latex gloves or latex-free gloves for health care workers allergic to latex, further protects health care workers (Wilburn 2005).

Replacement of mercury-containing thermometers and blood pressure devices or replacing incineration with safer alternatives for the destruction of medical waste, as advocated by organizations such as Hospitals for a Healthy Environment and Health Care Without Harm, are other examples of how to improve the environment of health care workers, patients, visitors and the wider community (Brody 2008). Patients, staff and visitors may also be exposed to numerous airborne chemicals, such as those emitted from building materials or building contents, including pesticides, plasticizers and fire retardants (Guenther & Vittori 2008). Disinfectants and sterilizing products can also be hazardous to health care workers, either through direct physical contact or by means of indoor air pollution. Greener cleaning products and improved indoor air quality can go a long way to improve the environment of health care workers.

Sometimes simple, low-cost techniques, such as rearranging the furniture, can improve ward environments (Baldwin 1985). In many hospitals, surfaces such as ceilings or floors are hard and sound-reflecting, rather than sound-absorbing (Ulrich 2006). Hospital noise induces staff stress and correlates with reported emotional exhaustion or burnout among nurses (Topf & Dillon 1988). The consideration of the acoustic environment in health care settings is gaining momentum. The transition from PVC flooring to no-wax alternatives, for example, is accompanied by improved acoustics (softer materials underfoot) and a reduction in inflammatory conditions in the feet of nurses (Guenther & Vittori 2008). Making surfaces less slippery and providing enough prominently placed handwashing facilities or alcohol gel hand rub dispensers next to staff movement or work paths, and within their visual fields, are other simple ways of making the environment safer (Ulrich 2006).

## Impact of design

There is an increasing volume of research from an architectural perspective on the ways that the built environment contributes to the healing of patients. Four features of hospital buildings that have traditionally been considered components of healing environments are: nature, daylight, fresh air and quiet (Van den Berg & Wagenaar 2006). The movement towards healing facilities has sometimes been described as Evidence-Based Design, an endeavour to create hospitals and other health care buildings informed by the best available design (Ulrich 2006). While the impact of the design of health facilities on patients has received increasing attention in recent years (see Chapter 12 by Glanville & Nedin), the impact on staff is far less well researched, and the impact on visitors seems to have been completely ignored (PricewaterhouseCoopers LLP 2004).

The design of hospitals is often dominated by the consideration of clinical functionality at the expense of the quality of the health care environment, neglecting the importance of a positive working ambience (CABE 2003).

In the United States, this can be traced to the focus on "patient-centred" care that has taken centre stage since the 1990s. A new paradigm, "relationship-centred care", introduced by Rachel Naomi Remen, attempts to shift from the focus on the patient to a focus on the relationship between care providers and patients, a significant differentiation (Suchman 2007).

Yet, healing environments and improvements in building design and the selection of materials not only affect patient outcomes, but also staff recruitment and retention, as well as operational efficiency and productivity of facilities (Guenther & Vittori 2008; Malkin 2006). There is compelling evidence that traditional approaches to the design of hospitals often erode staff morale and retention, and decrease the effectiveness with which care is delivered. On the other hand, improved design can enable staff to do their jobs more effectively, with less strain (Ulrich 2006). A postal survey of 265 Directors of Nursing and six focus groups with nurses in England in 2004 found that most subjects agreed that hospital design has an influence on workplace performance, as well as recruitment and retention (PricewaterhouseCoopers LLP 2004). Similarly, a survey of NHS staff in London showed that, when health workers were asked for suggestions to improve their working lives, "better pay" ranked only fourth on their "wish list", behind "more staff", "better working conditions" and "better facilities" (Zurn, Dolea & Stilwell 2005). However, it remains difficult to quantify the organizational and health benefits of sustainable building strategies, such as reduced staff illness and absenteeism, improved staff performance (when measured through reduced medical errors), reduced hospital-acquired infections, and improved staff recruitment and retention (Guenther & Vittori 2008).

While recognizing the limitations of the available evidence, it is possible to identify a number of ways in which the design of health facilities impacts on the staff working in them. To start with, the location of health facilities has important implications for the recruitment of nurses and other health care workers. Too often, hospitals are not located near where the staff live. The availability of regular public transport and staff parking for those who travel by car, both close to the main entrance of the hospital, positively influence staff recruitment (PricewaterhouseCoopers LLP 2004). Consideration of sustainable modes of transport is crucial in the design and location of new facilities. In the Boulder Community Hospital in Colorado, United States, the number of parking spaces is 25% below the city requirement and there are signed carpool spaces, as well as bicycle racks, cycle paths, showers and changing facilities that encourage employees to cycle or walk to work, thus enhancing ecological sustainability, reducing the carbon impact of the hospital and improving the health of employees (Guenther & Vittori 2008). In the context of climate change, it is crucial to consider the impact on the environment and the health of visitors, patients and staff that arises from the culture of car dependence and suburban sprawl and the reliance on car transport to hospitals that are being built in suburban areas (Guenther & Vittori 2008). Sustainable building strategies, such as those aiming for carbon neutrality, zero waste and persistent bioaccumulative toxicant (PBT) elimination simultaneously benefit patients, staff and local communities, while living up to the environmental responsibility of hospitals (Guenther & Vittori 2008). They will also need to take into account the upstream and downstream implications of health care buildings, for example, the distance that building materials have to be transported or occupational health in the manufacturing industry (Guenther & Vittori 2008).

Patients, visitors and staff are all part of the same hospital environment. Many of the factors that influence patient experience also impact on the people working in the hospital, such as the ability to control the immediate environment through ventilation or the availability of natural light (PricewaterhouseCoopers LLP 2004). One nurse noted in a focus group conducted in England: "It makes you happier to be working in a nice environment, pleasant view, sufficient daylight and the possibility of opening a window for fresh air" (PricewaterhouseCoopers LLP 2004). The CABE study also recognized the importance of the hospital's image in the community as a factor in recruitment.

Many design measures are beneficial for patients, staff and the environment. The quality and quantity of light in a health facility has a decisive effect on patients, medical personnel, maintenance workers and visitors (Horton 1997). There is some evidence from outside the health sector that sunlight penetration in the workplace has a direct effect on job satisfaction, intention to resign, and general well-being (Leather et al. 1998). A study of 141 nurses in a university hospital in Turkey found that daylight exposure resulted in less stress and higher satisfaction at work (Alimoglu & Donmez 2005). Providing natural daylight improves energy efficiency, patient outcomes and staff effectiveness (Guenther & Vittori 2008). While the positive effects of daylight on patient outcomes are well established, in particular in North America, where occupational health legislation did not prescribe daylight and many deep floor plates and buildings have been built, many health care workers spend their working days in artificially lit spaces. This applies particularly to those working in diagnostic and treatment blocks in hospitals (Pradinuk 2008). Increased daylight may increase initial capital costs but can lead to productivity gains in the long term, manifest through improved delivery of health care and in staff recruitment and retention (Pradinuk 2008).

Good design can also help to reduce medication errors. Errors decline steeply when interruptions or distractions are reduced or eliminated. Furthermore, dispensing errors can be lowered by providing appropriate lighting of work surfaces. Provision of a separate space with adjustable task lighting may reduce dispensing errors (Ulrich 2006). More generally, good quality staff environments impact positively on patient care (CABE 2003). Deep plan buildings, with a larger proportion of windowless rooms, have been associated with worse patient outcomes (Ulrich 2006).

Design innovations can result in reduced nosocomial infections, medical errors, patient falls and medication use by inpatients; increased caregiver productivity; reduced horizontal and vertical travel time and patient transfers; reduced energy consumption; and reduced costs for future layout modifications (Guenther & Vittori 2008). Single-acuity adaptable rooms, for example, not only reduce nosocomial infections, but also substantially reduce patient transfers, improve staff–patient communication and reduce medical errors and in-hospital medication costs (Guenther & Vittori 2008) (Box 5.1). At the same time,

---

**Box 5.1** *Acuity-adaptable rooms*

Acuity-adaptable rooms have been developed in response to the realization that patients often move through several beds during their stay in hospital to enable care to be provided that matches the intensity of their needs. Acuity-adaptable beds allow the patient to remain in the same bed, which is adapted to meet their changing needs.

A national demonstration project with 56 beds has been developed at Methodist Hospital, Indianapolis. Each room occupies 36 m$^2$ and consists of three areas: the family zone, the patient zone and the caregiver zone. The family zone includes a chair-bed, a refrigerator, an Internet connection, telephone with voicemail capability and a television/video cassette recorder. Each room includes substantial family space. Waiting areas include soothing features, such as an indoor garden and/or an aquarium, as well as useful items, such as a kitchenette and small lockers. Patients and their families also have access to computer-based information that is individualized to each patient.

All equipment and supplies are easily accessible, including acuity-adaptable headwalls and advanced computer technology located directly on the patient's bed, so that body weight and other vital data can be recorded without disturbing patients. Patients are admitted and discharged from the same room.

The staff zone has all necessary supplies, to minimize movement around the facility. Nursing stations with computer access and servers for supplies are decentralized. There is additional workspace for caregivers outside each patient's room. Emergency equipment, such as defibrillators, are concealed behind doors. The benefits of acuity-adaptable rooms seem to make up for the higher initial capital costs, such as for the medical equipment that is available in the room even in times of low acuity.

*Source*: Hendrich, Fay & Sorrells 2004.

however, single rooms may increase the distance between patients, resulting in increased physical requirements for staff (Van Enk 2006).

The ability of nurses to care for patients is influenced, inter alia, by the geographical dispersion of patients, the size and layout of individual patients' rooms, and technology (such as pagers or computers) (International Council of Nurses). In six focus groups of nurses conducted in England, having sufficient, flexible working space was mentioned as the most important factor enabling them to do their job effectively. The nurses identified as particularly important the layout and use of space, so that they could observe patients (PricewaterhouseCoopers LLP 2004). Conventional floor designs for patient care units, characterized by centralized nurse stations and centralized location of supplies, negatively affect patient safety by increasing staff walking and fatigue. Floor layouts with decentralized nurse stations and supplies, on the other hand, reduce staff walking and increase observation and care time for patients (Ulrich 2006).

Signage is important not only to patients and visitors, but also to staff, who may not know all areas of the hospital equally well or who may have to waste time giving directions to patients or other staff (Carpman & Grant 1997). Furthermore, residential accommodation and crèche facilities incorporated into the hospital design are important for staff recruitment and retention (PricewaterhouseCoopers LLP 2004). Health care workers also appreciate private space and areas reserved for them (PricewaterhouseCoopers LLP 2004). The availability and location of lockers, showers and canteens is also important for the well-being and performance of hospital staff.

## Improving performance

The performance of health care workers is influenced by many factors, often difficult to disentangle, including workplace conditions, pay, job satisfaction, progression opportunities and non-work issues (PricewaterhouseCoopers LLP 2004). While it has been recognized that productivity partly depends on whether health care workers are provided with the necessary equipment, pharmaceuticals and technology (Dieleman & Hammeijer 2006; Zurn, Dolea & Stilwell 2005), the impact of the built environment on staff performance has received far less attention. Yet, health care workers seem to be aware of how the design of health care facilities impacts their work. In a telephone survey of 500 nurses in English hospitals, 87% of interviewees agreed that working in a well-designed hospital would help them to do their job better (CABE 2003).

Little hard evidence is available so far on the trade-offs involved between higher capital costs and benefits in terms of patient outcomes and staff well-being and performance. Despite these caveats, current knowledge suggests that there is indeed a strong business case for designing better hospital environments. According to a model scenario of the US Center for Health Design, with oversized single-patient rooms, acuity-adaptable rooms and decentralized nursing stations, the additional costs up front were quickly recovered, partly as a result of lower nosocomial infections and lower nurse turnover (Berry et al. 2004). In the case of the Barbara Ann Karmanos Cancer Institute in Detroit, United States, the renovation of inpatient nursing units reportedly resulted in a reduction of the nurse attrition rate from 23.0% to 3.8% (Malkin 2006).

This example indicates that capital and labour can to some degree substitute each other. Capital investments can increase efficiencies and reduce the number of staff required for delivering care, and may also reduce overall staff costs; if staff turnover reduces, so does the cost of recruiting replacements (Hayes et al. 2006). In resource-poor settings, on the other hand, a more labour-intensive approach may be appropriate. In the Soviet Union, the Government tried to make up for the dearth of capital with high numbers of hospital beds and staff. In 1989, the Soviet Union had three times more hospitals and twice as many physicians per capita than the United States (Ahmedov et al. 2007). Labour was cheap and easily available, while capital was scarce (Afford & Lessof 2006). Medical and nursing schools were geared towards producing large numbers of staff and low pay encouraged a labour-intensive rather than capital-intensive approach (Afford & Lessof 2006).

Productivity and performance of staff can also be supported directly by good design. One important example of how capital investment can influence the workload of health care workers is the way the layout of health facilities determines walking distances. In far too many hospitals, corridors "seem to run to infinity" (Malkin 2006). In focus groups with nurses in the United Kingdom, long distances between different areas were noted as having a negative impact on nursing performance (PricewaterhouseCoopers LLP 2004). Canteens are often located far away from the working space, so that staff have to rush there and back during their meal breaks (PricewaterhouseCoopers LLP 2004).

In the design of Rhön Klinikum hospitals in Germany, much attention is paid to functional relationships (see the relevant case study in the accompanying case studies volume). One of the aims in the design of new hospitals is to reduce walking distances for nurses. Rhön Klinikum have therefore chosen to reject the organization of nursing departments according to medical disciplines, and instead organized them according to the level of nursing care: intensive, high, medium and low. The design of the hospitals is rather traditional and does not provide for acuity-adaptable rooms. Patients are moved through the different departments as their condition improves, and the hospital design is concentrated and compact.

In the case of the St Olav's Hospital in Trondheim (see the relevant case study in the companion volume), the hospital design and the use of ICT aims to promote staff comfort, satisfaction and job efficiency. The hospital estimates that it will require 10% fewer staff members than the former one to treat the same number of patients (Guenther & Vittori 2008).

The desire to reduce distances has, however, to be weighed against other desired outcomes. As mentioned earlier, there may be trade-offs between the provision of daylight and view versus clinical adjacency and minimizing walking distances. When walking distances should be minimized, this may require a more compact design and deep plan buildings, reducing the opportunities for natural daylight (PricewaterhouseCoopers LLP 2004).

Increased use of ICT will inevitably have important implications for health care workers. Telehealth in particular can replace human capital, as specialists can remain in their places of work (Dechter 2004). The effect of electronic patient records on the organization of work and on patient outcomes remains uncertain, with concerns about the time it takes to access the records (Kossman & Scheidenheim 2008).

Organizational culture and division of labour are often embedded within the built environment of health facilities. The design of hospitals may reflect the culture of management, while the management style can also be influenced or constrained by the design of an individual workspace (PricewaterhouseCoopers LLP 2004). Facility redesign is often coupled with major organizational change (Hamilton & Orr 2005), and patient-centred capital investments have major implications on the staff working there, for example by necessitating multidisciplinary care teams. The St Olav's Hospital in Trondheim, Norway, is designed in accordance with the American Planetree Model, which is based on a patient-centred approach to care and the creation of a healing environment (see, for example, Nolon, Dickinson & Boltin 1999). Rather than moving patients around the hospital, a team of specialists brings medical processes to each patient's room, a model that is similar to the acuity-adaptable rooms mentioned earlier, facilitating cross-specialty collaboration (Guenther & Vittori 2008).

## Involving health care workers in the design phase

There is substantial evidence that nurses are more likely to be attracted to, and perform better in, hospitals in which they can advance professionally, gain autonomy and participate in decision-making (Baumann et al. 2001; International Council of Nurses 2007a; PricewaterhouseCoopers LLP 2004). In "magnet hospitals" (facilities that are able to attract and retain staff comprising well-qualified nurses and consistently provide high-quality care) in the United States, nurses were found to be better placed to use their knowledge and expertise to provide high-quality patient care (Havens & Aiken 1999), partly because they were enabled to be autonomous and were empowered (Upenieks 2005), so benefiting from a participatory decision-making management style (Dieleman & Hammeijer 2006; International Council of Nurses 2007b).

These findings illustrate the importance of involving health care workers in all aspects of their work. The need for staff to have control over their work also applies to processes of change (Dieleman & Hammeijer 2006). However, in the construction of new hospitals, health care staff are only rarely consulted (Walenkamp 2006). Where consultations do take place, they often take on a pro forma character. In a telephone survey of 500 nurses in English hospitals in 2003, 99% of interviewees argued that it is important for them to be consulted on decisions about the design of hospitals, but over half (52%) believed that they do not at present have any influence on the design of hospital environments (CABE 2003). In focus groups conducted with nurses in the United Kingdom in 2004, participants noted that many consultations are purely nominal and the views of staff are not taken into account in the final design. They suggested that it would be better if the staff working in affected units were consulted prior to the start of the building work (PricewaterhouseCoopers LLP 2004).

There is indeed a strong case for involving health care workers in the design of new facilities. Examples of hospitals that have involved their staff in capital investment illustrate the benefits of a more participatory approach. In the case of a 68-bed acute care hospital in the United States that purchased new patient beds, the involvement of the employees, in the form of a representative team, was one of the success factors of the investment. After the purchase, the number of staff injuries and patient falls declined substantially, increasing nursing satisfaction and reducing nursing time (Hardy 2004). In the West Middlesex hospital in the United Kingdom, staff were engaged actively in the design of the new hospital. At every level, clinicians had their say on key components for each department, how they should work and what accommodation was needed, from the number of rooms to the number of beds (NHS 2003). The St Olavs Hospital in Trondheim, Norway, described in the companion case studies volume, underlines the benefits of involving staff in the design phase. As well as involving patients, the hospital planning process involved extensive staff participation, with more than 500 individuals participating in discussions on the new hospital. One result of this involvement is the "*sengetun*" ("bed-courtyards" for step-down care), reflecting a desire to minimize walking distances for nursing staff (see the relevant case study in the accompanying volume).

Improving the quality of buildings at the design stage can have important, long-term life-cycle benefits (see Chapter 8 by Bjørberg & Verweij). While it is essential that the design team consults with the medical staff (Markus 2006), other users of the building also need to be consulted, including housekeepers, lab technicians, food servers, engineers, risk managers and administrators (Guenther & Vittori 2008). Representatives of each hospital service, department or unit should be involved in this process. There are various ways of making the design of a hospital more participatory. It is possible to start with free-hand sketches of plans, then printing out each alternative developed during the meetings with staff, and inviting further suggestions and comments. It is particularly useful to build a full-size mock-up of each room during the conceptual design phase (Diaz 2006; Guenther & Vittori 2008). However, consultations need to be managed effectively, not to fall victim to idiosyncratic views or existing (and often sub-optimal) work processes. They need to get to the bottom of how staff work and be set in the context of the wider objectives of capital investment.

## Conclusions

This chapter has reviewed the available evidence on how capital investment impacts on health care workers. This is an issue that has been far less researched than the role healing environments can play in improving patient outcomes. It is striking how international organizations of health care workers have paid only limited attention to the ways the built environment enables or hinders "positive practice environments". In contrast, a number of "green" building tools for the evaluation of health care environments have started to be utilized to pay attention to patient and staff environments.

From the evidence available so far, it can be concluded that well-designed and sustainable hospitals and other health care facilities improve the health and well-being of health care workers and result in improved staff recruitment, retention and performance. Better equipment can reduce the risk of injuries and minimize the hazards to which health care workers are exposed, and better facilities are located nearer to where staff live, provide sufficient daylight and ventilation, and minimize walking distances. This is not only beneficial to health care workers, but also improves patient outcomes by reducing medical errors and hospital-acquired infections.

To ensure that new buildings improve the delivery of medical care and provide a healthy environment for staff, patients and visitors, it will be essential to involve health care workers in the design of new facilities. These initial investments in better designed and more sustainable health facilities promise to yield significant returns in the long term.

## References

Afford C, Lessof S (2006). The challenges of transition in CEE and the NIS of the former USSR. In: Dubois C-A, McKee M, Nolte E. *Human resources for health in Europe*. Maidenhead, Open University Press:193–213.

Ahmedov M et al. (2007). Uzbekistan: Health system review. *Health Systems in Transition*, 9(3):1–206.

Alimoglu MK, Donmez L (2005). Daylight exposure and the other predictors of burnout among nurses in a University Hospital. *International Journal of Nursing Studies*, 42:549–555.

Baldwin S (1985). Effects of furniture rearrangement on the atmosphere of wards in a maximum-security hospital. *Hospital and Community Psychiatry*, 36:525–528.

Baumann A et al. (2001). *Commitment and care: the benefits of a healthy workplace for nurses, their patients and the system. A policy synthesis*. Ontario, Canadian Health Services Research Foundation.

Berry LL et al. (2004). The business case for better buildings. *Frontiers of Health Services Management*, 21:3–24.

Brody C (2008). From towers of illness to cathedrals of health. In: Guenther R, Vittori G. *Sustainable health care architecture*. Hoboken, John Wiley & Sons:392–394.

CABE (2003). *Radical improvements in hospital design*. London, Commission for Architecture & the Built Environment.

Carpman JR, Grant MA (1997). Wayfinding. In: Marberry SO. *Health care design*. New York, John Wiley & Sons:275–292.

Collins JW et al. (2004). An evaluation of a 'best practices' musculoskeletal injury prevention program in nursing homes. *Injury Prevention*, 10:206–211.

Dechter M (2004). *Health capital planning review. Report*. Toronto, Canadian Council for Public–Private Partnerships.

Diaz JR (2006). Ways of working, attributes and recent projects of KMD. In: Wagenaar C, ed. *The architecture of hospitals*. Rotterdam, NAi Publishers:400–405.

Dieleman M, Hammeijer JW (2006). *Improving health worker performance: in search of promising practices*. Geneva, World Health Organization.

Guenther R, Vittori G (2008). *Sustainable health care architecture*. Hoboken, John Wiley & Sons.

Gunnarsdóttir S, Rafferty AM (2006). Enhancing working conditions. In: Dubois C-A, McKee M, Nolte E. *Human resources for health in Europe*. Maidenhead, Open University Press:155–172.

Hamilton DK, Orr RD (2005). Cultural transformation and design. In: Marberry SO, ed. *Improving health care with better building design*. Chicago, Health Administration Press:145.

Hardy PA (2004). Getting a return on investment from spending capital dollars on new beds. *Journal of Healthcare Management*, 49:199–205.

Havens DS, Aiken LH (1999). Shaping systems to promote desired outcomes. The magnet hospital model. *Journal of Nursing Administration*, 29:14–20.

Hayes L et al. (2006). Nurse turnover: a literature review. *International Journal of Nursing Studies*, 43:237–263.

Hendrich AL, Fay J, Sorrells AK (2004). Effects of acuity-adaptable rooms on flow of patients and delivery of care. *American Journal on Critical Care*, 13:35–45.

Horton JG (1997). Lighting. In: Marberry SO. *Health care design*. New York, John Wiley & Sons:166–179.

International Council of Nurses (2007a). *Positive practice environments. Fact sheet*. Geneva, International Council of Nurses.

International Council of Nurses (2007b). *Positive practice environments: quality workplaces = quality patient care. Information and action tool kit.* Geneva, International Council of Nurses.

International Council of Nurses. *Nurse : patient ratios. Fact Sheet.* Geneva, International Council of Nurses (http://www.icn.ch/matters_rnptratio.htm, accessed 27 February 2008).

Kossman SP, Scheidenheim SL (2008). Nurses' perceptions of the impact of electronic health records on work and patient outcomes. *Computers, Informatics and Nursing,* 26:69–77.

Leather P et al. (1998). Windows in the workplace. *Environment and Behaviour,* 30:739–762.

Malkin J (2006). Healing environments as the century mark: the quest for optimal patient experiences. In: Wagenaar C, ed. *The architecture of hospitals.* Rotterdam, NAi Publishers:258–265.

Markus CC (2006). Healing gardens in hospitals. In: Wagenaar C, ed. *The architecture of hospitals.* Rotterdam, NAi Publishers:315–329.

Milisen K et al. (2006). Work environment and workforce problems: a cross-sectional questionnaire survey of hospital nurses in Belgium. *International Journal of Nursing Studies,* 43:745–754.

Nelson A et al. (2006). Development and evaluation of a multifaceted ergonomics program to prevent injuries associated with patient handling tasks. *International Journal of Nursing Studies,* 43:717–733.

NHS (2003). *NHS Magazine, February 2003.* London, United Kingdom National Health Service.

Nolon AK, Dickinson D, Boltin B (1999). Creating a new environment of ambulatory care: community health centers and the Planetree philosophy. *Journal of Ambulatory Care Management,* 22:18–26.

Pradinuk R (2008). Doubling daylight. In: Guenther R, Vittori G. *Sustainable health care architecture.* Hoboken, John Wiley & Sons:326–331.

PricewaterhouseCoopers LLP (2004). *The role of hospital design in the recruitment, retention and performance of NHS nurses in England.* Belfast, PricewaterhouseCoopers LLP, in association with the University of Sheffield and Queen Margaret University College, Edinburgh (http://www.healthyhospitals.org.uk/diagnosis/HH_Full_report.pdf, accessed 27 February 2008).

Registered Nurses' Association of Ontario (2008). *Workplace health, safety and well-being of the nurse.* Toronto, Registered Nurses' Association of Ontario.

Rosenman KD, Reilly MJ, Schill DP (2003). Cleaning products and work-related asthma. *Journal of Occupational and Environmental Medicine,* 45:557–563.

Suchman AL (2007). Advancing humanism in medical education. *Journal of General Internal Medicine,* 22(11):1630–1631.

Topf M, Dillon E (1988). Noise-induced stress as a predictor of burnout in critical care nurses. *Heart & Lung,* 17:567–574.

Ulrich R (2006). Evidence-based health care design. In: Wagenaar C, ed. *The architecture of hospitals.* Rotterdam, NAi Publishers:281–289.

Upenieks V (2005). Recruitment and retention strategies: a Magnet hospital prevention model. *Medical-Surgical Nursing,* April:21–27.

Van den Berg A, Wagenaar C (2006). Healing by architecture. In: Wagenaar C, ed. *The architecture of hospitals.* Rotterdam, NAi Publishers:254–257.

Van Enk RA (2006). The effect of single versus two-bed rooms on hospital acquired infection rates. In: Wagenaar C, ed. *The architecture of hospitals.* Rotterdam, NAi Publishers:309–313.

Walenkamp GHIM (2006). Preventing surgical infection through better air quality in the operating room. In: Wagenaar C, ed. *The architecture of hospitals.* Rotterdam, NAi Publishers:181–189.

WHO (2006). *The world health report 2006. Working together for health.* Geneva, World Health Organization.

WHO Regional Office for Europe (2008). Health for All database (HFA-DB) [offline database]. Copenhagen, WHO Regional Office for Europe (July 2008 update).

Wilburn S (2005). *Occupational health and safety*. Arlington, VA, Health Care Without Harm (http://www.noharm.org/details.cfm?type=document&id=1194, accessed 3 September 2008).

Zurn P, Dolea C, Stilwell B (2005). *Nurse retention and recruitment: developing a motivated workforce*. Geneva, World Health Organization.

# Part three:
# Economic aspects of capital investment

Chapter 6

# Market competition in European hospital care

*Hans Maarse, Charles Normand*

## Introduction

This chapter investigates some elements of market competition in European hospital care. We use the term market competition as a broad concept, covering a diverse and hard to demarcate range of changes or reforms, such as the growth of the profit-making market, the rise of private entrants in hospital care, or the introduction of new models for hospital funding that seek better to relate payment to performance.

Market competition may have a profound impact on the structure of hospital care and hospital construction across Europe. For instance, it may induce growth of small hospitals that concentrate on a single specialty or at most a few specialist areas. Market competition may also call for new hospital designs that perform significantly better in terms of efficiency, flexibility, patient orientation and innovation than most current general hospitals.

The concept of market competition is ambiguous and a source of confusion (Paulus et al. 2003). For instance, does competition mean price competition, or is it sufficient that providers compete for volume contracts with uniform prices set by a central regulating body? Does it imply profit-making medicine? What is the scope of competition? Does it apply to all forms of hospital care or to only a few elective (non-acute) services?

We conceptualize market competition as the result of multiple developments in hospital care. It may be brought about by a government policy that is explicitly directed at creating competitive relationships. Pro-competition reforms are intended to increase the efficiency and innovativeness of hospital care, to improve its quality and to make hospital care more patient oriented. Examples of these reforms are the introduction of competitive bidding models or the elimination of barriers to entry into the hospital market by new providers. Market competition may also be stimulated by innovations that are not strictly speaking market initiatives. Developing hospital information systems to support performance measurement with the goal of improving the quality and efficiency of hospital care fits perfectly within a market reform, because information is also a precondition for informed choice and more effective price competition by providers. Furthermore, it would be wrong to view market competition only as the result of government reforms. The picture is usually more complicated. For example, "bottom-up" initiatives by private providers or local governments that privatize their public hospital may also elicit competition.

The concept of pro-competition reform is also misleading. It implies that market competition is a "single policy" that can be easily demarcated in time and scope. Such a conceptualization is entirely wrong. Across Europe, pro-competition policies have emerged over longer periods of time, consisting of a wide array of policy decisions in a highly political environment with many stakeholders. These decisions are incremental and often capricious and inconsistent. There is no linear pattern. Market reforms may be revoked later and planned reforms may be postponed or weakened. This pattern reflects the fact that market-oriented reforms remain controversial, with concerns over the impact on costs, equity in access to care, and the distribution of the financial burden. Policy-makers often follow a cautious strategy, both for reasons of political feasibility and to avoid policy risks.

We focus our investigation on a selected number of issues: changes in the public–private mix of hospital care; the role of new entrants in hospital care; the reform of the funding arrangements of hospital care; the introduction of new models for capital investments; and the development of information systems on hospital performance. Furthermore, we restrict our investigation to western Europe and take our illustrations mainly from four countries: England, Germany, Ireland and the Netherlands. In our view, this sample of countries gives the reader a good overview of the scope and impact of the trend towards market competition in European hospital care. Unfortunately, we cannot say much about the impact of market competition on hospital care because there is so little good evidence of its effects in the European context.

Finally, it is important to say a few words about the hospital versus other providers. Since the 1980s an increasing proportion of specialist care has been shifted from an inpatient to an outpatient (ambulatory) setting. Furthermore, one may expect a rise of single-specialty hospitals that compete with general hospitals in specific areas, a development that is already taking place in the United States and raises much controversy (Voelker 2003; Iglehart 2005; Guterman 2006). Despite the growing diversity in settings for the delivery of specialist care, we only discuss hospitals in this chapter.

## Changes in the public–private mix of hospital care

The public–private mix in European hospital care is diverse (Maarse 2006) (see Box 6.1). Whereas in various countries, including England and the Scandinavian countries, a largely public delivery model came into existence (Øvretveit 2001), other countries, including Germany, France and Ireland, developed a mixed structure of public and private hospitals. Most private hospitals in these countries are private non-profit-making (voluntary) agencies that were founded by voluntary associations. So far, France is the only European country with a sizeable profit-making sector. In 2000, approximately 38% of all hospitals in France were profit-making, accounting for 15% of the total bed volume. Most of the activity of profit-making hospitals is in the day care setting or short-term surgery (Bellanger 2004; Rochaix & Hartmann 2005).

The public–private dichotomy is obviously an analytical simplification that neglects much of the variety found in the real world of hospital care. This is illustrated, for instance, by the concept of private non-profit-making hospitals. In countries such as Germany, these hospitals, which are subject to the same regulatory and funding arrangements as public hospitals, are not even considered part of "the private sector". It is also difficult to differentiate clearly between non-profit-making and profit-making hospitals (Bradford & Gray 1986). Non-profit-making hospitals may also make substantial excess revenue and profit-making hospitals may lack an explicit profit-making motive (Øvretveit 2001).

However, the distinction between public and private hospitals is important. Many policy-makers consider structural changes in the public–private mix a necessary element of market competition. Privatization, by converting public hospitals into private agencies and extending the scope of profit-making medicine, is viewed as a precondition for market competition. This is not to imply, however, that market competition within the public sector is impossible. The creation of the so-called internal market in the NHS in England in the 1990s was an attempt to introduce some competition into a public hospital environment (Glennester 1998; Klein 1998; Le Grand 1999).

Since its inception in 1948, the NHS in England has had a mainly public delivery structure. At the same time, there has always been a relatively small private (independent) sector for mostly privately paid health care, currently accounting for approximately 10% of acute hospital beds. The reforms of the 1990s aimed to generate competition between NHS providers within the internal market. With that purpose in mind, most hospitals had been converted to "Trusts" by the end of the 1990s. Trust hospitals remained public bodies with a significant degree of public control and limited exposure to the consequences of failure. The creation of "Foundation Trusts" can be conceived

---

**Box 6.1** *Ownership and operation of health care organizations*

**Australia** – Public hospitals make up 70% of beds and the rest are in private hospitals. Commonwealth and state governments have sought in general to reduce their role in direct health service delivery and to increase the role of voluntary and profit-making providers. Primary care is privately provided.

**Austria** – In 1998, 60% of hospital beds were publicly provided by the states (*Länder*) and communities. A total of 16.3% of hospital beds were owned by religious orders; 7.8% were owned by health insurance funds; and 4.6% were operated by private entities. Primary care is provided by independent contractors who typically work in single practices.

**Denmark** – Hospitals are generally managed and financed by the counties (with the exception of a few private hospitals). In primary care, there are private self-employed contractors and community services, managed by municipalities.

**France** – So far, France is the only European country with a sizeable profit-making sector. In 2000, approximately 38% of all hospitals in France were profit-making, accounting for 15% of the total bed volume. The remaining hospitals are owned by the public sector or by foundations, religious organizations or mutual insurance associations. Self-employed doctors, dentists and medical auxiliaries work in their own practices. There are approximately 1000 health centres, usually run by local authorities or mutual insurance associations. Some of the staff are salaried.

**Germany** – A total of 37% of acute hospitals are publicly owned; 40% are private non-profit-making facilities; and 23% are private profit-making hospitals. Private profit-making providers dominate the rehabilitation sector, while the reduction in acute beds has largely been in the public sector. In primary care, private profit-making providers are mostly contractors, with a small number of salaried staff.

**Israel** – Approximately half of all acute hospital beds are government owned and operated. Another third of acute beds are owned by a health plan. Approximately 5% of acute beds are in private profit-making hospitals and the remainder are church affiliated and other voluntary, non-profit-making hospitals. Primary care physicians are employed by or contracted to health plans.

**Italy** – Hospitals are mostly publicly owned (61%), with 539 private hospitals (39%), which tend to be non-profit-making. Primary care is provided by private profit-making providers and by publicly owned local health units for more specialist ambulatory care.

**Luxembourg** – There is one private profit-making maternity hospital. Of the remaining hospitals, approximately half are run by local authorities and half by non-profit-making (mainly religious) organizations. In primary care, providers are self-employed and in

*. . . contd*

**Box 6.1** *contd*

competition with specialists. Much primary care nursing is provided by "medico-social centres" based on contracts with national and local authorities.

**The Netherlands** – All hospitals are private non-profit-making providers and there are no profit-making hospitals. Hospital planning and health insurance legislation have always contained a formal ban on profit-making hospital care. However, this is changing and policies are likely to lead to greater involvement of profit-making hospital provision.

**Norway** – Hospitals have traditionally been owned and run by counties and municipalities, with a small voluntary sector. Recently, some centralization of control has been established. In primary care, there is a public–private mix of contractors and employees.

**Poland** – In 2003 there were 72 non-public hospitals, compared to 732 public hospitals. Poland has decreased its hospital bed capacity substantially since the 1990s, and primary health care and family medicine have been strengthened since 1991. Outpatient specialized care is mostly based on private medical practices in large cities and independent health care institutions in other areas.

**Portugal** – In 2004 Portugal had 171 hospitals, 89 of which were public and 82 private – almost half of the latter belong to profit-making organizations. The reduction in acute beds has largely been in the public sector. In primary care there is a mix of public and private providers. There is a large independent private sector, which provides diagnostic and therapeutic services.

**Russian Federation** – Almost all hospitals are in public ownership. As in the Soviet period, there continues to be considerable overprovision of secondary and tertiary care. In rural areas, primary care is provided by health posts staffed by feldshers and/or midwives, while in urban areas primary care is provided by local polyclinics. In both cases, health care workers are state employees.

**Spain** – Hospitals are largely publicly owned, with a small number of autonomous and charitable hospitals. In primary care, most health care workers are state employees.

**Sweden** – Hospitals are largely independent public bodies owned and run by counties (often working in groups) and regional authorities. Primary care is largely publicly provided, with a growing private sector, including physiotherapy, district nurses and maternity services.

**Switzerland** – There is a mix of public, publicly subsidized and private hospitals. The public hospitals may be operated by the canton, associations of municipalities, individual municipalities or independent foundations. Primary care is provided by independent practitioners.

*Source*: *Health Systems in Transition* series reports of the European Observatory on Health Systems and Policies.

as the next stage in giving autonomy. They have more control over assets, are less financially regulated, can raise a certain amount of financial resources and are more accountable for success and failure (Newbold 2005). Strictly speaking, the introduction of Trusts cannot be considered privatization, but it may be seen as a step in the direction of a form of corporatization, although in the case of the United Kingdom there is a statutory lock on the assets (Pollock 2004). Another development is that the private sector has managed to extend its range of services since the 1990s, which now include critical care facilities and facilities for complex surgery and after-care (Higgins 2004).

Hospitals in Ireland are a mixture of public and private non-profit-making (voluntary) general hospitals. In contrast to the United Kingdom, voluntary hospitals were never brought formally into the public health care system (Wiley 2005). There is also a small private profit-making sector that mainly deals with privately paid health services. The difference between the public and voluntary sectors is mainly historical. In practice, there is little difference in terms of revenue funding and resources for capital development. The structure of the public–private mix has not changed significantly since the 1980s, although some smaller voluntary hospitals have been closed or have become part of larger public hospitals. There is no significant trend towards privatization in Irish hospital care.

Hospital care in Germany has traditionally been delivered by a mix of hospitals. Public hospitals have always coexisted with private non-profit-making (*freigemeinnützig*) and profit-making hospitals and there are now no significant differences in the way each type of hospital is regulated and recurrent expenses are funded. Similar to the French model, an important aspect of hospital care in Germany is that most profit-making hospitals enter contracts with health insurance funds and are thus not solely dependent on privately paid services. The structure of the public–private mix in hospital care in Germany has been undergoing some change since the 1990s. Whereas the proportion of public general hospitals declined from 47% in 1990 to 36% in 2004, the percentage of private profit-making hospitals grew from 15% to 24% (the percentage of private non-profit-making hospitals remained more or less stable). Over the same period, the percentage of beds in profit-making hospitals increased from almost 4% to 11%, compared to a decline in the public sector from 63% to 52% (Bundesministerium für Gesundheit 2006). Traditionally, many profit-making hospitals concentrated on only a few medical areas. This picture is changing, however, now that profit-making hospital chains, of which Rhön Klinikum, Sana, Asklepios and Fresenius are probably best known, are extending their market share by taking over significant numbers of general and even university hospitals (see the case study on Rhön Klinikum in the accompanying volume).

Various public owners (such as municipalities or pension funds) sold their hospital to a profit-making chain by means of a competitive bidding procedure. They saw privatization as the only option to increase hospital productivity and were no longer prepared to cover hospital deficits after the lifting of the full cost reimbursement principle in 1993. Another argument for privatization was the shortage of financial resources at the state (*Länder*) level for much-needed capital investments. Private chains have been in a better position to generate these capital resources.

Privatization by selling a public asset has not been the only option. Less radical options were awarding a contract to a private company to manage the hospital, or changing the legal structure of the hospital, without necessarily a change in ownership (Busse & Wörz 2004). A truly remarkable aspect of hospital privatization in Germany is its local or "bottom-up" character. It is not the result of an explicit federal policy to shift ownership from the public to the private sector. The degree of hospital privatization also varies across *Länder*, which suggests that privatization is influenced by contextual factors in each state.

In the Netherlands, at the time of writing all hospitals are private non-profit-making providers and there are no profit-making hospitals. Hospital planning and health insurance legislation have always contained a formal ban on profit-making hospital care. However, this will almost certainly change in the future. Lifting the ban on profit-making hospital care has been presented as a constituent element of the ongoing market reform in Dutch health care. Another policy issue is how to prevent hospital reserves accumulated in a protected "public" environment from leaking to the profit-making sector. To solve this problem, the introduction of a public undertaking as a new legal entity has been proposed. A public undertaking has a profit-making status, but its accumulated reserves can only be spent on health care. Interestingly, developments in the real world seem to outrun the Government's policy. There are several initiatives for commercial exploitation of hospitals and, following competitive bidding, a loss-making hospital was recently taken over by a private investment company.

In summary, in the four countries considered, hospital care is largely delivered by either public or private non-profit-making hospitals. France is the only country in Europe where a substantial profit-making hospital sector has come into existence, although the market share of profit-making hospitals is also increasing in Germany. With the exception of Germany, there has been little serious and consistent privatization. The Dutch Government is actively considering privatization by accepting profit-making hospitals as a further step towards a hospital market, but this policy is still at an initial stage.

## Rise of new providers

Most hospitals in Europe are general hospitals offering a wide array of acute and elective health services. The main trend over recent decades has been one of consolidation, with a decline in the number of general hospitals. A more recent development is the rise of new providers that are mostly private single-specialty organizations delivering routine hospital care. They have always been a part of the hospital landscape, but what is new is that their creation is now being encouraged by governments and that they are extending their range of services. These developments can be explained by several factors. The advance of medical technology has made it possible not only to treat more patients and a broader range of medical problems in an ambulatory setting, but also to do so in specialized stand-alone clinics. Long waiting lists in elective care also play a key role. Furthermore, new providers are assumed to increase productivity, to be more patient friendly and to enhance patient choice. New providers may also be able to adopt more efficient work practices, being less constrained by existing rules or traditions. There is also a link with market competition, because new entrants will boost competition.

The Netherlands presents a good example of this development. Until the late 1990s, it was government policy to discourage the establishment of "private clinics". However, a waiting list crisis in the late 1990s, as well as calls for more entrepreneurship and market competition in hospital care, created a different environment. The number of "independent treatment centres" grew from 31 in 2000 to almost 160 by the end of 2006. They are active in various fields, including ophthalmology, dermatology, maternity and child care, orthopaedic surgery, cosmetic surgery, radiology and cardiology. The new centres conclude contracts with health insurers for the reimbursement of the costs of health services covered by the new health insurance legislation (Bartholomee & Maarse 2006).

Although the number of new entrants looks spectacular, the volume of care they deliver is still only a small fraction of total hospital care. If we focus on the 8% of hospital care where price competition now exists (see "Hospital funding", later in this chapter), the centres covered 24.7% of the total turnover of dermatology; 8.4% of cosmetic surgery; and 3% of ophthalmology in 2006. These percentages are significantly lower for those hospital services which are still subject to central price regulation (Nederlandse Zorgautoriteit 2007b). It remains unclear to what extent new providers will alter the future landscape of hospital care. They may reinforce a trend away from general hospitals towards a model in which most elective (non-acute) care is delivered in single-specialty clinics. At a more fundamental level, the threat of competition may work as a powerful force for hospitals to redesign their internal organization in order to increase productivity, improve the quality of care and become more patient focused (see the Orbis case study in the accompanying volume).

A somewhat similar development can be observed in England where the Government started a Treatment Centre Programme in 2003 to provide extra capacity needed to decrease waiting times, increase patient choice, stimulate innovative models of service delivery, and step up productivity. Treatment centres are, as in the Netherlands, dedicated units for pre-booked day surgery and short-stay surgery, along with diagnostic procedures, in specialties such as ophthalmology, orthopaedics and for a range of other conditions. These include hip and knee replacements, hernia repair and gall bladder and cataract removal. Treatment centres are run by the NHS or commissioned from independent sector providers after selection from among preferred bidders. This process was largely led by central Government, and did not engage significantly with local priorities or views. By the end of 2006 there were 21 Independent Sector Treatment Centres (ISTCs) run by private providers and some 60 such centres run by the NHS. The creation of ISTCs fits into the Government's policy to establish firm public–private partnerships in the delivery of health care (Department of Health 2007). As in the Netherlands, it is too early to draw conclusions on their ultimate impact on the delivery of specialist services. However, there is some anecdotal evidence that ISTCs have not only increased patient choice and reduced waiting times for some specialties, but also had a significant effect on the responsiveness of existing providers and the spot purchase price (the price for immediate payment and delivery) in the private sector (Secretary of State for Health 2006). At the same time, there is concern about the quality of care and the value for money delivered by ISTCs (Wallace 2006).

The rise of new private provider organizations can also be observed in Ireland. The National Treatment Purchase Fund (NTPF) was established in 2002 by the Government as a response to the long waiting times for non-urgent treatment in public hospitals (Langham et al. 2003). The programme entitles all patients to free-of-charge treatment funded by the NTPF after waiting three months for admission to a public hospital for inpatient treatment. More recently, some categories of people waiting for outpatient treatment have also been eligible. The NTPF contracts mainly with private providers in Ireland and the United Kingdom. The limited data available suggest that the cost per procedure under the NTPF tends to be above the cost per case for similar procedures in public hospitals (Comptroller and Auditor General 2006), but the requirement to retain commercial confidentiality makes comparisons difficult. Moreover, the prices paid by the NTPF varied greatly for apparently similar work. Particular controversy arose over the purchase of "spare capacity" in public hospitals, since there is no clear definition of what is "spare". A concern was that hospitals could be paid twice to carry out the same procedure for the same patient and that there was an incentive not to treat the patient, if the patient might reappear as an NTPF patient with additional funding.

The situation in Germany is different. Germany has a long tradition of medical specialists working in private clinics, providing ambulatory medical care, whereas most hospitals provide only inpatient care. Thus, the delivery of inpatient care (in hospitals) has always been separated institutionally from ambulatory care (in private centres). Another aspect of specialist care in Germany is overcapacity. Because waiting times are particularly short, there is no reason to build up new capacity by means of new private medical centres. Against this background, the rise of new provider agencies has been much less pronounced than in the other countries under consideration. The emphasis in current policy-making is on breaking down the wall between inpatient and ambulatory care and on setting up networks providing integrated care to large categories of patients (such as patients with diabetes, COPD or heart failure). For that purpose, new legislation was enacted to encourage the establishment of new small-scale medical centres, in which hospitals and physicians in private practice collaborate with each other. An important problem facing these centres is the lack of integrated remuneration arrangements for hospital physicians and physicians working in private practice.

In summary, we can conclude that there has been an increase in new private providers in most of the countries considered, although the situation in Germany, with its traditional division between specialist care in hospitals and private practice, is different. General hospitals often consider the rise of new private centres as a threat to which they must respond in order to avoid a loss of market share.

## Hospital funding

Changes in hospital funding are also relevant. In European hospital care, there is a trend away from global budgets towards case mix-based funding. The new funding model is not a market reform itself, because it can be used to optimize the budget allocation process without any intention to introduce competition. However, case mix-based funding is a precondition for market competition.

The introduction of a new funding model in England, somewhat confusingly called Payment by Results (PbR) (Department of Health 2002) while really being payment by activity, is a good example of this. The new model is intended to solve the problems of contracting that came into existence during the internal market reforms in the 1980s and 1990s. A big problem with the so-called block contracts between commissioning agencies and hospitals was that they were insensitive to the volume and nature of activity. PbR has been introduced as a tool to help PCTs to purchase care from the most appropriate provider, whether in the public or private sector (Boyle 2005). HRG tariffs, which are the national average cost of inpatient care or day care for patients with a similar diagnosis, form the cornerstone of PbR. The tariff for each HRG includes all clinical and nonclinical costs. The introduction of PbR has been slower than the Government had envisaged at its launch in 2003. There were only 15 procedures covered by PbR in 2003, but this is planned to rise to 90% of hospital care by 2009. Another important aspect concerns the use of average costs for setting tariffs, as these do not provoke price competition and therefore provide only relatively weak incentives to improve efficiency. They are also insufficiently sensitive to capture highly specialized care. Thus, some specialized facilities, such as stand-alone orthopaedic facilities, are penalized because the case definitions fail to differentiate, for example, primary hip replacements from the much more complex and expensive second revisions. There is now an intention to move from average prices to a tariff more closely linked to evidence-based best practice for some of the higher volume HRGs.

Germany is also experimenting with a new funding model based on DRGs, with the aim of better allocating financial resources. As in England, it is a "learn-as-you-go system" that is expected to be fully implemented by 2009. The German DRG system applies, with a few exceptions, to all forms of inpatient care. In 2006 there were 914 national DRG cost weights, plus an additional 40 (non-national) cost weights. The German DRG system in principle excludes price negotiations between the health insurance funds (or private insurers) and hospitals. Cost weights are set nationally and the monetary value of a relative weight – the so-called base rate – is set at the state (*Länder*) level (Schreyögg, Tiemann & Busse 2005). Nevertheless, some price competition is developing. A few health insurance funds have agreed variable rates with provider networks for integrated care to specific groups of patients, in which the rate varies with patient volume.

Diagnosis Treatment Combinations (DTCs) are the Dutch approach to case mix-based hospital funding. In contrast to Germany and England, DTCs cover both inpatient and outpatient care. At the time of writing there are approximately 30 000 DTCs, but this number is expected to decrease significantly in the near future, as there is now consensus that the system is too complicated to function properly. DTCs are intended as a tool for price competition. In 2006 approximately 8% of hospital production (by value) was funded on the basis of negotiated DTC prices. Examples of hospital care for which price competition applies are cataracts, inguinal hernia, total hip and knee replacement and diabetes care. A recent evaluation by the Dutch Health Care Authority (Nederlandse Zorgautoriteit 2007a) indicated that price negotiations have indeed pushed down price increases somewhat, but it is unclear whether this is a lasting effect. The scope for price negotiations will be extended to 20% of hospital production in 2008, which is significantly less than the 70% the previous government had in mind (emergency care and the most complex clinical care remain excluded from competition).

An important argument for slowing down the implementation of price competition is concern about the complexity of the new funding system. Another concern is that health insurers are not yet able to function as an effective countervailing power in price negotiations and that hospitals may use competition to push up prices. There is also a lack of transparency. Competition requires that health insurers and patients are well informed about the performance of each hospital, but this condition has not yet been fulfilled. A further problem is how to avoid the possibility that the open-ended character of the new funding system will cause cost inflation. To reign in the growth of hospital expenditure, price competition will be complemented by yardstick competition for those hospital services which are beyond the scope of price competition (80% in 2008). Yardstick competition uses maximum prices (tariffs) that are set centrally by the Dutch Health Care Authority, and efficient hospitals are allowed to retain their revenue surplus. The new funding system creates a common, level playing field, because it applies both to hospitals and independent treatment centres.

In Ireland, the funding of hospitals has also undergone reforms. Since 1993 the funding arrangements have included an adjustment for the number and mix of cases. Whereas the main funding remains calculated on the basis of global budgets, a proportion (currently 20%) of inpatient and day-patient budgets is subject to change in the light of case mix calculations (Wiley 2005). The 2001 Health Strategy recommended raising this to 50% by 2007, but this target has not been achieved. Although there has been little formal assessment of this reform, it has been noticeable that more time and effort are being channelled into the recording and coding of activities. As with virtually all case mix payment systems, there are also concerns about gaming behaviour, with the classification of cases subtly shifting. However, to a large extent, the hospitals that are doing well under case mix funding also exhibit good financial performance, while those that are not include hospitals that have struggled to remain within budget.

Although the development of case mix-based funding models for hospital care can be regarded as a precondition for market competition, it is unclear to what extent these models will boost competition. This is partially due to the short time dedicated to gathering experience so far, and the limited scope of competition. Another critical factor is how the relationship between funding agencies and hospitals will evolve. What may be expected from contracting? Will funding agencies (such as health insurers or PCTs) be an effective countervailing power in negotiating contracts with hospitals so as to reward efficiency, innovation, quality of care and a patient-driven orientation? There are formidable barriers to effective purchasing, such as a lack of timely and reliable information on the costs and quality of care. Other obstacles to a pro-competition usage of case mix-based funding include difficulties with legal arrangements for contracting, the (regional) structure of the market for hospital care, user preferences, political circumstances and government interference.

## Hospital planning and funding of capital investments

The organization of hospital capacity planning and capital investments is another critical determinant of competition. A recent review (Ettelt et al. 2007) indicated that centralized models dominate hospital capacity planning in Europe (see Chapter 3 by Ettelt et al.). Governments are also directly involved in the funding of capital investments (see Chapter 7 by Dewulf & Wright). Centralized hospital capacity planning and government grants for capital investments are at odds with market competition. The market model requires hospitals to have considerable autonomy in making investment decisions. Whereas private investors make their own investment plans, seek capital resources to finance them and bear the financial risk of investments, hospitals in Europe, whether they are public or private non-profit-making facilities, operate in a completely different institutional setting. They are largely dependent on central or regional government decisions for the approval and funding of their investment plans.

Until recently, the Netherlands provided a good example of central planning. The Hospital Planning Act (1971) authorized the Ministry of Health to regulate hospital capacity in terms of service volume and activity. As part of the current market reform, the central planning model will be gradually replaced with a new model that gives hospitals more autonomy for planning and investments. The new planning legislation still requires hospitals to have a government licence, but that licence is, in principle, no longer intended as a planning tool, but as an instrument to safeguard quality of care and good governance. The new regulation makes hospitals responsible for their own capital investments. However, the Government retains its planning power in a few specialist areas and also remains authorized to intervene when access to hospital care is considered to be at risk.

The current market reform in the Netherlands also includes a significant revision of the regime for financing capital investments. Under the previous system the costs of rent and depreciation of government-approved investments were financed by a mark-up on the per diem rate over a 40-year period, so that neither hospitals nor banks incurred any financial risk – further accentuated by the Guarantee Fund for the Health Sector (*Waarborgfonds voor de Zorgsector*). Under the new arrangements, hospitals will receive a normative mark-up on case mix-based payments to finance their capital investments, which means that the scope for capital investments will depend on the volume of services delivered (see Chapter 8 by Bjørberg & Verweij).

The new system is expected to have important implications. Policy-makers believe that hospitals will be more aware of the costs of capital investments. Other implications of the new regime are that it may attract investment companies, venture capitalists, property companies or other private agencies that are searching for investment opportunities and new partnerships in health care. The new regime may also lead to hospital bankruptcies, which may affect the cost of capital. There are plans to phase in the new arrangements over a longer period of time to avoid serious disruptive effects.

The situation in Germany is different. Germany introduced the so-called dual financing system in 1972 which separates the funding of recurrent expenditure from capital investments (see Chapter 7 by Dewulf & Wright). Whereas the health insurance funds pay for recurrent expenditure and smaller investments, the states (*Länder*) are responsible for hospital capacity planning and the taxed-based funding of major capital investments (building and major reconstruction) through grants (hospital reserves are another source of funding). Profit-making hospitals may also opt to benefit from state funding, but sometimes prefer to make their own investment decisions instead of being subject to a time-consuming political and bureaucratic process (Busse & Riesberg 2004).

In Germany, there has been no pro-competition reform of hospital planning and capital investments so far. Policy proposals to replace the current dual financing model with a single financing model are politically contested. Most *Länder* are reluctant to support such reforms, because it would deprive them of political tools to influence health care within their territory. Another problem is the uneven distribution of the need for capital investment, creating an unequal starting point. Whereas some states have intensified their investments since the 1990s (particularly in the eastern part of Germany), investments in other *Länder* lagged behind. It is important to note that, while the privatization of public hospitals has increased the role of private investors, the increase in private investments has so far remained particularly limited (Deutsches Krankenhaus Institut 2005).

The English NHS also has some central control over capital developments. At the time of writing, smaller capital investments are planned by local PCTs within a framework set by the Department of Health. Larger investments require the approval of the Department of Health and projects involving investments of more than £100 million must be approved by the Treasury (Ettelt et al. 2007). Traditionally, hospital investments were financed by state grants. However, in the early 1990s the Government introduced an alternative model for capital investments, known as the PFI (see Chapter 7 by Dewulf & Wright). The privatization of capital investment funding has always raised much political controversy (Pollock 2004), but there are signs of growing frustrations. Many complain of the lack of flexibility in PFI contracts. Furthermore, there is mounting evidence that PFI brings only temporary budgetary relief (costs are shifted to the future) and that it appears to be quite an expensive tool for capital investments over a longer period of time (Atun & McKee 2005; McKee, Edwards & Atun 2006).

In Ireland, until recently, all capital developments (and indeed all replacements of equipment) were funded by the Government. As in the other three countries, hospitals competed in a not particularly transparent process for government funds. There has recently been a shift to encouraging (and in some cases requiring) private sector participation in funding capital investments in hospitals. It is too early to assess the impact of this change, but some early signs are not encouraging. There seems to be little willingness among private sector partners to bear the risks associated with hospital development projects and the processes have been slower than the public ones they are replacing. A crucial lesson here is that a system that has limited capacity to plan and manage capital projects may have even less capacity to manage a tendering and competitive process using private sector partners.

In summary, we conclude that hospital planning and capital investments evolved as part of the "public domain" in European health care. At the time of writing, the autonomy of hospitals in the Netherlands is being enhanced as part of the pro-competition strategy of successive governments, but its ultimate impact is still unclear. In Germany and England, there is still a strong involvement of government bodies in hospital capacity planning. The introduction of PFI in England has increased the role of private investors in hospital developments, but the role of PFI may have reached a plateau and its future is uncertain.

## Information on performance

In various countries, initiatives have been undertaken to acquire information on the performance of hospitals. Hospital performance information is not only an instrument to inform the general public and other stakeholders, but also a tool for improving the efficiency and quality of hospital care. Although not a market instrument itself, like case mix tariffs it can be regarded as a precondition for market competition, because purchasing is doomed to fail if the purchasing agencies do not have adequate information on hospital performance in terms of capacity, efficiency, waiting times, patient safety and clinical quality of care.

The number of initiatives to compile quantitative, standardized and comparative information on hospital performance is rapidly increasing. These initiatives are not only undertaken by government agencies, but also increasingly involve private organizations, such as Dr Foster in the United Kingdom, an independent provider of health care information.

In England, the Care Quality Commission (the successor of the Healthcare Commission and Commission for Health Improvement) has been charged with independent performance measurement of hospitals and other health and social care providers. The Commission tests compliance with minimum standards, and NHS providers, including hospitals, will be subject to an annual check against a wider set of standards. The Care Quality Commission, like the Healthcare Commission before it, will publish annual ratings of health care organizations' performance. Foundation Trusts are in addition subject to a separate assessment of financial performance. There tends to be significant public interest in these results.

A similar development can be observed in the Netherlands. The Health Care Inspectorate, the National Institute for Public Health and Environmental Hygiene and a number of private agencies are investing in information systems to inform hospitals, health insurers and the general public on the performance of each hospital. Some media also publish a detailed annual ranking of hospitals which informs the reader about the "best" and the "worst" hospitals. These rankings are based not only on structure and process indicators, but also include clinical outcome indicators. It is the intention of the Health Care Inspectorate to extend the use of clinical indicators in hospital performance measurement. The Inspectorate also visits each hospital once a year to discuss the hospital's scores on the performance indicators.

The call for greater transparency on the quality and costs of hospital care has also reached Germany. Publication of the results of quality assurance initiatives became obligatory in 2000 for nosocomial infections. Benchmarking of the quality of hospital care and ambulatory surgery is coordinated by the Robert Koch Institute, but is only slowly gaining acceptance. From 2005, hospitals are obliged by law to publish on their Internet home page data on their capacity (beds, human resources, medical equipment), as well as the range and volume of their services. However, they are not obliged to publish information on outcomes (Busse & Riesberg 2004) and publications that contain systematic and nationwide comparisons and rankings of hospital performance do not yet exist.

In Ireland, a new agency, the Health Information and Quality Authority (HIQA) has recently been established to take on responsibility for monitoring quality and safety. Most hospitals are already involved in quality assurance activities, such as accreditation, and there are regular audits aimed at reducing hospital infections. The HIQA has faced difficulties, since it was established at the same time that other major structural reforms were being introduced, and as yet there is no evidence of any impact on quality of care in the acute sector, although the agency has been more visible in terms of its quality audits of long-term care.

In summary, there is a call for more information on public policy performance (De Bruijn 2002). Against this background, the amount of information on hospital performance is rapidly increasing, and hospitals are increasingly required to account publicly for their performance. It can be expected that market competition will encourage this development further.

## Conclusions

This chapter investigated some aspects of market competition in European hospital care. Our overview has shown that there is no clear and coherent drive towards market competition across Europe. Our findings point to a remarkable gap between the rhetoric of market competition and what happens in the "real world". What we found was a diversity of reform activities in a broad range of areas which fit into a market approach, but are not necessarily market initiatives themselves. Policy initiatives to shorten waiting times by inviting private sector providers to compete for public funding or to relate hospital funding better to performance are examples of reforms with a positive impact on the development of a hospital market. The Netherlands is the only one of the four countries under consideration where we found a more or less consistent pattern of reforms to elicit market competition in hospital care, but the scope of these reforms is as yet highly uncertain.

Our overview illustrates the limited nature of market reform in Europe. For instance, with the exception of the Netherlands, price competition exists nowhere and, even in the Netherlands, its scope has so far remained particularly limited. Competition in all the countries described mainly concentrates on high-volume routine elective (non-urgent) care. Despite the rhetoric of market competition, the legal ban on profit-making hospital care has not yet been lifted in the Netherlands. Public planning of major hospital capital investments is still prevalent across Europe. The only country where the market share of profit-making hospitals has grown considerably is Germany, but this growth was not the outcome of a nationally orchestrated privatization policy. There was also a rise of new private entrants in hospital care in England, Ireland and the Netherlands, but their role in the delivery of specialist care should not be overstated. General hospitals still play a leading role in delivering specialist services to patients. It is too early to assess to what extent the rise of single-specialty private centres will alter the structure of the European hospital landscape.

Market reform in hospital care is no "big bang" process. Most reforms take many years and follow a cautionary approach. Governments are eager to avoid distortions in hospital care and to "learn by doing". Political conflicts about market reforms also help to explain their incrementalist nature, and there is still little consensus on the appropriateness of market reforms in hospital care or in health care in general.

It is difficult to make valid predictions about the future of market reforms across Europe. Health care policy-making is an embedded activity that is heavily influenced by wider developments in public policy-making. In many countries, one can observe a trend towards market competition in public domains. Public procurement procedures are increasingly being organized to get more value for money (see Chapter 7 by Dewulf & Wright), and this trend will also impact on health care policy-making. The prospects for market competition in health care are likely to vary with the type of care being delivered. Market competition is most likely to extend into areas of high-volume routine elective care where there is reasonable consensus on the definition of good health care and where the degree of medical risks is limited. It is unlikely to extend rapidly into complex and emergency care.

Future market competition for hospital care also depends on values. Although there are many and notable differences in the way values are translated into concrete arrangements, it is fair to say that hospital care in western Europe has a tradition of universal access, equal treatment and a fair distribution of the financial burden. It is plausible to assume that the policy legacy of these values will set limits to market competition in hospital care. From this perspective, it comes as no surprise that the scope of market competition has so far remained limited. The policy challenge for the future is how to preserve public values in a market competition model.

A final important factor concerns the impact of market reforms. As yet, there is only scant evidence on the effects of market reforms. There are still many unanswered questions. For instance, do profit-making hospitals outperform public hospitals in terms of efficiency, quality of care, innovative power or patient focus? Does market competition reduce waiting times? What is its impact on administrative costs? Do funding models based on pay for performance elicit "creep", that is, the tendency to be classified as more complex so as to attract higher fees (Nassiri & Rochaix 2006)? To what degree is the private sector willing to bear risks in hospital care? To what extent does private capital penetrate into hospital care and create tensions between patient value and shareholder value? How can the public sector collaborate effectively with the private sector in public–private partnerships?

The absence of clear answers to these and other pertinent questions means that much of the current debate on market competition is dominated by a priori arguments from all sides of the political spectrum. We argue for more systematic research to see what works and what does not, and on the implications this has for capital financing models.

## References

Atun R, McKee M (2005). Is the private finance initiative dead? *British Medical Journal*, 331(7520):792–793.

Bartholomee Y, Maarse H (2006). Health insurance reform in the Netherlands. *Eurohealth*, 12(2):7–9.

Bellanger M (2004). Modernization instead of privatisation in French health care. In: Maarse H. *Privatization in European health care: a comparative analysis in eight countries*. Maarssen, Elsevier:63–77.

Boyle S (2005). Payment by results in England. *Euro Observer*, 7(4):1–4.

Bradford H, Gray BH (eds) (1986). *For-profit enterprise in health care*. Washington, DC, National Academy Press.

Bundesministerium für Gesundheit (2006). *Statistisches Taschenbuch Gesundheit 2005*. Berlin, Bundesministerium für Gesundheit.

Busse R, Riesberg A (2004). *Health Care Systems in Transition: Germany*, 6(9):1–234.

Busse R, Wörz M (2004). The ambiguous experience with privatization in German health care. In: Maarse H. *Privatization in European health care: a comparative analysis in eight countries*. Maarssen, Elsevier:79–95.

Comptroller and Auditor General (2006). *Annual report 2005*. Dublin, Stationery Office (http://audgen.irlgov.ie/documents/annualreports/2005/2005_Report_Eng.pdf, accessed 21 October 2008).

De Bruijn H (2002). *Managing performance in the public sector*. London, Taylor and Francis.

Department of Health (2002). *Reforming NHS financial flows. Introducing payments by result*. London, United Kingdom Department of Health.

Department of Health (2007) [web site]. General information about treatment centres. London, United Kingdom Department of Health (www.dh.gov.uk, accessed 3 July 2007).

Deutsches Krankenhaus Institut (2005). *Krankenhaus Barometer*. Düsseldorf, Deutsches Krankenhaus Institut.

Ettelt S et al. (2007). Capacity planning in health care: reviewing the international experience. *Euro Observer*, 9(1):1–5.

Glennester H (1998). Competition and quality in health care: the UK experience. *International Journal for Quality in Health Care*, 10(5):403–410.

Guterman S (2006). Specialty hospitals: a problem or a symptom. *Health Affairs*, 25(1):95–105.

Higgins J (2004). Incrementalism in UK policy-making on privatization in health care. In: Maarse H. *Privatization in European health care: a comparative analysis in eight countries*. Maarssen, Elsevier:153–167.

Iglehart J (2005). The uncertain future of specialty hospitals. *New England Journal of Medicine*, 352:1405–1407.

Klein R (1998). Why Britain is reorganizing its National Health Service – yet again. *Health Affairs*, 17(4):111–125.

Langham S et al. (2003). Addressing the inverse care law in cardiac services. *Journal of Public Health Medicine*, 25:202–207.

Le Grand J (1999). Competition, cooperation, or control: tales from the British National Health Service. *Health Affairs*, 18(3):27–39.

Maarse H (2006). The privatization of health care in Europe: an eight-country analysis. *Journal of Health Politics, Policy and Law*, 31(5):981–1014.

McKee M, Edwards N, Atun R (2006). Public–private partnerships for hospitals. *Bulletin of the World Health Organization*, 84(11):890–896.

Nassiri A, Rochaix L (2006). Revisiting physicians' financial incentives in Quebec: a panel system approach. *Health Economics*, 15(1):49–64.

Nederlandse Zorgautoriteit (2007a). *Ziekenhuismonitor [Hospital monitor]*. Utrecht, Nederlandse Zorgautoriteit [Dutch Health Care Authority].

Nederlandse Zorgautoriteit (2007b). *Ziekenhuiszorg [Hospital care]*. Utrecht, Nederlandse Zorgautoriteit [Dutch Health Care Authority].

Newbold D (2005). Foundation Trusts: economics in the post-modern hospital. *Journal of Nursing Management*, 13(5):439–447.

Øvretveit J (2001). *The changing public–private mix in Nordic health care: an analysis*. Gothenberg, Nordic School of Public Health.

Paulus A et al. (2003). Market competition: everybody is talking but what do the say? *Health Policy*, 64(3):278–289.

Pollock A (2004). *NHS Plc. The privatization of our health care*. London, Verso.

Rochaix L, Hartmann L (2005). Public–private mix for health in France. In: Maynard A. *The public–private mix for health*. Oxford, Radcliffe:151–160.

Schreyögg J, Tiemann O, Busse R (2005). The DRG reimbursement system in Germany. *Euro Observer*, 7(4):4–6.

Secretary of State for Health (2006). *The Government's response to the health committee's report on independent sector treatment centres*. London, United Kingdom Secretary of State for Health.

Voelker R (2003). Specialty hospitals generate revenue and controversy. *Journal of the American Medical Association*, 289(4):409–410.

Wallace W (2006). Independent sector treatment centres: how the NHS is left to pick up the pieces. *British Medical Journal*, 332:614.

Wiley M (2005). The Irish health system: development in strategy, structure, funding and delivery since 1980. *Health Economics*, 14:169–185.

Chapter 7

# Capital financing models, procurement strategies and decision-making

*Geert Dewulf, Stephen Wright*

## Introduction

The health sector in many European countries is changing rapidly, not least in the way that public administrations tackle obtaining and paying for the assets needed to deliver services. The mechanism by which assets are delivered crucially impacts not only on the assets themselves, but also on the services provided from them. Traditionally, sources of capital for investment were dominated by public sector "equity". The growth of competition in the health sector and the consequences of EU policies on procurement are pushing hospital boards and ministries of health to implement new financing models and to rely more heavily on private capital and expertise (see Chapter 6 by Maarse & Normand). As an increasing number of public–private partnerships are introduced, there is a growing need for evidence that these new schemes are truly delivering "value for money" and are ultimately supportive of health care delivery.

This chapter provides an overview of procurement strategies and capital financing models and develops a framework for making strategic decisions on what models deliver best value for health care delivery. The chapter starts with an overview of different procurement strategies. It then describes current developments in financing of capital investment in Europe and elaborates on the role of contracts and cooperation in the various financing structures. Finally, the chapter turns to a discussion of the question of "value for money" and of strategic issues in the future delivery of health services, in particular as they relate to hospitals.

## Procurement strategies

Procurement comprises the full range of activities related to the purchase of assets or services. There are several ways in which health care services or assets can be procured. The method used for procurement is sometimes linked intrinsically to the system of providing finance, but is otherwise separate. Winch (2002) makes a distinction between four types of procurement:

- maintain in-house capability

- appoint a supplier

- launch a competition (often used for selecting architects)

- issue an invitation to competitive tender.

Today, in most European countries, public sector procurement policies stress the importance of competitive tendering. This trend is reinforced by EU guidelines on transparency and probity in procurement. Most services are procured by means of a competitive tendering procedure. According to EU requirements (from June 2005), for all projects exceeding the value of €5.923 million (excluding value-added tax) a competitive tendering procedure is required. Competitive tenders may be open to all bidders or released only to a list of selected companies. Five methods can be distinguished (Bing et al. 2005):

- open competitive tendering

- invited tendering

- registered lists

- project-specific pre-qualification

- negotiated tendering.

In addition to the growth of competitive tendering, we can observe a general trend towards the contracting out of health services. Throughout Europe, health care provision is no longer seen as the sole responsibility of governments. In the United Kingdom, for instance, market mechanisms were introduced with the stated goals of extending patient choice, delegating responsibilities to service providers, increasing value for money, improving the quality of services and rewarding NHS staff for being responsive to local needs and preferences (Montgomery 1997). Increasingly, the way services and facilities are procured is changing from a traditional approach, in which risks and revenue were retained by the public sector, towards concession contracts, where risks and revenue are, in theory, transferred to the private sector.

**Table 7.1** *Different procurement schemes*

| Procurement system | Management | Procurement process | Risks | Funding |
|---|---|---|---|---|
| Traditional procurement | Public | Public actor puts one or more works out to tender | Risks and responsibilities for public actor | Costs and revenues for public actor |
| Innovative procurement | Public | Public actor puts output-specified question for overall solution out to tender | Design, build and/or maintain risks for private actor | Costs and revenues: lump sum for public actor, variable sum for private actors |
| Public–private partnership: concession contracts | Public | Public actor puts a service question out to tender, rewarded with a concession | Design, build, finance and maintain/operate risks for private actor | Costs and revenues: lump sum for public actor, variable sum for private actors |
| Public–private partnership: joint venture contracts | Public–private | Joint procurement and shared responsibility | Public–private shared | Cost and revenues: public–private shared |
| Privatization | Private | Public tasks and competences are transferred to the private sector | Risks and responsibilities for private actor | Costs and revenues for private actor |

*Source*: Bult-Spiering & Dewulf 2006.

Bult-Spiering and Dewulf (2006) make the distinction between various procurement schemes, with different roles and contributions of the public and private parties (Table 7.1).

Within public–private partnerships, several contract forms can be distinguished:

- design, build, finance and operate (DBFO)
- design, build, finance and maintain (DBFM)
- build, operate and transfer (BOT).

These public–private partnerships differ in three ways from the traditional form of procurement (Ball, Heafy & King 2000; Bult-Spiering & Dewulf 2006).

- Life-cycle responsibility. The private agent is responsible for the entire life-cycle of the provision.

- An output specification is used, in which the public principle defines the services required rather than the precise form of the assets underlying the service.

- Risks are transferred from the public sector to the private sector.

There is a trend towards more integrated contracts, but this may conflict with EU guidelines for competitive tendering. New procurement routes, such as partnering and concession contracting, may become even more difficult to establish in a situation in which price is not the only or is only a secondary selection criterion (Winch 2002).

A tender procedure normally contains the following stages:

- market consultation or request for information
- request for (pre-)qualification
- invitation to tender or request for submission of a proposal
- tender evaluation and short-listing
- negotiation with short-listed tenderers
- selection of the tender, award of concession and financial close.

The competitive tender procedure is often criticized for the high transaction costs involved. One major reason is the length of the tender procedure. The tender process for public–private partnership projects in the United Kingdom in 2005, for instance, took an average of approximately 27 months before "financial close" of the contracts concerned took place. The average procurement time for the (smaller) projects within the NHS Local Improvement Finance Trust (LIFT)[4] initiative was 21 months (HM Treasury 2006). Today, some observers are expecting that new EU legislation will increase the bidding costs by 2%, since it requires that short-listed bidders work out more detailed proposals. The Government of the United Kingdom has apparently offered additional payments to consortia in some recent PFI procurements to cover the additional costs of the "competitive dialogue" process (Donnelly 2007). To lower the transaction costs, governments in various countries are standardizing procedures and contracts. Standardization is clearly a way to speed up the tender process.

## Financing models

Within the health systems of Europe, where financing and, to a lesser extent, health service provision are dominated by the public sector, most of the financial resources for capital or services are ultimately supplied by the State. However, various arms of the State are involved, including the local, regional, national and supra-national levels. This complexity means that payment for assets and services can be delayed. This section reviews how capital assets are paid for, either at the point of construction or over time.

---

[4] LIFTs are property-based public–private partnership structures to develop primary care facilities and associated medical (such as chiropody or dentistry) and commercial (such as pharmacy) premises.

## Public sector equity

Existing, traditional capital sources for investment in Europe are dominated by public sector "equity".[5] However, this term is misleading, because there is limited resemblance to the private sector understanding of the concept of equity. In broad terms, in the case of public sector equity, the value of the estate does not have to be accounted for, nor must a financial return on this equity be delivered to public shareholders. There is now a movement to do precisely that: accounting for depreciation of the value of the assets, and potentially placing capital charges on the balance sheet of the public sector enterprises concerned. This is sometimes introduced as part of a package to create independently managed trusts.

The classic case of "free" public capital for investment has been seen in Germany, a social health insurance system. In Germany's dual system (*duales System*), the states (*Bundesländer*) offer funds to various hospital service providers, whether publicly owned (for example by municipalities), the profit-making private sector (for example, Rhön Klinikum, which is reviewed in the accompanying volume of case studies, or Fresenius), or the non-profit-making private or voluntary sector (for example, Caritas or Red Cross), as long as the facility concerned is accredited by the regional hospital plan (*Krankenhausplan*) of the state (*Bundesland*) concerned.

## Public sector debt

There seems to be increasing use of public sector debt, when there is at least nominally the requirement to pay interest. The real differences in terms of behavioural incentives in the public sector between debt and equity are in practice not particularly great. Much depends on whether there is a "soft" or "hard" budget constraint. If, in reality, the entity concerned will face no sanctions by overspending (soft budget constraint), then debt is effectively being written off. Most autonomous communities (*Comunidades Autónomas*) in Spain, for example, do not practise disciplined budgeting procedures in the health sector and the consequences of exceeding budget allocations may therefore simply not be severe (at least in the short to medium term).

The treatment of debt within administrations can differ considerably. In the Netherlands, debt on the balance sheets of independent regional hospital trusts, raised from whatever source (typically the commercial banking sector), has hitherto been amortized by law over a 50-year period, a practice that is now changing (see Chapter 6 by Maarse & Normand). Given that many assets

---

[5] Traditional private sector equity is a form of financing which gives rise to ownership rights in the entity concerned and bears the first risk of loss of capital; the return earned ("dividends") is a function of performance rather than being guaranteed as in the case of debt. Public sector equity shares these features in an attenuated form.

become redundant over a period much shorter than 50 years as a result of demographic, epidemiological, technological factors, or those related to the life of the asset, many hospitals carry "phantom assets" on their balance sheets, which have long since ceased to be used for their original purpose, or have even been demolished. This means that there is still a debt amortization stream, even though a replacement asset is also very likely to be on the balance sheet (and being amortized in its turn) unless one or other party steps in to buy it off. The clear – but glib – solution is to match accounting lives to functional lives, but this is extremely difficult *ex ante*, and more so given that the technical life of a health care asset can often be extended indefinitely (with the structure concerned, however, becoming progressively less well suited to delivery of appropriate care). Procedures that allow functionally defunct assets to be written off are clearly desirable.

## Growing areas of health sector finance

There are three financing routes that are of growing significance for the health sector in Europe: EU grants, various forms of public–private partnership, and privatization.

### European Union grants

The main EU Structural Funds are the ERDF, the Cohesion Fund and the European Social Fund, each of which has different eligibility criteria. These are in addition to Framework Programme 7 funds for research and development, or assistance to candidate or association countries, such as in the western Balkan countries. This chapter discusses the use of Structural Funds as support to EU Member States in obtaining various forms of infrastructure in the so-called "convergence countries" of the EU (see Box 7.1). This is essentially another form of public sector equity, although with special features.

In past rounds of Structural Funds support, the health sector was not entirely excluded, but was certainly not prioritized. In contrast, the health sector has been included explicitly in the "New Financial Perspectives 2007–2013". The total of New Financial Perspectives grants paid by the European Commission across all sectors to the countries concerned between 2007 and 2009 will amount to approximately €347 billion. It is possible to estimate that transfers to the order of 2–5% could flow into the health sector. This would then amount to approximately €1.0–2.5 billion per year. Given that the total capital investment made by the health sector in Europe amounts currently to approximately €35 billion per year, the resources potentially available as EU regional aid would be perhaps 3% of annual gross fixed capital formation in the health sector.

**Box 7.1** *John Paul II Hospital in Krakow, Poland*

In recent years, the John Paul II Hospital in Krakow has been developing new facilities and modernizing existing ones. The extension of the hospital and the equipment of several wards and administration units have been financed from various sources, including the hospital's own resources and the central government budget. However, the most important investments were totally or partially funded by the EU. Medical equipment was purchased within separate projects and major investments encompassed refurbishment and reconstruction.

In 2007 the hospital had two projects under way that were co-financed by the EU within the framework of the Structural Funds Integrated Regional Operational Programme:

- digitization of the echocardiographic and mammographic system (EU funding 75%; hospital funding 25%); and

- an e-Hospital – creation of a digital platform for medical data and teleconsultation (EU funding 75%; hospital funding 25%).

Implementation has resulted in major alterations of the hospital structure, including the introduction of new diagnostic and therapy modalities and an increased focus on the continuity and complementarity of treatments. The support from EU programmes has been essential for the development of the hospital. Most initiatives would have been pursued anyway, but it would have taken much longer and they would have been more limited in scope.

*Source*: Case study in the accompanying volume.

This is considerable, and all the more so given that it will be focused on the "convergence countries", which are poorer than the EU average and often quite small.

It should be noted that the section of the European Commission responsible for approving countries' suggestions for allocating Structural Fund money is the Directorate-General Regional (DG-Regio). This Directorate-General deals with all sectors, including transport, environment and energy, and its expertise is in country liaison, rather than sectoral policies. Historically, the Directorate-General of the Commission with principal responsibility for the health sector (DG-Sanco) has not been involved in decisions on capital investment in infrastructure, even when hospitals were funded (the most important recipient of capital investment in the health sector). There is clearly a need to ensure that EU regional aid resources are used wisely.

## Public–private partnerships

In political discussion and in the media, there is much confusion about what constitutes a public–private partnership. A popular working definition, from the Institute for Public Policy Research, United Kingdom, is that "a public–private partnership is a risk-sharing relationship between the public and private sectors based upon a shared aspiration to bring about a desired public policy outcome" (Institute of Public Policy Research 2001). It could be said that a project is a public–private partnership if there is a long-standing operational responsibility throughout the life of the project, such as in the DBFO schemes. The public sector ceases to own assets (a stock), but rather contracts for services, including accommodation services (a flow) to be provided to it.

Public–private partnership is often used as a synonym for privatization. However, a public–private partnership is best regarded as a temporary, albeit long-term, project, while privatization tends to be permanent. In that sense, therefore, privatization is the polar opposite example of a public–private partnership (Fig. 7.1).

The term public–private partnership includes a wide variety of different forms and schemes, ranging from fully public to fully private (Bennett, James & Grohmann 2000; Savas 2000). In health care, the term public–private partnership often refers to a concession contract (including in cases of privatization). A concession awards a company full responsibility for the

**Fig. 7.1** *Spectrum of public–private partnerships*

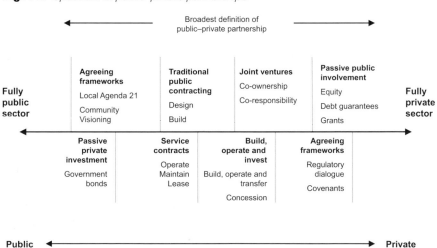

*Source*: Bennett, James & Grohmann 2000.

delivery of services from an asset, including the operational activities, although in health care this does not usually include clinical services. Yescombe (2002) has visualized the relationship between the different actors in a concession project (Fig. 7.2).

**Fig. 7.2** *Some main relationships among actors in a concession project*

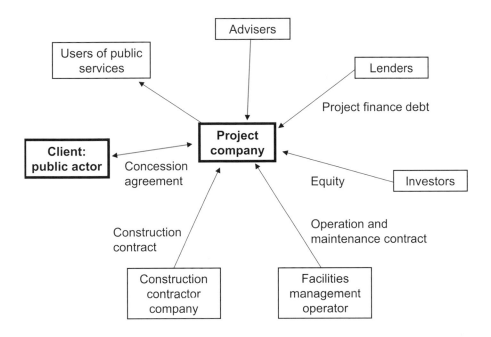

*Source*: Based on Yescombe 2002.

The most widely cited example of a public–private partnership model is the United Kingdom PFI programme, which was started by a Conservative government, but considerably extended by the Labour administration that came to power in 1997. Strictly speaking, PFI is where the United Kingdom central Government offers special dedicated credits for financing; public–private partnerships can also encompass the situation where a local administration contracts for a service without central government financial support. PFI has been used in various sectors, including roads, bridges and tunnels, defence, justice, air traffic control, public administration, education and health. In the case of health, the PFI programme is a massive initiative which will renew a substantial proportion of the entire health estate of the United Kingdom. The mechanism, tailored in different respects, is also being used in France, Italy, Portugal and Spain. There are also public–public partnerships (for example, Hospital de Asturias in Spain), which, by transferring responsibility for estate deliverables to a dedicated, but still public agency, attempt to sharpen performance incentives.

There are important differences in the scope of public–private partnerships in different jurisdictions. Accommodation public–private partnerships (United Kingdom PFI, France, some public–public partnerships in Spain) supply only the structure of the buildings, sometimes along with various types of equipment, including medical equipment. Other model systems include accommodation and medical services public–private partnerships, such as the current Portuguese model, with "InfraCo" and "ClinCo" operating as special purpose companies, each with parallel (although variably configured) shareholdings and with different contract lifespans. Finally, there are whole-population service models (such as the Alzira model in Spain – see the relevant case study in the accompanying volume). Most of these public–private partnerships relate to the acute hospital sector (an exception is the Coxa hospital in Finland, for elective joint surgery, also discussed in the accompanying case studies volume). By their nature, public–private partnerships are most commonly used in countries with an NHS, as many countries with a social health insurance system already have independent (including private) hospitals. France does, however, use public–private partnerships: the Regional Hospital Agency (*Agence Régionale de l'Hospitalisation*) management units are branches of the Ministry of Health in Paris and now, in some cases, (such as in Caen or Sud Francilien) they contract for accommodation services.

Overall, there are many pros and cons of public–private partnerships in health. Some, such as life-cycle planning, output-based specification of service delivery, and allocation of risks to those parties best able to carry them, are not as such intrinsic to public–private partnerships, although they fit naturally with this model. On the other hand, the United Kingdom PFI is often criticized, for example on the grounds that it had caused bed reductions, although these were not directly attributable to the PFI scheme. The central Government sometimes plans explicitly for bed rationalization, and private finance simply happens to be the vehicle that delivers it. Furthermore, the financial costs of a newly built hospital often have to be balanced by reductions in both capital and operating costs, necessarily achieved by reducing capacity irrespective of the financing route. On balance, integrated private sector design and operation should aspire to improve performance, and government reports imply some modest achievements in this respect (see, for example, National Audit Office 2003).

Public–private partnership, as currently conceived in Europe, is essentially a DBFO structure, and based on "project finance". Project finance, should, in fact, be better thought of as "limited recourse finance", as project finance is in strict definitional terms "non-recourse". In practice, for funders there is usually a "second way out" (or a third), and they do not have to rely on the cash flow generated by the asset concerned. For example, in the United Kingdom there is the "Residual Liabilities Act", which imposes on the Secretary of State an obligation to buy out the senior debt (debt that has priority for repayment in a liquidation situation) in the event of several potential causes of project default.

The financing of public–private partnerships usually involves 10% equity and 90% debt or debt-like instruments. With such a structure, it is apparent that public–private partnerships are, in effect, just another way of raising debt finance. The State could have taken this debt onto its own balance sheet. Public–private partnerships do not then generate "fresh" resources for the health sector, as the debt ultimately has to be reimbursed. The burden is not moved permanently to some other party, but rather only shifted in time. It is often a key political imperative for governments to move finance for public–private partnerships off their balance sheets. Conventionally, and in an accounting sense, this can be achieved if there is "enough" risk transfer. There are Eurostat rules to this effect, and in practice about 20% risk transfer is generally the minimum. In an economic sense, however, the resources to support the project will still need to be made available at some time by the public sector.

The discount rate of the senior debt (debt that has priority for repayment in a liquidation scenario) issued by a public–private partnership special purpose vehicle (a company that is created solely for a particular financial transaction or a series of transactions) is usually 2–3% more expensive than public debt. It can be argued, however, that the true economic cost to society is theoretically the same, although with distributional implications (in that private, rather than public, owners of the capital are reimbursed). This derives from Arrow and Lind (1970), who argue that the cost of capital in a privately financed contract reveals the true cost of risk in carrying out the activity (even if the public sector can then pool risk, justifying lower discount rates). Allowing for the risk transfer computation in the "public sector comparator" (see subsection "Contracts and cooperation", this seems on balance a reasonable summary. However, given that interest rates in PFI, being commercial lending rates, are factually higher than with government funding, this has led to propositions that the Government will supply finance for schemes developed by the private sector, that is, the scheme is then a design, build and operate (DBO) scheme.

Originally, project finance had been developed in the 1930s for oil, gas or power projects in the United States. Similarly, the PFI instrument was first used for the heavy infrastructure sectors (water and transport). In order to secure adequate risk transfer, some degree of market or demand risk has to be borne by the private sector partner within the public–private partnership. In cases such as the energy or transport sectors, it is not enough merely to bear the operational risk, since the technical issues and cash flow exposed in maintaining, for example, a road, tend not to be large relative to the discounted total net present cost of the project. In the case of a road, bridge or tunnel, the transferred market risk has historically been usage of the facility: tolls, set to repay total net present cost where charges for road use apply, and "shadow" tolls where they do not. In the case of social infrastructure, such as health care (and areas such as education, justice and defence), the assets involved are operationally much more complex. Public administrations have therefore almost invariably chosen to achieve the desired extent of risk transfer via delivered performance and the availability of space and equipment, rather than demand risk (that is, the number of patients passing through the facility, something which is essentially outside the control of the facility provider). In fact, apart from trivial issues such as car parking or hospital retail facilities, demand risk is positively excluded from almost all hospital public–private partnerships.

A major problem is that long-term planning is difficult, because health care is changing fast. The impact of the shift of services into the community on the number of beds required in the hospital sector, for example, is difficult to predict. Consequently, there is a high chance that the health care authority will become locked into a long-term contract for buildings and services that are no longer appropriate. In the case of the West Middlesex hospital in the United Kingdom, some flexibility is incorporated in the contract and bed numbers can be varied according to changes in demand (Bult-Spiering & Dewulf 2006). However, in many cases, the flexibility demanded of the private sector partner in the normal PFI/public–private partnership contract is strictly limited, as evidenced by the rushed introduction of extra "descoping" (the strategic abandonment and/or weakening of objectives) chapters just before signature of some recent contracts, when it became obvious that costs were too high and beds would need to be taken out of the schemes concerned. In general, it can be said that there are asymmetric incentives in public–private partnerships: easily quantifiable and able to be captured in terms of cost-containment over time for the private partner; and more nebulous and difficult to achieve in terms of quality gain – including asset flexibility – over time for the public authorities.

With regard to equity finance, the sources of funds in a typical health care public–private partnership are construction and facilities management companies, together with financial institutions. The debt used to be supplied by commercial or investment banks, together with the EU's European Investment Bank, but increasingly, the bond markets are major players, creating tradable debt instruments which are usually structured from the start to have a certain risk profile – and are not necessarily of the highest quality. Insurance, mainly "monoline" companies (that is, involved in a single type of business, in this case the insurance of project finance debt), has often been brought in to enhance credit by guaranteeing bond debt repayments, thus again transferring the responsibility for the risk to those entities which have an appetite for it, although with the turmoil evident in credit markets at the time of writing, not necessarily the digestive capacity. Italian public–private partnerships retain a substantial public funding proportion (20–50%), because of the features of Italian procurement law (Finlombarda 2006). Some other vehicles could be used to lessen the apparent drain of profits to the private sector, such as the "non-profit-making distributing organization" used in some United Kingdom school PFIs. Refinancing at some stage after operations have started is a sensitive political issue, and United Kingdom government guidance now indicates that public–private partnership negotiations should consider from the start the split of any potential gains if the original equity holders sell out after the initial period.

## Privatization

It could be argued that, given the weight of the public sector in the health arena of all European countries, including the CEE countries moving away from the communist Semashko system, the examples of privatization are close to a de facto "permanent" public–private partnership. In Germany, for example, the private hospital companies such as Rhön Klinikum (see the corresponding case study in the accompanying volume) and Fresenius are licensed to build and operate hospitals within the hospital plan of the respective state and only receive payments for patient treatments from the publicly regulated health insurance companies on this basis. They operate within what amounts to a concession model. In some cases these private companies take free investment funds from the *Länder*. In other cases, funds are raised on a corporate basis, as in any other sector (equity and debt), and the companies sometimes argue that the commercial cost of these funds is offset by the extra freedom of action provided by not taking state funds. One case which exposes the grey area between public–private partnerships and privatization is the Alzira model in Spain (see Box 7.2).

## Contracts and cooperation

Transactions between awarding authorities and service providers are governed by contracts. In the economic literature, the debate on how to govern projects is based on a "contract-centred approach" (Madhok 1995), with a focus on the project organization's structure and the chosen type of contract. A contract can be seen as a mutual commitment between two or more organizations, which defines the obligations of these organizations.

---

**Box 7.2** *The Alzira model (Spain)*

The Hospital de la Ribera is now a Spanish pioneer of the public–private partnership model, by which a private company is awarded a contract to build and run a public hospital. In the Spanish context, this is called an "administrative concession" or the "Alzira model". The private company responsible for providing the medical care is UTE-Ribera (*Union Temporal de Empresas*, Temporary Union of Companies – Ribera). The hospital was built in Alzira and currently has a catchment area of nearly 245 000 inhabitants.

Initially, in 1999, the Alzira model was designed to offer hospital care at the Hospital de la Ribera. However, it was soon realized that the hospital needed to collaborate with the primary care sector and should coordinate and integrate medical care in the whole health area of the respective health department. A second Alzira model was therefore created in 2003, which established integrated private management within the health department for both primary care and hospital care. The terms of the administrative concession were also changed in 2003 to make the public–private partnership less profitable and politically more acceptable. This change put a limit on the potential annual profit and ensured that any benefits over this limit would be returned to the local government, while at the same time ensuring the financial survival of the concessions.

*Source*: Case study in the accompanying volume.

---

The role of explicit contracts is increasing in most sectors of European societies. In the health sector, the development of quasi-markets has already led to a contractual culture (McHale, Hughes & Griffiths 1997). Throughout Europe, governments are stimulating market dynamics by splitting health care purchase from provision. Health reforms have pursued the separation of policy, regulation and monitoring functions on the one hand and delivery of services on the other (Pavignani & Colombo). As a result, the health sector is becoming increasingly more of a playground for lawyers and legal firms. In the United Kingdom, the amount of litigation involving commercial contract disputes increased shortly after the introduction of the NHS internal markets in the early 1990s.[6]

Contract governance has been restricted further by EU guidelines on public procurement, which aim for increased transparency. For good reasons, these rules make it impossible for public authorities to deal with service industries based only on trust or past experience. A study of research and development agreements found that contracts can afford to be less "complete" when parties have an ongoing business relationship (Ciccotello & Hornyak 2000). For the most part, however, publicly procured contracts are not based on soft criteria,

---

[6] Vincent-Jones (1993), cited in McHale, Hughes & Griffiths 1997, p. 197.

such as trust and prior dealings, but are in practice dominated by hard criteria, defined characteristically as the lowest price.

Partly due to the increasing litigation in the health sector, contracts are often based on classical economic theory, which stresses the importance of "term specificity" as the prime indicator for the "completeness of the contract". A contract should *in principle* be complete, since this reduces both the uncertainty faced by decision-makers and the risks stemming from opportunism on both sides (Williamson 1985). Term specificity concerns how specific and detailed the contract terms are. While most contracts in construction are based on fixed-price models, renegotiation during the execution of the contract is confined to changes in the product or term specification (Bajari & Tadelis 2001).

Technical, political or economic developments may in time force the awarding authority to revise its output specifications (see the relevant case study in the accompanying volume). Moreover, most contracts are based on a static rather than a dynamic model of the sector. Specifications are rooted in fixed (often current) demands and usually only inadequately take into account the dynamic environment in which hospitals operate. A clear example from the United Kingdom is the use of the "public sector comparator" as an instrument to assess value for money in public procurement processes. The public sector comparator is meant to compare the full costs and, to the degree to which they can be defined, benefits of the public sector version with the public–private partnership alternative. However, it is difficult to assess what would have happened in the event that a hospital had been built by the public sector instead of the public–private partnership alternative. One should clearly take into account that, in the United Kingdom, there has been little alternative to the PFI, since health authorities have fixed annual budgets and therefore no guarantee over future funds. In other words, comparing contracts on their level of performance is like comparing apples with pears, or as the Deputy-Director of the United Kingdom National Audit Office, Mr. Coleman, described the public sector comparator: "pseudo scientific mumbo jumbo" (National Audit Office 2002). The public sector comparator, apart from being expensive to develop and maintain during the bidding period, is thus usually a static measurement of value based on current performance criteria, and often does not allow for flexibility to deal with future uncertainties.

Long-term contracts, such as public–private partnership contracts, tend to be "incomplete", due to information shortcomings and transaction costs. Indeed, the longer the contract, the less information we have, and it is then either impossible or infinitely costly to describe each possible event during the lifetime of the contract, however desirable that might be in theory (De Fraja 2002). What we do know about the future is that the state of the world is unlikely to be as it is assumed at the time of the contract. This is especially the case in the health sector, the dynamic characteristics of which make it more difficult to specify future contingencies when compared to heavy infrastructure sectors such as energy, water or transport.

In addition to term specificity, a "complete" contract should in some sense also include "contingency adaptability", which is the ability to deal with unanticipated contingencies (Luo 2002). Contingency adaptability involves having mechanisms to respond contractually to future problems, conflicts and contingencies. In the case of hospitals, for instance, a truly complete contract would deal with changes in the number of patients, driven by epidemiology or demography, or with new medical technologies, and the relevant guidelines should in principle account for these. In fact, such uncertainties are normally not dealt with appropriately in actual contracts.

Many studies have been carried out on the impact of the contract length on the behaviour of providers. During long-term contracts, according to Lindenberg (2000), providers are confronted with many unforeseeable temptations to "cheat and deviate in some way from the contractual agreements". According to the author, partners in a contract should focus on a process to eliminate mistrust, rather than rely on the legal details of the contract performance. In other words, successful contract management has more to do with the realm of cognitive social psychology than transaction cost economics or jurisprudence. What is at stake here is not trust in the sense of "blind faith", but rather reliance or so-called "weak solidarity", where self-interest has been harnessed to create appropriate long-term and reciprocal behaviours (see also Nooteboom 2002). In practice, however, most contract disputes in health care are solved in litigation (especially in Anglo-Saxon law) or arbitration (much continental, "Roman" law), and focus on the written specifications of the original contract.

Another important development is the pressure for standardization, often indicated by the need for transparency and the desire to lower transaction costs. Standardized contracts may be conducive to trust, in that they increase the confidence in contracting as an organizing principle (Vlaar, Van den Bosch & Volberda 2007). However, long-term projects often need tailor-made contracts.

Certain commentators have raised several arguments against contracting for health services (Pavignani & Colombo):

- transaction costs in contracting are high because, in addition to the procurement costs, costs are incurred for monitoring and evaluating the contract;

- competition between providers is often limited, since long-term contractual relationships usually prevail and opportunistic behaviour of providers could be the result;

- the ability of an operator to enter or leave the health market is limited; and

- long-term contracts lock public funds for a specific use, limiting the flexibility for reallocating resources to address efficiency or equity problems.

In summary, both economic and sociological considerations determine the success of a project. Or, as one author put it: "Without contracts, cooperation will lack an institutional framework to proceed. Without cooperation, contracts cannot encourage long-term evolutions" (Luo 2002).

## Value for money and strategic aspects of capital decisions

Is there an optimal way to procure or finance? There is no clear-cut answer to this question. Most evaluations are based on perceptions of stakeholders (see, for example, National Audit Office 1999) or on anecdotal evidence.

Some evaluations are positive. In the case of the West Middlesex hospital, the concession scheme led to a reduction in construction time. In only 18 months, the new hospital was constructed. Other important benefits of the case were the price certainty and allocation of risk to the private sector (National Audit Office 2002).

However, value for money in asset decisions is difficult to assess. It should be centred on the ability of the asset to deliver the required core (medical) services. In particular, the nature of procurement or financing should not distort judgements on the optimum method of life-cycle delivery of services – "the procurement tail should not wag the services dog". Value should be defined as value for the end user. In the case of the West Middlesex hospital, unlike many other concession schemes, the end user (here the staff) was heavily involved. It is reported that medical personnel were engaged in the design from the start, so that the needs of staff and patients would not be dictated solely by architects, accountants and surveyors. At every level, clinicians had their say on key components for each department, how they should work and what accommodation was needed, from the number of rooms to the number of beds (NHS 2003). It must be recognized, however, that there is a dilemma, in that most public sector clients will only ever build one hospital, so that they are not experienced in balancing the various and often conflicting considerations.

Value for money should also be related to the degree to which ancillary services and facilities support the core service, such as health care delivery in hospitals. One important performance criterion is the level of efficiency. Blanc-Brude,

Goldsmith & Välilä (2006) distinguish two forms of efficiency: productive efficiency and allocative efficiency. Productive efficiency refers to achieving the best outcome for the hospital; with the funds available, for instance by reducing operating and maintenance costs. Allocative efficiency refers to the value of the hospital compared to other possible uses of the resources, for example by maximizing the health gain associated with the hospital. Some investments may lead to a higher productive efficiency but to a lower allocative efficiency (in other words doing the wrong thing well). In the case of hospitals, one could argue that some investments lead to lower maintenance costs, but a less clinically effective or patient-friendly hospital. The second type of efficiency (allocative) is more difficult to assess, but is probably of greater strategic importance.

Another important criterion is the way risks are managed. Edwards and Shaoul (2003) found, perhaps not surprisingly, that the amount of risk transferred to the private sector in health concessions was almost exactly the amount required to bridge the gap between the cost of concessions and traditional procurement. In light of the length of contracts and the dynamic environment in which hospitals operate, the analysis of risk allocation is extremely important. Some risks can be quantified and transferred to the provider, but many risks are shared and non-quantifiable (see the relevant case study in the accompanying volume).

Creating flexibility is an important way to manage these risks. It is not only important that the contract specifications match current demands, but that the contract can continue to meet future health care needs. We can distinguish three forms of flexibility: technical, financial and contract flexibility.

The strategic choice of the form of contract should be determined by the answer to two basic questions (Smit & Dewulf 2002).

- Do the intended facilities and services create an added value to the core activities?

- Do the providers have the competences to provide the services?

The options resulting from these two questions are illustrated in Fig. 7.3.

In this regard, we can make a comparison with organizational strategies for outsourcing. Activities that have low added value to the organization and are not part of the core activities may be contracted out easily, so therefore a concession contract could be signed (Smit & Dewulf 2002). The problem is how to determine what a public value is. As Savas (2000) indicated, changes in social values lead to changes in how society determines what is a worthy collective good and what is not. In other words, the public interest axis is not a static but rather a dynamic one, influenced by a changing context. A joint

**Fig. 7.3** *Added value and core competences*

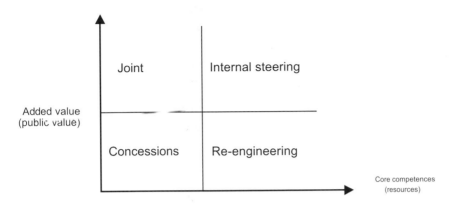

*Source*: Smit & Dewulf 2002.

venture would then be a more suitable solution than a simple concession. A joint venture could be seen as a strategic alliance in which both parties accept the idea of shared risk and reward.

In addition to internal governance considerations, we have to look at the possibilities available in the market. The duration and structure of the contract will depend on the quality of the services provided by private parties, as well as the way these parties can safeguard the public interests. As in the case of the LIFT structures, portfolio partnerships aim to generate more flexibility and commitment to facilitate meeting dynamic local needs. Moreover, the traditional measurement of value for money does not pay much attention to the issue of use flexibility, and consequently the awarding authority confines itself to specifying easily measurable contingent terms rather than focusing on contingency adaptability. Social scientists go so far as to stress that sociological virtues of cooperation or building relationships (Madhok 1995) are more important than the contract itself. These norms create flexibility that helps mitigate hazards associated with contracts.[7] The social and emotional bond between partners is extremely important (see the earlier discussion on "trust").

A strategic issue in today's contracting is how much flexibility one needs. In developing a health facility such as a hospital, there is a need to define what is the core portfolio and which part of the portfolio must be flexible. Gibson and Lizieri (1999) make a distinction between the core portfolio, the first periphery portfolio and the second periphery portfolio. The core is what adds the greatest value. In its case, property managers will often decide to own the property or to take out a long lease. For the core portfolio, only functional flexibility is

---

[7] Dyer & Smith 1998, cited in Luo 2002, p. 906.

needed, that is, it needs to be adaptable for a range of uses. The first periphery portfolio is that portion of the ancillary services that needs to fluctuate with the business activity, as with numerical flexibility (for example changing number of beds). The second periphery of facilities and services requires particularly short-term flexibility. These are the facilities that support high-risk or uncertain activities; such services require financial flexibility, often in the form of short-term leases (Dewulf, Depuy & Gibson 2003). For each individual hospital, what is defined as core or periphery may be different.

## Conclusions

The implementation of new financing models has significant implications for hospital management and governments, which are often not foreseen or foreseeable. Relying on private resources could, for instance, have far-reaching consequences in terms of risk and flexibility. Contracts between public administrations and private consortia heavily rely on contract completion, that is, contracts based on well-defined and fully comprehensive output specifications. Such contracts should reduce uncertainty and opportunism, although in reality information shortcomings and transaction costs prevent full achievement of this ideal. The health sector is changing fast, due to financial, technological and demographic developments. Therefore, public–private partnership contracts should move beyond term specificity to include contingency adaptability, in order to secure the required asset flexibility. They should also be structured in such a way as to provide the right incentives for all parties to cooperate.

Value for money is conceptually critical, but exceedingly difficult to measure. It should be firmly based on the ability of assets to be flexible (technically, financially and in terms of contract) so as to deliver core (medical) services and compatible ancillary services (such as facility management). This requires identification of the core competences of the public and private sectors.

## References

Arrow K, Lind R (1970). Uncertainty and the evaluation of public investment decisions. *The American Economic Review*, 60:364–378.

Bajari P, Tadelis S (2001). Incentives versus transaction costs: a theory of procurement contracts. *The Rand Journal of Economics*, 32:387–407.

Ball R, Heafy M, King D (2000). Private finance initiative – a good deal for the public purse or a drain on future generations? *Policy Press*, 29:95–108.

Bennett E, James S, Grohmann P (2000). *Joint venture public–private partnerships for urban environmental services*. New York, Public Private Partnerships for the Urban Environment (PPPUE).

Bing L et al. (2005). The allocation of risk in PPP/PFI construction projects in the UK. *International Journal of Project Management*, 23:25–35.

Blanc-Brude F, Goldsmith H, Välilä T (2006). *Ex ante construction costs in the European road sector: a comparison of public–private partnerships and traditional public procurement*. Luxembourg, European Investment Bank.

Bult-Spiering WD, Dewulf G (2006). *Strategic issues in public–private partnerships: an international perspective*. Oxford, Blackwell Publishing.

Ciccotello CS, Hornyak MJ (2000). Cooperation via contract: an analysis of research and development agreements *Journal of Corporate Finance*, 6:1–24.

De Fraja G (2002). *PPP and contractual incompleteness: a theoretical economist's view*. York, University of York.

Dewulf G, Depuy L, Gibson V (2003). Porftolio management. In: Best R, Langston C, De Valence G. *Workplace strategies and facilities management*. Oxford, Butterworth and Heinemann:206–219.

Donnelly L (2007). NHS pay private companies for failed PFI bids. *Sunday Telegraph, 7 May 2007* (http://www.telegraph.co.uk/news/main.jhtml?xml=/news/2007/05/06/nhs06.xml, accessed 23 August 2007).

Edwards P, Shaoul J (2003). Partnerships: for better, for worse? *Accountability Journal*, 16:397–421.

Finlombarda (2006). *Survey of project finance in the health care sector. Fifth edition*. Milan, Finlombarda.

Gibson V, Lizieri C (1999). New business practices and the corporate real estate portfolio: how responsive is the UK property market? *Journal of Property Research*, 16:201–218.

HM Treasury (2006). *PFI: strengthening long-term partnerships*. London, HM Treasury.

Institute of Public Policy Research (2001). *Building better partnerships*. London, Institute of Public Policy Research.

Lindenberg S (2000). It takes both trust and lack of mistrust: the workings of cooperation and relational signaling in contractual relationships. *Journal of Management and Governance*, 4:11–33.

Luo Y (2002). Contract, cooperation and performance in international joint ventures. *Strategic Management Journal*, 23:903–919.

Madhok A (1995). Opportunism and trust in joint venture relationships: an exploratory study and a model. *Scandinavian Journal of Management*, 11:57–74.

McHale J, Hughes D, Griffiths L (1997). Conceptualizing contractual disputes in the National Health Service internal market. In: Deakin S, Mitchie J. *Contracts, cooperation, and competition*. Oxford, Oxford University Press:195–213.

Montgomery J (1997). Control and restraint in National Health Service contracting. In: Deakin S, Mitchie J. *Contracts, cooperation, and competition*. Oxford, Oxford University Press:175–194.

National Audit Office (1999). *Examining the value for money of deals under PFI*. London, The Stationery Office (Report of the Comptroller and Auditor General, HC 739, Session 1998–1999).

National Audit Office (2002). *The PFI contract for the redevelopment of the West Middlesex University Hospital*. London, United Kingdom National Audit Office (Report by the Comptroller and Auditor General, HC 49 Session).

National Audit Office (2003). *PFI: Construction performance*. London, United Kingdom National Audit Office (Report by the Comptroller and Auditor General, HC 371 Session 2002–2003, 5 February 2003) (http://www.nao.org.uk/publications/nao_reports/02-03/0203371.pdf, accessed 21 August 2007).

NHS (2003). *NHS Magazine, February 2003*. London, United Kingdom National Health Service.

Nooteboom B (2002). *Trust: forms, foundations, functions, failures and figures*. Cheltenham, Edward Elgar.

Pavignani E, Colombo A. *Health action in crises. Module 7: Analysing patterns of health care provision*. Geneva, World Health Organization (http://www.who.int/hac/techguidance/tools/disrupted_sectors/module_07/en/, accessed 22 August 2007).

Savas E (2000). *Privatization and public–private partnerships*. New York, Chatham House.

Smit M, Dewulf G (2002). Public sector involvement: a comparison between the role of the government in private finance initiatives (PFI) and public private partnerships (PPP) in spatial development projects. In: Montanheiro L, Berger S, Skomsøy G. *Public and private sector partnerships: exploring cooperation*. Sheffield, Sheffield Hallam University Press:451–463.

Vlaar PWK, Van den Bosch F, Volberda HW (2007). On the evolution of trust, distrust and formal coordination and control in interorganizational relationships: towards an integrative framework. *Group & Organization Management*, 32(4):407–429.

Williamson OE (1985). *The economic institutions of capitalism: firms, markets, relational contracting*. New York, The Free Press.

Winch GM (2002). *Managing construction projects*. Oxford, Blackwell Publishing.

Yescombe ER (2002). *Principles of project finance*. London, Academic Press.

# Chapter 8

# Life-cycle economics: cost, functionality and adaptability

*Svein Bjørberg, Marinus Verweij*

## A strategic perspective on asset investment

Previous chapters have discussed the rapidly changing context of health care. Capital assets in the health sector exist in a dynamic and rapidly changing environment, with far more risks and competition than in the past. In most European countries over the decades, health assets – square metres – have been "free" for health care providers. Whether the country had a national health service or a social health insurance system made little difference. Once a capital project had been approved, the expense was covered from the government budget or from insurance funds, and the providers ran little or no risk.

In the near future, however, in many European countries capital assets will no longer be cost- or risk-free for health care providers. In the Netherlands, the Government is planning to include the cost of capital in output pricing mechanisms (Netherlands Board for Health Care Institutions 2007a). There is a clear rationale for doing this, as output pricing should cover the total cost of the product. In other sectors of the economy the price of property has always been an integral part of the product price.

In the health sector, however, the situation is worrying. There seems to be too little awareness of the cost and benefit of capital investment, and concepts such as life-cycle economics of buildings are underdeveloped. The comparative ease of availability of capital and the absence of a rigorous market in public provision of care have masked the need for progress. In addition, in many countries the debate has focused on catching up with backlog maintenance, rather than on developing a forward-looking approach that considers the real cost of capital assets in the future. Often, maintaining old, failing buildings is far more expensive in the long run than building anew. This is where life-cycle costing can be a particularly valuable instrument (Dowdeswell 2006). This chapter makes the case for a more widespread use of the life-cycle costing model. This model does not only allow comparison of different strategic scenarios, it also helps to take better account of the relationship between capital investment and the process of health care delivery.

## Shifting incentives

The traditional risk-free financing of capital assets in the health sector has a number of characteristics.

- There is a financial split between investment funding lines and recurrent expenditure. This means that there was never a strong incentive to consider the efficiency and recurrent costs of buildings.

- As capital assets are "free", there is an inherent upward pressure to procuring more square metres, with the Government or its asset agency often acting as countervailing power.

- In many cases, the primary target has been to keep capital projects within budget and time. This could easily jeopardize the long-term functionality and efficiency of facilities.

- The functional lifespan of a health building is usually far shorter than its technical lifespan. In practice this has often meant holding on to dysfunctional health buildings for far too long (Netherlands Board for Health Care Institutions 2007c).

The rapidly changing context and the increasingly risky environment confront the providers with completely new questions. Drawing on the case studies from across Europe that are published in the companion volume, it seems that future developments will need to be characterized by the following considerations.

- It is not so much the initial investment that counts, but the costs of the building over its life-cycle.

- It will no longer be a question of seeking the largest and most prestigious health building, but rather a search for the optimal facility. A hospital with too much inflexible floor space could find itself at a disadvantage from a competitive point of view.

- There will be a strong incentive to have buildings with "shrinkage and growth" flexibility to permit fluctuations in production in a volatile environment.

- So far, capital assets in health have been fairly unique, with limited possibilities for alternative use. In a more competitive environment, the long-term market value of assets will become far more important. Residual value will profit the provider, once the asset is no longer functional as a health building and needs to be sold.

- There will also be a strong drive towards closer integration with care processes outside of hospitals.

It is rather strange that the debate about the life-cycle costs of health buildings was sparked by market reforms. Even if buildings are fully publicly funded from the government budget, the life-cycle expenditure will be charged to the taxpayer in one way or another. Inefficient buildings are particularly expensive to run. The Norwegian Government has therefore established a long-standing policy of calculating the life-cycle costs of all major public infrastructure projects (Government of Norway 2006) (Table 8.1).

- Capital cost (investment): €6500

- Costs in use (management, operation and maintenance (MOM)) per year: €130

- Costs to business (primary business, such as health services) per year: €2570.

**Table 8.1** *An example of the ratio between capital costs, "costs in use" and "costs to business" (in €/m²)*

| Lifetime (in years) | Capital costs over the lifetime (X) | Costs in use over the lifetime (Y) | Costs to business over the lifetime (Z) | Ratio X:Y:Z |
|---|---|---|---|---|
| 30 | 6 500 | 3 900 | 77 100 | 1 : 0.6 : 11.9 |
| 40 | 6 500 | 5 200 | 102 800 | 1 : 0.8 : 15.8 |
| 60 | 6 500 | 7 800 | 154 200 | 1 : 1.2 : 23.7 |

*Source*: Bjørberg S, Multiconsult, personal communication, 2007.

The ratio between capital costs, costs in use and costs to business (which depends on the number of years in the life-cycle and the way costs are calculated) is often used to show that the initial building costs are small in comparison to the overall costs to business (the recurrent expenditure) during the life-cycle. This is a crucial point. In the earlier example, the annual cost to business is €2570, which implies that after approximately 2.5 years the accumulated cost is as high as the initial investment.

Economizing on investment budgets, as is so often carried out in order to remain within government targets, could prove to be particularly costly in terms of cost to primary business during the life-cycle. A straightforward example is economizing on investment to reduce the energy consumption of a health facility. In many cases these investment cuts will turn out to be "penny wise, pound foolish". Where economizing on the capital investment affects the primary business, the impact could be even more detrimental. The importance of the building to the primary business of a health facility should not be underestimated. This principle is particularly well understood by the Rhön Klinikum group in Germany (Fig. 8.1).

**Fig. 8.1** *Key principles of Rhön Klinikum*

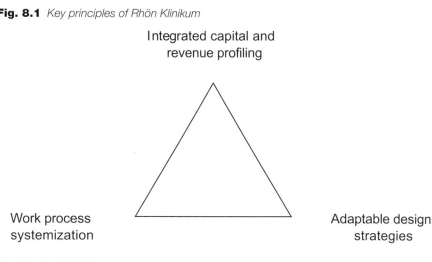

*Source*: Dowdeswell 2006.

## Are hospitals unique buildings?

Why is a hospital built as it is? There has been a trend over recent decades towards concentrating care provision in large health facilities and compounds (University Medical Centre Groningen 2006; Wagenaar 2006). This has been driven partly by professional factors: different medical disciplines are encouraged to work together in a multidisciplinary context to enhance the quality of care. However, other factors are also at play. New ICTs, for example, make communications far easier than in the past, while the shortage of building land in many European cities necessitates other solutions. The approach in Europe has often been based on the assumption that a hospital is a unique item of property that is suitable for few other functions. But are health assets really so unique?

The Netherlands Board for Health Care Institutions has developed a model that divides the hospital into four different segments, listed here (Netherlands Board for Health Care Institutions 2006b) (typical figures for the percentage of floor space are shown in parentheses):

- A "hot floor" with all the capital intensive functions unique to the hospital, including the operating rooms, diagnostic imaging and intensive care facilities (24%).

- Low care nursing departments where, in addition to care, the residential function plays a primary role. This asset is similar to a hotel (27%).

- All office facilities, administration, staff departments and outpatient units. An important question is why many of the outpatient functions could not be housed in normal office-type facilities. This commonly occurs in the United States and Australia (36%).

- A fourth segment – factory – concerns production line functions that are not part of the primary process, such as laboratories and kitchens. These are particularly suitable for outsourcing (13%).

The different segments each comprise substantial parts of the surface area of a general hospital. Thinking along these lines offers new avenues for building more flexible health assets in the future.

Not only are the investment costs per square metre particularly different for the four segments; the technical life-cycles are also different. On average, the costs of a square metre of hot floor are twice as high as those of offices. In addition, the life-cycle of the hot floor is much shorter than that of the office. In calculations made when developing this model, the initial investment costs of hospitals built appropriately for the four segments could be as much as 10–15% lower than the traditional all-in-one approach. Furthermore, the model offers the potential to further normalize health assets: nursing departments could be built for eventual use as hotels, while offices and outpatient departments could be built as offices. The residual asset value will be much enhanced if the asset is not specific to health care functions. There are already some examples of this model being used in a "campus" setting, such as the Albert Schweitzer hospital in Dordrecht (Netherlands), and the plans being made by the Bernhove hospital (Netherlands) for a new site in Uden. Within the campus area of the hospital, we see differentiated zones for the hot floor, office, factory and hotel functions, with building types differentiated accordingly. This will make a future exit-strategy, if needed, much easier and enhance the residual value of the property.

Lastly, within a more volatile context, providers will need flexibility to deal with production fluctuations. The approach will differ according to the segment. Research in the Netherlands has shown that the hours in which operating theatres are actually in use are not much more than 20% of the total hours in the week (Netherlands Board for Health Care Institutions 2005b). An increase in production should therefore not be addressed primarily by building more theatres, but by using them for more hours, as many commercial providers do. This also applies to outpatient facilities. In this case the use of normalized assets may be an alternative solution to the required "shrinkage and growth" flexibility. Many larger health care providers have a portfolio of health real estate that, when well managed, can create flexibility in itself.

## The Core Hospital

The prizewinning entry of the Dutch design competition "Future Hospitals: competitive and healing" was the "Core Hospital" by Venhoeven/Guthknecht (Netherlands Board for Health Care Institutions 2005a). Their unique approach to the hospital of the future was to ask: which functions absolutely need to be in the core hospital building, and which functions could be located elsewhere? Their conclusion was that only a little over 50% of the traditional floor area was needed, closely related to the hot floor functions. Other functions were located elsewhere (Fig. 8.2).

**Fig. 8.2** *The Core Hospital*

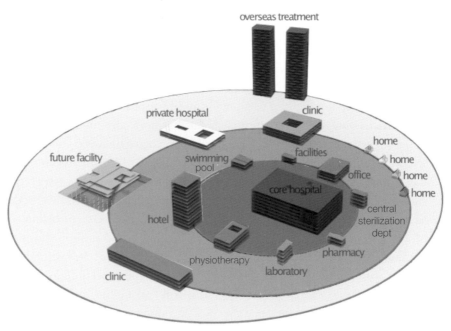

*Source*: Netherlands Board for Health Care Institutions 2005a.

Their motive for this approach was driven by an urban planning perspective. In many European cities, land is in such short supply that the building of new inner city hospitals has become virtually impossible. In many cases, hospitals have been moved to the periphery of cities. The model of the Core Hospital makes it easier to build hospitals in inner cities.

This approach is a natural extension of the segments model discussed earlier. Further research on the segments model has focused on those medical and organizational relationships between hospital functions which are so important that they need to be physically positioned within the "hot floor" area. It was seen earlier that the hot floor area in a general hospital comprises 24% of overall floor space. However, if related functions are taken into consideration, the hot floor area increases to 46% of overall floor space. Fig. 8.3 shows an extreme "segmented" model, while Fig. 8.4 shows a more realistic hybrid model.

**Fig. 8.3** *An extreme segmented model*

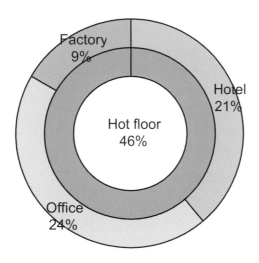

*Source*: Netherlands Board for Health Care Institutions 2007b.

The results come particularly close to the Core Hospital analysis. In both cases, the conclusion is that the highly specific hospital functions that need to be co-located cover only about half of the floor area traditionally projected for a general hospital.

These conclusions provide new perspectives for future network- and campus-type hospitals that allow a much more differentiated approach to assets.

## The Rhön Klinikum approach

One of the case studies in the companion volume describes the Rhön Klinikum company in Germany (see the relevant case study in the accompanying volume). Rhön Klinikum is one of the fully private companies operating within a public social insurance system. It is able to undertake a high level of capital investment, and still make a profit, by combining three important principles:

**Fig. 8.4** *A hybrid model*

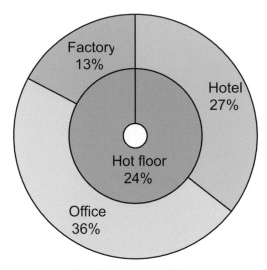

*Source*: Netherlands Board for Health Care Institutions 2007b.

- a tightly controlled and monitored operational fiscal policy

- a compact and flexible building concept

- strong systematization of care processes through the use of care pathways.

Its level of capital investment is nearly threefold higher than in traditional German hospitals. However, this investment is returned through more intensive production and higher profits. Investment decisions are guided by down-to-earth, well thought-through business cases. A more competitive health environment with integrated output pricing does not therefore necessarily mean that capital investment will slow down; it may be accelerated if there is a sound business perspective.

The other lesson to be learnt from this case is the benefit of close integration between the building and the primary process. The design of Rhön Klinikum hospitals is not particularly unusual, but much attention is paid to functional relationships. One of the principles is that every metre a nurse walks unnecessarily costs money. Rhön Klinikum have therefore chosen to abolish nursing departments according to medical disciplines, and instead organized the work according to the level of nursing care: intensive, high, medium and low. Patients are moved through the different departments, as their condition improves. This makes a concentrated and compact hospital design possible and shows how design and primary process can be integrated.

## Looking forward: life-cycle planning

As mentioned earlier, there is often a focus on catching up with "backlog maintenance". One of the consequences is that the existing infrastructure is implicitly taken as the model for future strategies. Life-cycle costing offers an opportunity to calculate the cost of an asset on the basis of forward-looking scenarios. Developing scenarios is therefore an essential prerequisite for effective life-cycle cost analysis. The power of the tool is its ability to compare different strategic scenarios.

Sustainable construction is one element of a worldwide movement devoted to sustainable development (see Chapter 12 by Glanville & Nedin). As changes in functional requirements emerge increasingly quickly, sustainable construction will need to adapt its functions over time. Life-cycle planning means that the whole life of a building should be planned, from the early design phase, throughout the operational life of the building, to demolition. This may sound simple in theory, but is particularly challenging and complicated in practice. Life-cycle planning involves economic analysis of both costs and income, analysis of the environmental impact, and analysis of the social impact on users, the local community and society.

The life-cycle economy comprises all economic aspects (costs and income) during the lifetime of the facility, both related to the building and to the primary business. Life-cycle costs are defined as the costs related to the construction, management, operation and development of the building over its lifetime, as well as to the costs of the primary business using the building. The level of investment, depreciation rates and interest rates need to be considered. It is also necessary to identify the consequences of the investment on building-related management, operation, maintenance and development (such as upgrading and refurbishment). For example, investing in high-quality cladding solutions can in many cases prove profitable (low life-cycle costs), due to lower maintenance and operation costs over the lifetime, even though the initial investment cost is higher than for other alternatives. Life-cycle costs also include facility management (services and supplies for the primary business). Investment costs, costs of the building in use and costs of the primary business make up the total life-cycle costs. If the business is to make a profit, these costs should be lower than the life-cycle income. Life-cycle value includes, in addition to life-cycle economics, issues such as the environmental and social impact of the building.

## Adaptability

Adaptability is crucial in a life-cycle perspective, in order to maintain the functionality of the asset and thereby contribute to a positive value over the life-cycle. The period between each refurbishment is called the service life period. This is the period when the use of the building is more or less static. If the service life period is the same as the whole lifetime of the building, there is no need for adaptability. If the service life period is particularly short, then the need for adaptability is particularly important. For some buildings, the use can be particularly static, for example for an opera hall or a library. The use in hospital buildings, on the other hand, is particularly dynamic, with high demands for adaptability. The service life period has to be taken into consideration in the design phase, so that the required level of adaptability can be determined (Fig. 8.5).

**Fig. 8.5** *Short and long service life period*

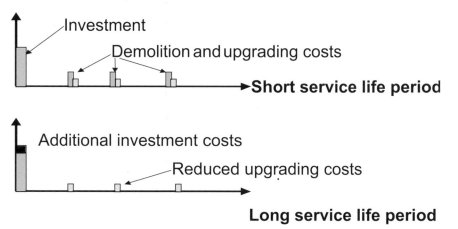

*Source*: Bjørberg S, Multiconsult, personal communication, 2007.

*Note*: Service life period is the period of time with no changes in the building.

If the service life period is short (for example 5–10 years), investment in adaptability will be worthwhile, whereas if the service life period is long (for example 60 years), investment in long-lasting solutions will be advantageous. Adaptability has three major dimensions:

- flexibility – the possibility of changing layout, that is, the space distribution

- generality – the possibility of changing functions

- elasticity – the possibility of changing volume.

Different levels of adaptability can be distinguished. In the classification system shown in Fig. 8.6, Level 0 indicates high adaptability requirements and Level 3 represents low adaptability requirements. For each level, demands within flexibility, generality and elasticity can be specified. Figure 8.6 illustrates the need for adaptability in different categories of buildings. This also demonstrates

**Fig. 8.6** *Examples of adaptability requirements*

## Level of adaptability

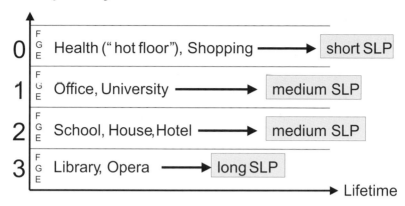

*Source*: Bjørberg S, Multiconsult, personal communication, 2007.

*Notes*: F: flexibility; G: generality; E: elasticity; SLP: service life period.

that the demands within a hospital can be divided into different levels of adaptability (the "hot floor" requires Level 0, the office requires Level 1, the hotel requires Level 2).

The same approach can be used to classify the adaptability of existing buildings. Figure 8.7 illustrates how the "hot floor" of a hospital dating from 1950 now only satisfies the demands of Level 2. Refurbishment of this space for further use as a "hot floor" in a modern-day hospital, where the requirements are at Level 0, is hardly practical or economically feasible. A building that does not meet the demands of its core business may give rise to extra costs due to the lack of functionality. In the outdated hospital building, health production will generally be less effective than in a more modern building, for example due to poor logistics or a space distribution that is impossible to rearrange.

When using this methodology, it is necessary to be aware of the requirements that need to be fulfilled at each level. In pursuit of this goal, a number of thematic matrixes have been developed in Norway (Table 8.2).

## Life-cycle costs

It is necessary to clarify the relationship between life-cycle costs, annual expenses, lifetime costs and annual costs, as shown in Fig. 8.8 and Fig. 8.9:

• annual expenses – what needs to be paid each year; this can differ from year to year;

**Fig. 8.7** *Low adaptability of a hospital hot floor built in 1950*

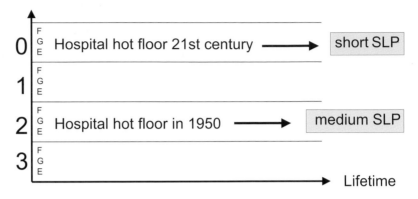

Level of adaptability

*Source*: Bjørberg S, Multiconsult, personal communication, 2007.

*Notes*: F: flexibility; G: generality; E: elasticity; SLP: service life period.

- life-cycle costs – investment costs plus annual expenses plus residual costs (demolition);
- lifetime costs – net present value of life-cycle costs;
- annual costs – annuity of lifetime costs.

The phrase "costs in use", mentioned earlier, with key figures from Norway (Table 8.1), is equivalent to the annuity costs for MOM.

Annual expenses include the costs of management, operation, maintenance, development and service throughout the period of use, including the costs when the period of use has ended (demolition). If the net present value of these costs is added to the capital costs, this gives the lifetime costs. The annual costs are calculated as an annuity, which means that they are assumed to be the same amount every year. All costs are calculated according to the value they have in the year of calculation.

These costs occur at different times throughout the lifetime of the building. First, there are the investment or capital costs. During the period of use, there are comparatively stable MOM costs, as well as periodic costs such as replacements of building elements or large redevelopment and upgrading projects. These may arise perhaps only once during the lifetime of the building, but maybe more often. Finally, in the end there will be demolition and disposal costs. To make all these costs homogeneous and compatible, they have to be discounted to the same time period. The calculation will be based on:

- costs and intervals of actions

**Table 8.2** *Example of a classification matrix*

| Key performance indicators | Adaptability | | | |
| --- | --- | --- | --- | --- |
| | **Level 0** | **Level 1** | **Level 2** | **Level 3** |
| Internal walls, doors and windows | Walls, doors and windows easy to mount and take down. Few technical installations in walls. Standardized connections. | Some walls, windows or doors rigidly connected to other elements, but mainly easy to change plan layout. | Walls, doors and windows difficult to move. | Heavy and rigid internal wall construction and many partitions. |
| Loading capacity | | | | |
| Dead load | Floors can handle extensive dead loads (e.g. storage). | Floors can handle most activities. | Limits for heavy dead loads. | Strict dead load limitations. |
| Live load | Floors can handle extensive live loads (e.g. fitness centre). | Floors can handle most activities. | Limits for activities with considerable movements (e.g. fitness centre). | Strict live load limitations. |
| Snow-load | | | | |
| Emergency exits | Emergency exits are satisfactory according to current regulations and standards for several different building purposes. | Conversion to new solutions and current standards and regulations can be made with reasonable ease. | Considerable deviation from the requirements for current standards and regulations or to adapt to new use. Mending possible within a practically and economically justifiable framework. | Mending not possible within a practically and economically justifiable framework to meet current regulations and standards. |
| Furniture | Furniture is easy to fit into most parts of the building, is easily adapted to equipment and technical installations and is easy to move around. | Furniture can mostly be moved and fitted into new rooms and solutions. | Most of the furniture can be moved around, but moving is heavy and furniture is not adaptable. | Extensive use of stationary furniture. Heavy, large and difficult to move. Old furniture, which is difficult to adapt to new technical solutions. |
| Conflicts between building elements (open building) | Little conflicts between the different main building elements. Easy to maintain and replace separately. | Main building elements can be replaced and maintained separately. | Bad planning for element separation. | Rigid connections between different building elements. |

*Source*: Larssen AK, Multiconsult, personal communication 2007.

**Fig. 8.8** *Net present value*

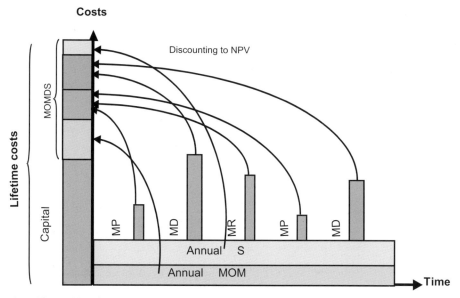

*Source*: Thorsnes T, Statsbygg, Norway, personal communication, 2007.

*Notes*: NPV: Net present value; MOMDS: Management, operation, maintenance, development and service; MP: Periodic (preventive) maintenance; MD: Development and maintenance (periodic or/and replacement); MR: Replacement (part of maintenance); MOM: Management, operation and maintenance.

- real rate of return for discounting
- estimated lifetime of the building.

Figure 8.9 shows the annual cost model. All costs throughout the lifetime are calculated at net present value (the sum of investment and net present value of future costs). This total net present value of lifetime costs can be put back as an annuity over the same period of time, resulting in estimated annual costs. The result is particularly sensitive to the rate of interest used in the calculations. In the public sector in Norway, these annuity costs are the minimum rent to be paid to maintain the technical level of the building. The question of how to choose the appropriate discount rate is important, as it affects the overall costs of particular projects and the decision regarding which projects should be pursued.

## Practical use of life-cycle costing

Life-cycle cost calculations can be used to evaluate different designs, materials, components, systems, rebuilding options, additions and improved or altered operations. The calculation is done in several steps, starting by identifying the main purpose of the calculation and deciding on the different parameters (such

**Fig. 8.9** *Annual cost model*

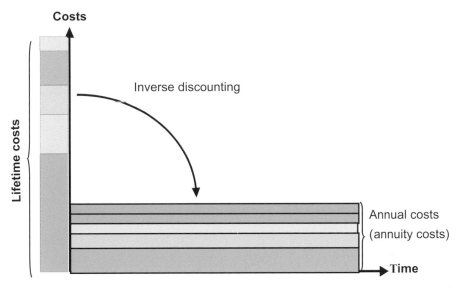

*Source*: Thorsnes T, Statsbygg, Norway, personal communication, 2007.

as facility lifetime and interest rates). A recently published report describes a methodology consisting of 15 steps (Davis Langdon Management Consulting 2007).

Life-cycle cost calculations are commonly performed at different levels, depending on the aim of the calculations and the phase of the lifetime. It should be borne in mind, however, that the main purpose of these calculations has normally been to estimate the future consequences of investment, rather than to obtain the lowest possible life-cycle cost. The level of calculation will always depend on available information related to the phases of the project, as shown in Fig. 8.10.

**Fig. 8.10** *Levels of calculation of life-cycle costs*

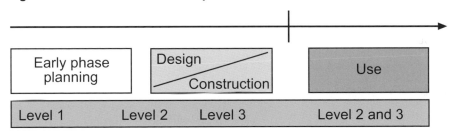

*Source*: Bjørberg S, Multiconsult, personal communication, 2007.

## Level 1

Calculations at this level are suitable at the initial planning stage of a project. Level 1 analysis gives a rough estimate of the life-cycle costs and the annual costs of projects. The result can be used to inform investment analysis. A systematic, operation-oriented design process is the most important tool to produce buildings with sound lifetime economics. To carry out a Level 1 analysis, the following information is required:

- location
- type of building and area
- discount rate and expected service life (calculation period).

Because of the limited information about the building, calculations at this level are carried out on the basis of rough estimates for management, operation, maintenance, development and service.

## Level 2

Calculations at this level are appropriate in the planning phase. At this level, the goal is to find project solutions that fall within the framework set in the preliminary phase of the project. A final determination of the cost framework will be carried out on the basis of sketch project calculations. To carry out a Level 2 life-cycle cost analysis, the following information is required:

- location;
- type of building, sketches and areas;
- construction programme with specified technical standards for materials, components and main systems and
- discount rate and service life period (calculation period).

Calculations at this level are normally based on a cost classification system; some countries have developed national standards for this (examples are the Norwegian NS 3454 and the Dutch NEN 2748 account plan). Classification systems also form the base for benchmarking during the phase when buildings are in use.

## Level 3

Calculations at this level are appropriate in the main project phase. The purpose of calculations at this level is to check the estimates from earlier phases, as well as to assess alternative solutions that might enhance the cost–effectiveness of the project in the short or long term. During the project phase, considerable savings can often be achieved through modest investments in planning. If the result is a well-planned and well-designed project, the need for additional investment at a later stage will be reduced. To carry out a Level 3 analysis, information on the following items is required:

- structure, materials and installations;

- measurable quantities for the different parts of the building as a basis for calculations;

- relatively certain price information;

- discount rate and service life;

- intervals assumed for periodic maintenance or replacements;

- assumed size of operational staff and management; and

- the energy budget.

This type of calculation provides estimates of intervals between maintenance activities and replacement of building elements, as well as costs for each activity. By using net present value computation, all costs payable at different stages in the lifetime of the building are expressed in a single amount at today's value.

To obtain a good estimate of the lifetime economic picture at an early stage of the project, it is necessary to focus on the most important cost elements, as listed here.

- *Capital costs:* are influenced by the area and the shape of the building, the type of construction, the type of materials and the choice of technical installations. Capital costs always have to be viewed in the context of operational and maintenance costs, planning for future reconstructions, expansions and new technical installations.

- *Operational and minor maintenance costs:* quality materials, technical installations and easy access to components are essential factors influencing this type of costs.

- *Cleaning services:* there should be surfaces and materials that facilitate cleaning, limited disruption of floor space by walls, columns and other dividers, and an entrance area designed to allow removal of dirt on the way in.

- *Energy costs:* several measures can be implemented to reduce energy use and therefore also energy costs. Different sources of energy can be considered. The design of facades and windows will play a major role in energy efficiency.

- *Development costs:* if the building will have a short service life period, as in the case of "hot floors" in hospitals, it must be highly adaptable. This will often require additional investments and have a major impact on business costs.

## Depreciation

There is uncertainty about future needs for change, but what is certain is that requirements will change. Design of new buildings should be based on three main principles if they are to be sufficiently adaptable.

1. There should be a separation of building parts and components with different service lifetimes.

2. Foundations, vertical as well as horizontal load-bearing structures, facades and roofs should have maximum technical lifetimes.

3. Inner components, such as ceilings, inner walls, partitions, floorings and elements of technical systems have to be designed and assembled in a way that makes them easy to remove and change. The position of the main technical systems should not be affected by changes in space distribution.

One of the issues in life-cycle cost discussions is the distinction between capital costs and maintenance costs. According to today's principles of accounting, the building is often depreciated as a whole, including technical installations. By decomposing building elements and depreciating them separately, some of the replacement costs will be included in the capital balance. Depreciation is a complex subject, but the theoretical ideal is to have a depreciation period equal to the expected service life of each of the installations. This requires separate depreciation periods for different components and systems.

## Case study example: life-cycle costs in practice

An example is drawn from a typical situation in the Netherlands in which, after several mergers of hospital organizations, the current hospital has two city sites close to each other (Netherlands Board for Health Care Institutions 2006a). The hospital is confronted with three long-term options: whether or not to concentrate the organization at one site, to retain and reassign the present oversized buildings, and/or accept large operational losses.

The site on which the main hospital is located is particularly spacious and therefore has a low building density on the ground. The main building is a typical Breitfuss-type (literally translated "wide foot") structure from the 1970s, in which a tall building block with nursing functions is placed above a flat building block with treatment and outpatient functions, with a floor area of about 65 000 m². Adjoining this building is a newer outpatient wing of about 8000 m², which has been in use for several years. The second hospital facility is located on a site with limited space. The main building dates from the early 1960s and has a floor area of about 30 000 m², while an extension of some 10 000 m² was added only recently.

Architecturally, the functional quality of the older buildings on both sites is poor: both main buildings are in need of refurbishment. The functional quality of the new buildings is good. Five scenarios were explored in the study (Table 8.3).

Scenarios 2 to 4 assume that the secondary site is transformed into a day hospital, with the old building at this site being disposed of. A hospital with exclusively single-bed rooms will then be developed on the main site. While this approach fits comfortably into the existing high-rise buildings, in terms of the size of wards, it also leads to oversizing in terms of space.

**Table 8.3** *Scenarios for developing the hospital*

**Scenario 1**

Completely new replacement on one site

End result: 81 000 m²

**Scenario 2**

- Main site: retain recently built wing; demolish and replace the old buildings (64 000 m²)

- Secondary site: retain and refurbish recently built wing; dispose of main building

End result in total: 82 700 m²

**Scenario 3**

- Main site: retain recently built wing; strip top off high-rise building; renovate retained older parts, construct new nursing ward

- Secondary site: retain and refurbish recently built wing; dispose of main building

End result in total: 87 700 m²

**Scenario 4**

- Main site: retain recently built wing; renovate old building, construct replacement building

- Secondary site: retain and refurbish recently built wing; dispose of main building

End result in total: 98 700 m²

**Scenario 5**

- Main site: retain recently built wing; renovate entire old building

- Secondary site: retain recently built wing; renovate main building

End result in total: 111 200 m²

*Source*: Netherlands Board for Health Care Institutions 2006a.

A life-cycle cost calculation was carried out by the authors for each scenario. Figure 8.11 shows the total capital costs and the sum of the MOM costs (running costs related to the building) over the life of the five scenarios.

Reflecting the fact that it envisages a complete replacement of all buildings, Scenario 1 calls for the highest investment. Scenario 5 requires the least investment, due to the limited new construction and renovation. However, because of the differences in both the floor area in each scenario and the technical quality of the resulting buildings, the MOM expenses show the exact opposite. The difference in MOM expenses across the various scenarios is striking.

Figure 8.12 shows the sum of the annual capital costs and MOM expenses. Scenario 2 generates the lowest annual cost, followed closely by Scenario 3. Scenario 1 turns out to be more expensive, due to the particularly high initial investment costs, which are not fully compensated for by reduced MOM expenses. Scenario 4 and in particular Scenario 5 yield the highest annual burden, due to the profligate use of space, the high MOM expenses resulting from poorer technical quality, and the substantial capital costs involved even in these scenarios.[8]

**Fig. 8.11** *Investment and management, operation, and maintenance costs of the five scenarios*

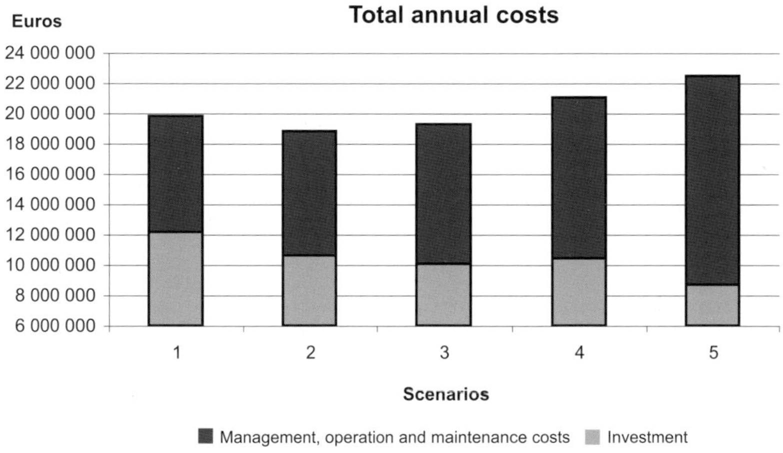

## Conclusions

Investment in health care assets calls for a strategic forward-looking approach. With growing competition in many European countries, health is taking on some of the features of an ordinary commercial sector. Consequently, capital investments will call for sound business cases that take not only the initial investment into account, but also the costs over the whole life-cycle. The life-

---

[8] It should be pointed out, however, that the cost calculations are illustrative, and eventual results will depend on (among other factors) the discount rate chosen.

**Fig. 8.12** *Total annual costs of the five scenarios*

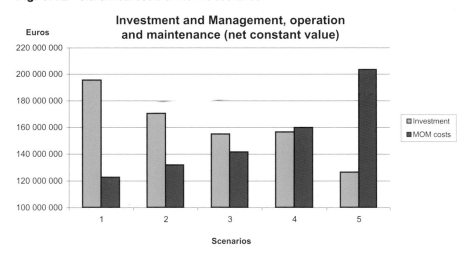

cycle costing model is a powerful instrument to compare different strategic scenarios. Its use in the health sector is still in its infancy, but there is a strong case for applying it more widely, thus yielding a much better understanding of the relationship between capital investment and the process of health care delivery.

## References

Davis Langdon Management Consulting (2007). *Life cycle costing as a contribution to sustainable construction: a common methodology.* London, Davis Langdon Management Consulting.

Dowdeswell B (2006). *The role of life cycle costing in capital investment in health care facilities* (Report No. 601). Utrecht, Netherlands Board for Health Care Institutions, European Health Property Network.

Government of Norway (2006). *Norwegian legislation on public procurement. Revised 2006 by Ministry of Government Administration and Reform.* Oslo, Government of Norway (http://www.regjeringen.no/en/doc/Laws/Acts/Lov-om-offentlige-anskaffelser.html?id=440597, accessed 17 October 2008).

Netherlands Board for Health Care Institutions (2005a). *Future hospitals: competitive and healing. Competition report.* Utrecht, Netherlands Board for Health Care Institutions (http://www.bouwcollege.nl/smartsite.shtml?id=2065, accessed 17 August 2007).

Netherlands Board for Health Care Institutions (2005b). *Optimization of operating room capacity, English summary.* Utrecht, Netherlands Board for Health Care Institutions (Report No. 580) (http://www.bouwcollege.nl/Pdf/CBZ%20Website/English/Summaries/Hospitals/english_580.pdf, accessed 17 August 2007).

Netherlands Board for Health Care Institutions (2006a). Life cycle costing (LCC): lucrative and crystal clear. *In Perspectief,* October:1–8 (http://www.bouwcollege.nl/smartsite.shtml?id=4896, accessed 17 August 2007).

Netherlands Board for Health Care Institutions (2006b). Slimmer omgaan met vastgoed [A worse handling of real estate]. *In Perspectief,* November:1–4 (http://www.bouwcollege.nl/Pdf/CBZ%20Website/Publicaties/In%20perspectief/InPerspectief16.pdf, accessed 17 August 2007).

Netherlands Board for Health Care Institutions (2007a). *Analyse van de effecten op instellingsniveau van de introductie van NHC's in de ziekenhuiszorg [Analysis of the effect on health care institutions of the introduction of the normative estate component (NHC) in hospital care].* Utrecht, Netherlands Board for Health Care Institutions (http://www.bouwcollege.nl/smartsite.shtml?id=654, accessed 17 August 2007).

Netherlands Board for Health Care Institutions (2007b). *Building differentiation of hospitals – layers approach.* Utrecht, Netherlands Board for Health Care Institutions (http://www.bouwcollege.nl/smartsite.shtml?id=6726, accessed 21 May 2007).

Netherlands Board for Health Care Institutions (2007c). Quality mapping of general hospital buildings. *In Perspectief,* 19 April:1–8 (http://www.bouwcollege.nl/smartsite.shtml?id=5803, accessed 17 August 2007).

University Medical Centre Groningen (2006). *The architecture of hospitals.* Conference proceedings, April 2005. Groningen, University Medical Centre Groningen.

Wagenaar C (ed.) (2006). *The architecture of hospitals.* Rotterdam, NAi Publishers.

Chapter 9

# Facility management of hospitals

*Kunibert Lennerts*

## Introduction

All countries in Europe face the challenge of finding sustainable sources of funding in response to upward pressure on health care expenditure. Hospitals account for a substantial proportion of overall health expenditure, with facility management costs making up 20–30% of expenditure on hospitals. However, facility management costs have so far failed to attract significant attention from health care providers and policy-makers in many countries. There is surprisingly little comparative information on facility management costs of hospitals and even less is known about how to take account of these costs when designing new hospitals. This chapter describes the experience of a study that has been ongoing since 2001 that has quantified facility management costs and related them to the medical services provided by hospitals. It argues for a more transparent accounting of facility management costs, which may be a step towards substantial cost savings. It also emphasizes the need to consider facility management costs in the design of new facilities.

There are several factors that seem to distinguish hospitals from many other business ventures. First, they are facilities which are open 24 hours a day, 7 days a week; second, they produce particularly complex services; and third, a mistake in a hospital can cost a life. These characteristics create exceptional operating conditions, generating a range of objectives that are much more complex than those that are contained in the profit-maximizing vision of most business ventures. Hospitals must also constantly update their equipment to meet the highest technical and safety standards, even though this can come at exorbitant prices.

What possibilities does the field of facility management offer? In many ways hospitals are moving in the direction of becoming health production industries. A greater number of patients are being treated every year, while the number of beds in hospital facilities is steadily decreasing. This is being achieved by reducing significantly the length of hospital stay and by treating many more patients on an ambulatory basis. Throughout Europe, this demands better coordinated treatment and greater efficiency, increasing the importance of facility management.

How can this greater efficiency be achieved? Approximately 20–30% of hospital costs are not related to core processes, that is, health services performed in order to cure patients. All remaining services can be considered non-core processes and can be defined as falling within the facility management process (Lennerts et al. 2003; Lennerts et al. 2005). In Germany, the volume of these processes corresponds to approximately €18 billion annually (Statistisches Bundesamt 2006).

Core processes and facility management processes thus both contribute to the patient's path through the hospital facility. From this patient-focused perspective, a comprehensive model can be developed to estimate facility management costs and to relate them to activity, based on case-mix measures, such as DRGs. The required information for these calculations can be generated by using a facility management product model for all facility management services.

This chapter presents the results of the research project "Optimization of processes in hospitals" (OPIK), established in 2000 at the University of Karlsruhe, Germany, in cooperation with 30 hospitals and industry partners. A total of 28 of the hospitals are located in Germany, with one each in Luxembourg and Switzerland. Although primarily focused on Germany, the approach is likely to be suitable for hospitals in other countries that have appropriate information systems, irrespective of location or size of hospital. This chapter describes how the results of the research project were used to optimize facility management, in particular by benchmarking performance.

## Facility management

The European Standard on facility management (CEN/TC 348), drawn up by the European Committee for Standardization in 2006 (European Committee for Standardization 2006), states that:

> Facility Management is developing in various European countries. Driven by certain historical and cultural circumstances, organizations and business areas have built different understandings and approaches. In general, all organizations,

whether public or private, use buildings, assets and services (facility services) to support their primary activities. By coordinating these assets and services, using management skills and handling many changes in the organization's environment, Facility Management influences its ability to act proactively and meet all its requirements. This is also done to optimize the costs and performance of assets and services. The main benefits of Facility Management approaches in organizations are:

- a clear and transparent communication between the demand side and the supply side by dedicating persons as single points of contact for all services, which are defined in a Facility Management agreement;

- a most effective use of synergies amongst different services, which will help to improve performance and reduce costs of an organization;

- a simple and manageable concept of internal and external responsibilities for services, based on strategic decisions, which leads to systematic in- or outsourcing procedures;

- a reduction of conflicts between internal and external service providers;

- an integration and coordination of all required support services;

- a transparent knowledge and information on service levels and costs, which can be clearly communicated to the end users;

- an improvement of the sustainability of an organization by the implementation of life-cycle analysis for the facilities.

This standard defines facility management as the integration of processes within an organization to maintain and develop agreed services which support and improve the effectiveness of its primary activities. Facility management therefore covers and integrates a particularly broad range of processes, services, activities and facilities. The distinction between primary activities and support services depends on the organization. With regard to health facilities, as already noted, all services not related directly to patient care can be defined as facility management services or products (although of course this depends on what is considered direct patient care, which may vary). Facility management aims to provide integrated management at strategic and tactical levels to coordinate the provision of agreed support services (facility services). This requires specific competences and distinguishes the facility management from the isolated provision of one or more services (Fig. 9.1).

**Fig. 9.1** *Facility management model*

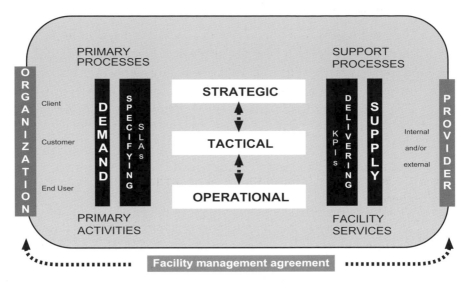

*Source*: European Committee for Standardization 2006.

*Notes*: SLA: Service level agreement(s); KPI: Key performance indicators.

## Clinical pathways in hospitals

Clinical pathways were developed widely in the late 1980s as a basis for activity-based cost management, especially in the United States, following the introduction of the DRG system, which offered a means of specifying the product of health care (Strobel 2004). Coffey and LeRoy (2001) define clinical pathways as an optimized sequence of interventions by health care workers in response to a diagnosis. The core element of the clinical pathway is the standardization of procedures. By extension, this offers a basis for standardizing the utilization of facilities in hospitals, taking account of the differing needs of each department.

## Cost allocation for facility management in hospitals

The delivery of health care in a hospital involves many "customers". The ultimate "customer" is the patient, whose interests are represented by a purchaser of care, such as a sickness fund, but there are also intermediate customers who, in terms of facility management, assume greater importance. These are the clinical units that deliver care and which are supported by those managing the facilities. The clinical units utilize the facilities of the hospital and, in some countries, it is their work that generates the revenue for the hospital, with income based on the number of patients treated, adjusted for case-mix, typically using a system such as DRGs. The challenge is how to link the clinical activity (and related revenue) to the facilities being used.

The OPIK research project has developed a cost allocation system for facility management which is based on the idea of products that can be measured in terms of value and quantity. Through this system, transparency is generated and the customer–provider relationship is strengthened. The project has shown that it is possible to generate savings without any negative impact on the quality of core clinical processes.

## The link between clinical pathways and facility management

The OPIK project focused on the link between primary care processes and facility management costs (Diez, Lennerts & Abel 2007). Figure 9.2 shows graphically a patient's stay as a sequence of time intervals in different functional spaces within the hospital. Depending on the nature of each of the space units, different quantities and qualities of secondary services are needed. Costs can then be allocated to the patient according to the utilization of space units.

**Fig. 9.2** *DRGs and use of functional space units*

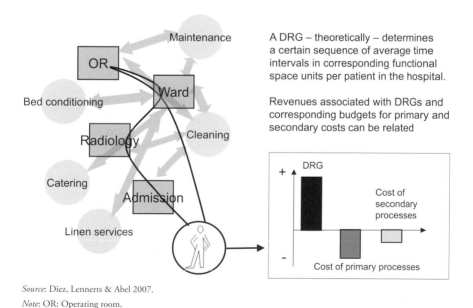

*Source*: Diez, Lennerts & Abel 2007.
*Note*: OR: Operating room.

Primary and secondary costs must be differentiated. Whereas hospitals in some countries mostly have detailed data on the use of primary services (such as the direct cost of treating different types of patient), data on the use of secondary services, such as the cost of medical and nonmedical infrastructure, are often scarce (Deutsche Krankenhausgesellschaft 2002). Hospitals may not allocate these costs to functional units, but instead combine them in an overhead category. These costs are then allocated by means of a formula, such as patient days in each unit. In this way, the relationship between the amount of facility management services and functional units becomes blurred.

The direct allocation of costs to each functional unit allows for a more accurate cost allocation and therefore a usable product model has to be developed for the secondary services.

## Transparent facility management using a product model

The product of facility management is the delivery of services (European Committee for Standardization 2005) in response to needs (Gabler 2000). Taking the definition of quality developed by the European Committee for Standardization (2005), it becomes clear that the product is the service delivered to the customer by the service provider. As the aim of facility management is to provide optimal support to the core process of a business, the requirements of facility management are defined by the primary processes it supports.

A set of criteria for products supplied was compiled. These are (Lennerts, Abel & Pfründer 2004):

- services need to be performed for the benefit of the customer
- it must be possible to define a comprehensible basis for allocation
- the effort to acquire the quantities needed must be reasonable
- the customer should be able to influence the quantity of the product.

To develop a product "catalogue", two principles came to the fore. On the one hand, the product needs to be measurable in a way that costs can be allocated to it. On the other hand, the product is a service that is necessary for the performance of core processes. These considerations can be illustrated using the example of an operating room.

In terms of facility management, the main requirement for performing an operation is space, which therefore is the basic product of facility management. Because of the need for high security and hygiene standards, the construction of operating rooms involves a high degree of specification and tends to be expensive. Furthermore, the accompanying technical equipment must be maintained in an absolutely reliable condition, as do the characteristics of the space itself, such as ventilation and communication systems. During the operation, medical gases, electrical power and heating are required; the surgeon requires an appropriate set of sterile instruments; and, following the operation, surgical waste must be disposed of.

Drawing on models from thermodynamics, the operating room can be regarded as an open system, where different products cross the system border (Fig. 9.3). Corresponding to the criteria set out earlier, the quantity should be easy to measure and it must be possible to establish the monetary value of the product.

**Fig. 9.3** *Performance of facility management services for an operation*

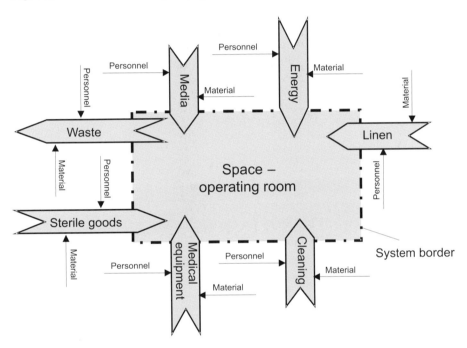

The basis of this model is the customer–provider relationship. A medical unit, as the recipient of facility management services, can be equated with a zoned space. This zoned space requires facility management services, which are provided by different facility management units. By assigning facility management products to cost centres, while defining zoned spaces as the service recipient, a simple customer–provider relationship emerges between the service recipient on the primary side and the service provider on the facility management side. The individual facility management units can thus be represented by cost centres, to which responsibility for certain processes and products can be assigned (Braun 1999). This allows for process-oriented cost allocation. The cost centre provides its product for other cost centres and procures necessary products from other cost centres for its own production.

**Table 9.1** *Classification of the 29 facility management products in Germany*

**Product list – cost proportions**

| Allocation basis: floor space in m² | Allocated on quantity basis | |
|---|---|---|
| outside facilities | waste disposal | ton of waste |
| operation | bed conditioning | bed |
| building maintenance | information technology services | personal computer |
| technical maintenance | fleet management | vehicle |
| basic rent | hygiene advice | analysis |
| cleaning | maintenance of medical equipment | value |
| pest control | cooling service | kilowatt-hour |
| security | broadcasting services | television |
| | catering | meal |
| **Order-related allocation** | sterilization service | sterile unit |
| | power supply | kWh |
| office supplies | telephone services | extension |
| caretaker services | patient transport | transport |
| reprographics services | heating supply | kWh |
| mail services | laundry services | ton linen |
| removal services | water supply | m³ |

In Germany, the authors have concluded that it is possible to represent the entire range of services performed for the benefit of customers in hospitals through 29 facility management products, although this number might be slightly different in other countries. The 29 facility management products can be clustered into three categories. The first cluster consists of products that can reasonably be assigned using space as the basis for allocation. The second cluster comprises products that can be quantified numerically, although data and system constraints mean that some products that can, in theory, be quantified must be allocated on a space basis. The third cluster is generated by products that are only utilized or carried out at the request of the customer or are not used on a regular basis. For these products, the customer is charged on the basis of products ordered. An overview of the product classification is given in Table 9.1.

## Optimization potential

The optimization of secondary processes can take a number of forms. In addition to cost savings from optimization of individual facility management activities, savings can also be achieved from improved coordination of primary and secondary processes. Benchmarking with other health care facilities offers a means of identifying processes that can be improved.

A key goal is to provide the best working environment for the core process, orienting facility management processes specifically towards the medical work flow. Detailed process analysis makes it possible to reduce friction between primary and secondary processes. It also makes it possible to guide optimization of clinical pathways, ensuring that they are patient-oriented and based on the optimal layout for patient treatment and movement. All of these different approaches have been analysed and tested within the OPIK project.

## The "Optimization of processes in hospitals" research project

The OPIK research project was launched in 2001. The University of Karlsruhe, Germany, in cooperation with the Professional Association of Hospital Engineering (*Fachvereinigung Krankenhaustechnik*, or FKT), selected 30 hospitals and facility management service providers to participate in the project. The project is entirely financed through private funds, made available by the participating service providers. The objective of the research is to analyse the business processes in the participating hospitals, with a focus on the interaction between primary (medical) and secondary (facility management) business processes. The hypothesis of the OPIK partnership was that a real potential for savings cannot be generated by focusing on single processes or steps within processes. Instead, a more holistic approach would be needed, based on a comprehensive framework for analysing business processes.

This allowed for the extensive analysis of processes in hospitals and the generation of a detailed process matrix, enabling the establishment of far-reaching standards for the performance of facility management services. The project seeks to create a basis for the introduction of efficient, holistic facility management structures and processes for German hospitals (Lennerts et al. 2003; Lennerts et al. 2005).

## Benchmarking of overall facility management performance

In order to determine the relative importance of the costs of facility management products, an ABC (or Pareto) analysis was carried out (Fig. 9.4). This chart has two scales. The left-hand scale, ranging from 0% to 50%, applies to the bars in the chart, which show the relative values of facility management products. The right-hand scale, ranging from 0% to 100%, applies to the curve and indicates the accumulated costs of facility management products.

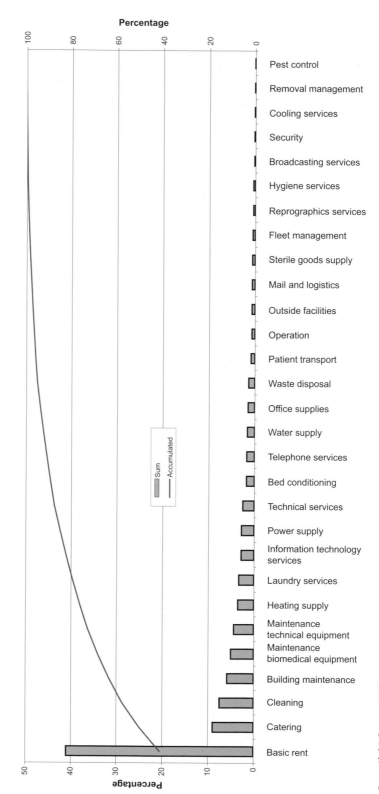

**Fig. 9.4** *ABC analysis of facility management costs*

*Source:* Abel & Lennerts 2005.

The ABC analysis demonstrates that a large number of facility management products contribute only marginally to overall costs. By far the biggest share of overall facility management costs is due to the basic rent or capital cost of available space (that is, annuitizing the capital cost over the lifetime of the facility). Almost 41% of facility management costs can be attributed to this element, followed by catering (8.62%), cleaning (7.49%), maintenance (building maintenance 6.33%, maintenance of biomedical equipment 5.07% and technical maintenance 4.48%), heating supply (3.45%) and linen services (3.14%). These eight facility management products account for 79.35% of overall costs, almost reaching the 80% threshold that is commonly used in ABC analyses to identify the most important categories of items. With regard to Fig. 9.4, it is possible to allocate about 60% of the facility management costs to space-related products, 35% to quantity-related products and 5% to order-related products. It therefore makes sense to start the process of optimizing the facility management process with the correct allocation of square metres to the different cost centres.

## Results of benchmarking

To illustrate the use of this approach in benchmarking, results are shown for all hospitals included in the study. Standard deviation was used as a measure of the statistical dispersion of the savings potential, which assumes that the dispersion of product prices is a result of the different ways in which services are performed. To ensure that this is the case, two requirements need to be met. On the one hand, the average needs to rest on a statistically valid basis; on the other hand, data on unit costs and product quantities must be valid. The examination of the facility management product portfolio of all participating hospitals produces the results shown in Fig. 9.5. This graph indicates the relative importance of the cost share of the various products and their associated savings potential. Taken together, these two indicators clarify where the greatest cost savings can be achieved.

Figure 9.5 shows that the maximum impact factor with regard to overall facility management costs of all hospitals included in the study can be found in the basic rent (12.8%), followed by building maintenance (4.8%), catering (3.7%) and cleaning (3.2%).

At the level of the individual hospital the picture becomes much more detailed.

Figure 9.6 shows a hospital with a high potential for savings.

**Fig. 9.5** *Portfolio analysis of all participating hospitals*

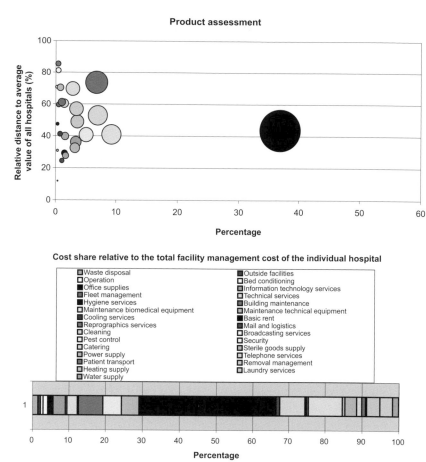

Source: Abel & Lennerts 2006.

The graph shows three areas with an impact factor of over 5%. These are the basic rent, with an impact factor of 6.9%; catering, with an impact factor of 6.6%; and technical services, with an impact factor of 5.2%. Achieving these savings would result in a reduction of overall facility management costs of 18.7%. The complete results of the analysis of hospital X are shown in Table 9.2.

In summary, the results suggest the potential to save over 24% of facility management costs in this hospital (subject to detailed examination of the processes involved). This approach is helpful in selecting processes that should be considered for optimization. The higher the cost share, the greater the impact on overall facility management costs will be.

**Fig. 9.6** *Portfolio analysis for a hospital with a high savings potential*

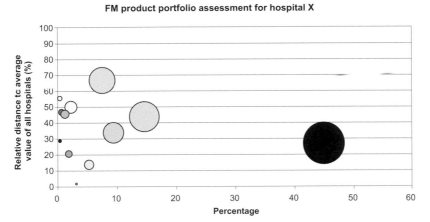

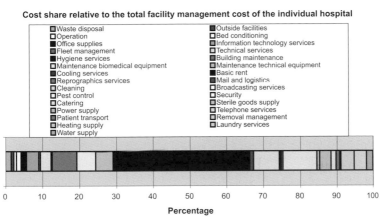

*Source*: Abel & Lennerts 2006.

Another result of the analysis is a price that can be allocated to each product. For example, it is possible to calculate a price for the basic rent and all space-related costs. This price per square metre can be adjusted for the nature of the space. The DIN standard 277 (Deutsches Institut für Normung 2005) subdivides the net floor area of German hospitals into seven subgroups. These are:

1. DIN 1: residential floor area

2. DIN 2: office floor area

3. DIN 3: production and laboratory floor area

4. DIN 4: storage and distribution floor area

**Table 9.2** *Results of the analysis of the hospital shown in Fig. 9.6*

| Product | Cost share (%) | Savings potential (%) | Impact factor (%) |
|---|---|---|---|
| Basic rent | 44.9 | 15.3 | 6.9 |
| Catering | 14.6 | 44.9 | 6.6 |
| Technical services | 7.5 | 69.8 | 5.2 |
| Cleaning services | 9.4 | 25.3 | 2.4 |
| Bed conditioning | 2.2 | 31.4 | 0.7 |
| Supply of sterile goods | 1.2 | 57.0 | 0.7 |
| Maintenance of biomedical equipment | 5.2 | 9.2 | 0.5 |
| Water supply | 1.8 | 23.5 | 0.4 |
| Copy and print services | 0.7 | 50.4 | 0.3 |
| Linen services | 3.1 | 6.0 | 0.2 |
| Broadcasting services | 0.4 | 57.0 | 0.2 |
| Hygiene services | 0.4 | 17.6 | 0.1 |

*Source*: Abel & Lennerts 2006.

5. DIN 5: education and culture

6. DIN 6: healing and nursing floor area

7. DIN 7: other utilization.

In a second step, the treatment area, for example, can be subdivided into different types of utilization. A sample of different types of utilization and respective prices is given in Table 9.3.

**Table 9.3** *Space prices per cluster in all participating hospitals*

| Utilization | Price (€) |
|---|---|
| DIN 1 – Live and lounge | 7.99 |
| DIN 2 – Office space | 14.48 |
| DIN 3 – Production, hand- and machine work, experiments | 28.80 |
| DIN 4 – Store, distribute, sell | 10.04 |
| DIN 5 – Education and culture | 22.47 |
| DIN 6 – Rooms with general medical equipment | 19.81 |
| DIN 6 – Rooms with special medical equipment | 30.18 |
| DIN 6 – Rooms for operations, endoscopy and delivery | 88.39 |
| DIN 6 – Rooms for radiology | 46.42 |
| DIN 6 – Rooms for radiation therapy | 87.38 |
| DIN 6 – Rooms for physiotherapy and rehabilitation | 14.59 |
| DIN 6 – Patient rooms with general equipment | 27.66 |
| DIN 6 – Patient rooms with special equipment | 64.64 |

## Benchmarking operating room performance

To benchmark operating room performance, real time performance data were collected on both planned and emergency operations. The primary process in the operation is typically structured through the steps accounted for by DRGs, as exemplified in Fig. 9.7. After the patient has been called from the accommodation ward, s/he arrives in the functional unit "operation" (end of black time span, start of first white block). The patient will then be transferred from the bed onto an operating table. This is the start of the patient's presence in the unit, which ends with the second white block in the chart, when the patient is placed back in bed and the period in the anaesthetic recovery room begins. The presence of the patient in the operating room is calculated as the sum of the operation time and the pre- and post-operative preparation time, resulting in an "overall operation time".

The second time span that is relevant for the utilization of the operating theatre, and therefore for facility management costs, is the "operation procedure time" (defined as the interval between the first incision and the final suture), marked in horizontal stripes in Fig. 9.7. Data on these two time intervals are collected in most of the hospitals covered by the OPIK study and could therefore be used in the analysis of facility management processes.

There can be more patients in the unit than there are operating theatres. To optimize workflow and maximize utilization of theatres, it is common to maintain a queue of patients. The overall operating time may therefore overlap between patients being operated on in the same operating theatre. The definition of operation procedure time determines the core activity of the operating medical staff, excluding preparation activities. The procedure time only takes place in the operating theatre, where only one patient can be at any one time.

## Results of a case study of six hospitals

The allocation model has been applied in a case study of six German hospitals. The sample of hospitals includes three different sizes of hospital. Two each were in the ranges 300–350 beds, 550–700 beds and 1200–1300 beds, as shown in Table 9.4.

**Table 9.4** *Size of selected hospitals, according to bed numbers*

| Hospital | 1 | 2 | 3 | 4 | 5 | 6 |
|---|---|---|---|---|---|---|
| Number of beds | 310 | 1300 | 317 | 695 | 555 | 1273 |

*Source*: Diez, Lennerts & Abel 2007.

**Fig. 9.7** *Time intervals of the primary operating theatre process*

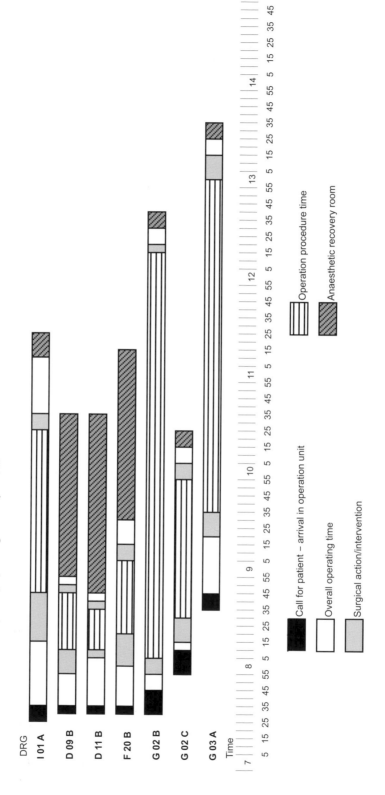

*Source:* Diez, Lennerts & Abel 2007.

Using the definitions set out earlier, the facility management cost for each functional unit operation was estimated for the years 2004 and 2005, with the data on performance of operations collected according to the DRG to which each patient was allocated.

When combined with the dimensions of the operating room unit and the daily utilization schedule established by the operating room management, this analysis indicates greatly varying operating room costs per minute across the six hospitals, ranging from €0.60 per minute to €1.74 per minute. The results are shown in Fig. 9.8, which also depicts capacity-related figures. Operating costs are mainly influenced by daily working hours and available space, but also by facility management performance (Diez, Lennerts & Abel 2007).

**Fig. 9.8** *Cost per OR minute (performance-related)*

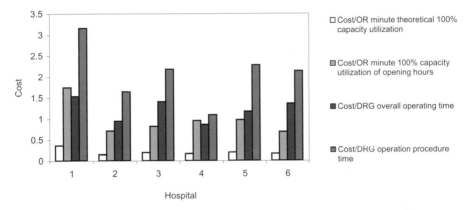

*Source*: Diez, Lennerts & Abel 2007.

*Notes*: OR: Operating room; DRG: Diagnosis-related group; The facility management cost of the functional unit per minute has been calculated as the facility management cost per year in relation to the overall operating time.

Figure 9.9 indicates that the space related to the operating theatres in hospital 1 is about 50% larger than in Hospital 2. The reason may be that large hospitals with many operating theatres can make more flexible and efficient use of the space available, especially in relation to supporting spaces, such as changing rooms, lockers and storage. On average, the space per operating theatre in the six hospitals was 157 m². This figure is similar to the results obtained by Chai (2000), who analysed the floor plans of 39 German hospitals and found an average floor space of the functional unit operating theatre of 160 m². When considering Hospital 4, it can be seen that not only is the space per operating theatre relatively large, but also the daily working hours are relatively short. While the effects of these two factors are to some degree compensated by good facility management performance, Hospital 4 still has the third highest cost per operating minute (see the second columns for each

**Fig. 9.9** *OR space dimensions and daily working hours*

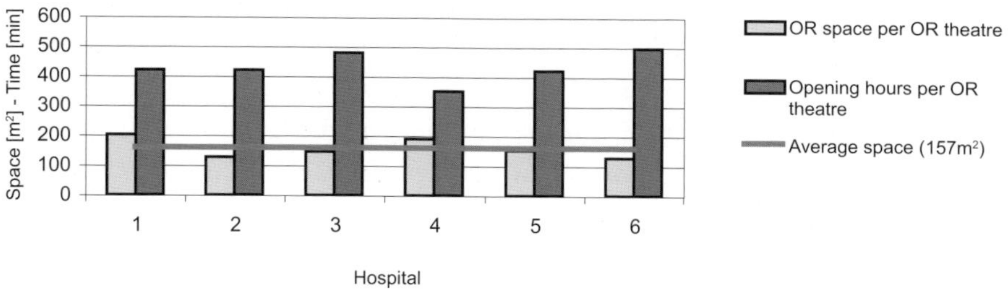

*Source*: Diez, Lennerts & Abel 2007.

hospital in Fig. 9.8). Obviously, poor efficiency in the utilization of space has a considerable influence on the eventual cost. Further investigations should be undertaken to analyse the impact that changes of these parameters cause, as well as to analyse the relationship between space for operating activities and space for supporting functions within operating units.

By combining facility management costs and primary process data, individual prices per minute have been calculated, as shown in Fig. 9.8. The operating room cost per minute per DRG ranges from €0.86 to €1.53 per minute. When using the procedure time as the cost allocation basis, prices per minute differ even more, ranging from €1.09 to €3.15 per minute, with Hospital 4 coming out at lowest cost.

An overview of the workflow in the operating room unit can be gained when comparing these figures. In Hospital 4 the lengths of operating (procedure) time and overall operating time are similar, which contrasts with Hospital 1. There are two possible interpretations of this: Hospital 1 may have a particularly slow work flow, in which the preparation of patients takes a lot of time, or they may have an extended holding area policy, with patients waiting and considerable overlaps.

Further work is needed to capture data on primary processes. Improved operating room management systems are facilitating this (Bethge 2004). In all cases, a distinction has to be made between having patients on hold, activity involving the patient, and the use of the operating theatre itself, as well as between fixed and variable facility management costs in the operating room unit.

# Conclusions

The challenge posed by upward pressure on health care costs is evident not only in Europe, but also all over the world. There is a clear need to maximize the efficiency of health care facilities. Facility management costs in hospitals account for 20–30% of overall hospital expenditure. By improving the relevant processes, it is possible to reduce costs without negatively affecting the quality of the core business.

The OPIK research project presented in this chapter has generated a model for facility management that can be used elsewhere in cost and process benchmarking. Furthermore, the project has produced a tool that makes it possible to check rapidly the costs of facility management in a hospital, so as to identify the key cost drivers that should be optimized, without wasting time on other elements that will not generate significant savings.

By combining data on activity (using the DRG system), it is possible to specify the optimal layout of a hospital in terms of, for example, the number of operating theatres or the size of food preparation areas. By connecting facility management products with the primary medical process, it becomes possible to compute the benefit of a facility management product as a share of the supported DRGs. This makes it possible to pay providers of facility management services on the basis of medical services, rather than according to cleaning or technical support, for example. Their income is then linked to the fortunes of the hospital, creating an alignment of incentives. Where there are public–private partnerships, this innovative approach permits a fairer distribution of risks while introducing the possibility of changing facility management costs, in line with changing medical activity.

This chapter has argued for more transparent accounting of facility management costs. However, there is surprisingly little comparative information available on the facility management costs of hospitals in Europe. Even less is known about how to take account of these costs when designing new hospitals. Filling these evidence gaps promises to generate substantial cost savings.

# References

Abel J, Lennerts K (2005). Cost allocation for FM services in hospitals. In: Lennerts K. *Facility management*. Berlin, VDE Verlag GmbH:531–541.

Abel J, Lennerts K (2006). A new method for the fast identification of savings potentials in FM in health care. In: Lennerts K. *Facility management*. Berlin, VDE Verlag GmbH:389–397.

Bethge J (2004). Benchmarking im OP – Zahlen, Daten, Fakten. In: Busse T, ed. *OP-Management – Praxisberichte*. Heidelberg, Economica, Verlagsgruppe Hüthig Jehle Rehm GmbH:105–119.

Braun S (1999). *Die Prozesskostenrechnung*. Berlin, Verlag Wissenschaft und Praxis.

Chai C-G (2000). *Entwicklung von betrieblichen und baulichen Konzeptionen für die Funktionsstelle Operation in allgemeinen Krankenhäusern unter besonderer Berücksichtigung der ambulanten Operationen.* Marburg, Tectum Verlag.

Coffey J, LeRoy S (2001). Clinical pathways: Linking outcomes for patients, clinicians, payers and employers. In: Kongstvedt PR. *The managed health care handbook, 4th edition.* Gaithersburg, MD, Aspen Publishers:521–538.

Deutsche Krankenhausgesellschaft (2002). *Handbuch zur Kalkulation von Fallkosten.* Version 2.0, 31 January. Siegburg, Deutsche Krankenhausgesellschaft, Spitzenverbände der Krankenkassen & Verband der privaten Krankenversicherung.

Deutsches Institut für Normung (2005). *Areas and volumes of buildings – Part 2: classification of net ground areas (utilization areas, technical operating areas and circulation areas).* Berlin, Beuth Verlag GmbH (DIN standard DIN 277-2:2005-02).

Diez K, Lennerts K, Abel J (2007). Performance-based facility management cost risk assessment for OR units in hospitals within a diagnosis-related grouping system. In: Schalcher H, Wehrmüller T, eds. *Proceedings of the 6th EuroFM Research Symposium, 26–27 June 2007.* Zurich, Swiss Federal Institute of Technology and Wadenswill, University of Applied Sciences:77–88.

European Committee for Standardization (2005). *Quality management systems – fundamentals and vocabulary.* Brussels, European Committee for Standardization (ISO standard DIN EN ISO 9000:2005-12, 2005).

European Committee for Standardization (2006). *Facility management – Part 1: terms and definitions 2006.* Berlin, Beuth Verlag GmbH (CEN standard prEN 15221-1:2006).

Gabler (2000). *Gabler Wirtschaftslexikon.* Wiesbaden, Verlag Dr. Th. Gabler GmbH.

Lennerts K, Abel J, Pfründer U (2004). Space as a cost producing unit in hospitals. In: Bröchner J, Haugen, TI. *Proceedings of the third European Research Symposium in Facilities Management.* Trondheim, Norwegian University of Science and Technology Faculty of Architecture and Fine Art:89–96.

Lennerts K et al. (2003). Reducing health care costs through optimized facility-related processes. *Journal of Facilities Management,* 2(2):192–206.

Lennerts K et al. (2005). Step-by-step process analysis for hospital facility management: an insight into the OPIK research project. *Facilities,* 23(3):167–175.

Statistisches Bundesamt (2006). *Kostennachweis der Krankenhäuser – 2004.* Wiesbaden, Statistisches Bundesamt (Fachserie 12 Reihe 6.3).

Strobel U (2004). Clinical Pathways – Integration und Bedeutung für das OP-Management. In: Busse T, ed. *OP-Management – Praxisberichte.* Heidelberg, Economica, Verlagsgruppe Hüthig Jehle Rehm GmbH:237–268.

Chapter 10

# The economic and community impact of health capital investment

*Jonathan Watson, Simona Agger*

## Introduction

This chapter examines the relationship between capital investment in the health sector and the communities in which it takes place. Within the EU in recent years there has been growing recognition of the importance of sustainable development, especially at the regional level. This has been reflected in the EU's Cohesion Policy, the increasing engagement by regional organizations in determination of priorities for Structural Fund investments and in the implementation of thematic and regional programmes. In the 2007–2013 round of funding, Structural Funds explicitly included investment in the health sector, with particular emphasis on health infrastructure. Although of most importance in the 12 Member States that have joined the EU since May 2004, these developments have wider implications, and particularly for those countries on the path to EU membership and those that, while not seeking membership, are emulating EU policies, including several countries of the former Soviet Union.

The greater responsibilities being placed on regional authorities have clear implications for investment decisions. These are moving beyond a focus on the most efficient way to invest in health infrastructure to broader considerations of the cost–effectiveness of different models of service design and delivery and of the added value that they bring to the region. Yet, at the time of writing only very few studies provide relevant evidence on the wider economic impact of capital investment in the health sector or that offer insights on the effects of inadequate capital investment, a situation pertaining in many countries of the former Soviet Union.

Given the limited data available, much of this chapter is conceptual in nature. However, to the extent possible, it draws on a range of sources, including Eurostat data, the case studies contained in the companion volume, analysis by the European Health Property Network (Erskine, Dowdeswell & Watson 2006) and the work of the Health ClusterNET. It challenges policy-makers at the regional and national levels to consider how to achieve added value from capital investment in the health sector, and argues that the "windfall" of EU Structural Funds provides a huge opportunity for changes in health systems to feed into wider social development, mediated by effective health sector investment. It begins by describing the Structural Funds and the place of health within them.

## The European Union's Structural Funds

Regional development is now a key priority for the EU, with integrated, sustainable and balanced development central to the Community Strategic Guidelines for Cohesion (2006). The priority given to regional development can be understood in the light of data collected by the European Spatial Planning Observatory Network (an EU agency for supporting territorial development). The level of development can be proxied by gross domestic product (GDP) per capita, adjusted for purchasing power and then used as the key variable for determining whether regions (at the NUTS-2 level (Nomenclature of Territorial Units for Statistics)) are eligible for support. In 2005, in the whole of the EU's (EU27) 268 NUTS-2 regions, per capita GDP ranged from 24% of the EU27 average in the north-east region of Romania to 303% in inner London in the United Kingdom (European Commission 2005).

The EU's Cohesion Policy recognizes the importance of sustainable action at regional level, if the EU as a whole is to achieve the Lisbon strategy.[9] It takes a more strategic approach to growth and to socioeconomic and territorial cohesion than its predecessor, and there is a stronger involvement of regions and local players in the preparation and implementation of programmes. It makes funds available to four categories of region: convergence regions (with a GDP per head below 75% of the EU average), phasing-out regions (that no longer qualify for full convergence funding, but would have done without enlargement), phasing-in regions (that no longer qualify for full convergence

---

[9] At the Lisbon Summit in March 2000, the EU set out a new strategy, based on a consensus among Member States, to modernize Europe. This became known as the Lisbon Strategy. The Lisbon Strategy was simplified and relaunched in 2005.

funding, and would no longer qualify even if enlargement had not taken place), and competitiveness and employment regions (that do not fall into any of the other categories). Within the Structural Funds total of €347.4 billion for the 2007–2013 period, 81.5% has been allocated to the Convergence objective (convergence and phasing-out regions); 16% to the Competitiveness and Employment objective (including phasing-in regions); and 2.5% to the European "territorial cooperation" objective.

The Convergence objective, which dominates expenditure by Structural Funds, seeks to promote growth in the least developed regions as a means of promoting convergence with the more developed regions in the EU. There are 84 convergence regions in 17 Member States, and these comprise a total population of 154 million. By definition, these regions have a per capita GDP of less than 75% of the EU average. A further 16 regions, comprising 16.4 million inhabitants and with GDPs only slightly above the threshold, are in the "phasing-out" stage. Cohesion funds are also available for countries where the GDP is under 90% of the EU average (EU12, Greece, Portugal and part of Spain). The amount available under the Convergence objective is split as follows: €199.3 billion for the convergence regions, €14 billion for the "phasing-out" regions and €69.5 billion for the Cohesion Fund, the latter applying to 15 Member States.

Investment priorities are set out in 27 National Strategic Reference Frameworks (NSRFs) agreed between the Member States and the European Commission in 2007 and applied through national thematic and regional operational programmes. Traditionally, these have focused on economic and social development, and while these remain key, especially to the achievement of the renewed Lisbon Strategy, there has also been a commitment to prioritize investment in some other areas, such as the environment and transport infrastructure. Critically, the role of health in generating economic wealth and prosperity has now been recognized in the 12 cohesion priorities for investment identified by the EU for 2007–2013. It is also reflected in Principle 2 "Health is the greatest wealth" of the EU's Health Strategy Together for Health (2007) (European Commission 2007). Health systems are seen as potential drivers for economic and social regeneration, especially when they are an integrated part of sustainable development and where there is a legacy of underinvestment, as in some of the poorer regions in Bulgaria, Romania, Poland and Hungary. Health systems are thus seen as one element of a larger, interlinked set of social and economic activities (Fig. 10.1).

The majority of health infrastructure investment using Structural Funds will be allocated to the convergence/phasing-out regions. However, Member States have differed in the extent to which they have used Structural Funds to invest in the health sector. The sum total of health investments for the 2007–2013 period

**Fig. 10.1** *Links between health sector investment and three areas of economic and social policy*

**Government and governance:**
balanced and integrated policies

**Health sector investment**

**Local communities:** education, employment and services

**Health sector supply chain:** procurement, outsourcing, capital investment, research and development

has been calculated at approximately €5 billion, or 1.5% of the total amount of Structural Funds (European Commission 2007). However, this can be considered an underestimate, as it only captures direct health sector investment, drawing mainly on ERDF funding in particular for health infrastructure investment. It does not include indirect health sector investments led by other sectors, such as urban regeneration led by local governments that results in better access to health and social services for marginalized social groups. It also fails to take account of investments outside the health sector that lead to social, educational, environmental and economic gains. These can contribute to better health outcomes, which in turn can enhance economic development, resulting in an upward investment spiral of economic and health performance.

The greatest share of direct health sector investment within the Structural Funds is on health infrastructure, designed to modernize health care facilities and services. This is clearly identified within budget allocations set out in NSRFs and (regional) operational programmes (Watson 2008; European Commission 2007). However, there is little evidence about how (and if) the available funds will be spent during the 2007–2013 period. It is particularly unclear whether there has been sufficient attention to developing strategies for health systems and, specifically, hospital master plans. Furthermore, it is not clear whether there has been adequate investment in the capacity required for project option appraisal to inform investment planning and decisions.

## Integrating health into sustainable development

Sustainable development can be thought of as integrating three core goals within one framework: economic growth, social stability and environmental protection (Whitford & Potter 2007; López-Casasnovas, Rivera & Currais 2005; SERI 2008). There are a growing number of examples where such integrated frameworks are being implemented. For example, the northeast of England has integrated health priorities under the umbrella of sustainable economic growth models, while in Western Australia integrated assessment frameworks inform regional sustainability strategies (Jenkins 2003; Buselich 2002).

Such integrated frameworks may be easier to achieve at regional level, as argued by the Sustainable Europe Research Institute (SERI). Regional administrations, untroubled by distractions such as defence and foreign policy, are often able to make quick decisions (SERI 2008). As pilots, they may become the triggers for larger-scale developments.

The health sector is increasingly recognized as an important element in these frameworks, reflecting the concept of health in all policies (Ollila et al. 2007), supported by growing evidence on the contribution of health to economic growth in Europe (Suhrcke et al. 2005). In parallel, there is growing interest in the inclusion of health-related indicators in models of sustainable development (López-Casasnovas, Rivera & Currais 2005). This will facilitate quantification of the socioeconomic and environmental consequences of investment in health infrastructure.

The potential dividend from health sector investment at regional or local level is twofold. First, it can be used to improve health services, leading to better access, enhanced productivity and more cost-effective use of resources. This represents conventional policy wisdom. However, there is another compelling set of policy goals. These relate to the potential contribution of health sector investment to economic regeneration. In this scenario, targeted health sector investment in deprived areas or those with relatively low economic output:

- contributes to economic regeneration;
- strengthens social cohesion;
- increases employment prospects where matched by inclusive employment policies; and
- raises the skill base in regional and local labour markets.

The connections between health capital investment and regional development might be best considered by looking at the concept of "sustainability". Health capital investment does not operate or impact in isolation. In terms of policy choices and investment decisions, there is a real need to move beyond a narrow economic focus on cost-efficiency to the more relevant question of how to achieve more added value from health capital investment with:

- capital assets that are more flexible and can adapt to evolution and innovations in service design;

- increasing the economic competitiveness of local small and medium-sized enterprises; and

- better employment opportunities that improve labour market access for people from vulnerable social groups (a priority of the EU's Lisbon Strategy and Cohesion Policy).

The ability to align health sector investments with sustainable development is a key challenge for regional health policy. It will help to identify where investments can be made that are likely to result in sustainable growth and major health gains by acting on the broader determinants of health. This takes regional health policy and health sector investments (where power and political influence is vested in bricks and mortar, as well as service provision) beyond traditional boundaries (Watson & Lamprecht 2004; Watson & Lamprecht 2002; Glaister et al. 2000).

A key question, therefore, is how health sector investment will deliver added value beyond providing and improving service provision. As noted earlier, there is growing evidence that significant economic benefits can be achieved by improving health, not only in developing countries, but also in developed ones (Suhrcke et al. 2005). In economic terms, health services are clearly important because they have a direct impact on population health (Nolte & McKee 2004), and thus indirectly on the productivity of the workforce and national wealth (López-Casasnovas, Rivera & Currais 2005). However, the health sector also matters because it represents one of the most important economic sectors and one of the largest service industries. According to WHO estimates, its output in 2005 accounted for 8.9% of GDP in the EU and 7.7% in the (much) wider WHO European Region (WHO Regional Office for Europe 2008). The performance of the health sector affects the competitiveness of the overall economy via its effect on labour costs, labour market flexibility and the allocation of resources (Suhrcke et al. 2005; López-Casasnovas, Rivera & Currais 2005).

## Health facilities and their environments

Hospitals and other health facilities are part of the wider social and physical environment. In cities, this environment is not simply a group of buildings and streets. It includes a complex grouping of activities and functions, which have their roots in history and which give meaning to the urban space. The settings dedicated to health care have acquired many meanings. They are places of work and of economic production, but they are also places offering settings for education and social integration.

In recent years, the process of renewing the hospital infrastructure in many European countries has raised the question of whether new hospitals should be built or whether old ones, often placed in the city centre, should be rehabilitated. Milan and Verona, in Italy, opted to keep the old location. These decisions were informed by a recognition that the hospitals symbolized values of community culture and solidarity. "It is where you sign a sort of social contract with your community" (Geddes de Filicaia 2006). In other instances, the old locations did not permit rehabilitation or the possibility of introducing new technologies, so new hospitals were constructed at different locations. Whichever approach is taken, it is important to recognize the relationship between the hospital and its environment. In the Netherlands, there has been a competition for the selection of the best project envisaging the hospital of the future. The winner of the competition stressed the urban setting of their hospital and flexibility, with special attention paid to the entire life-cycle of the infrastructure (see Chapter 8 by Bjørberg & Verweij). In Italy, a "decalogue" has set out 10 guiding principles for new acute hospitals (Italian Ministry of Health 2001):

1. humanization: focus on the person;

2. urbanization: integration within the territory and within the city;

3. social relations: sense of belonging and solidarity;

4. organization: effectiveness, efficiency and perceived well-being;

5. interactivity: complete and continuous health care to be provided through the network of social and medical services;

6. appropriateness: correct treatment and appropriate use of resources;

7. reliability: safety and security;

8. innovation: innovation in diagnostics, therapies and communication technologies;

9. research: clinical and scientific progress;

10. training: professional and cultural training and continuous education.

While Verona and Milan provide examples of where old hospitals have been renovated in urban areas, there are also examples from elsewhere in Italy of entirely new hospitals being constructed in urban settings. In Tuscany, their location has been described as a "bridge" between the old cities and recent suburban developments. In Naples, the location of the new hospital Ospedale del Mare has been chosen as a means of contributing to the rehabilitation of a slum area.

## The hospital as part of a larger system

Within a region the acute hospital is part of a larger system. This can be thought of as a matrix with two dimensions: a "vertical" one, setting out the relationships among different levels of the system, from community facilities to acute hospitals and specialized referral centres; and a "horizontal" one, linking facilities at the same level, such as acute hospitals. In considering the relationship of hospitals with the regions in which they are situated, two aspects are therefore important. The first relates to the multisectoral set of relationships that the health infrastructure creates with its environment. This includes physical parameters, such as where the health infrastructure is located and its specific geographical and natural characteristics, and is also concerned with the impact that investment in health capital has on community life, not only in the health domain, but also in the economic, social and cultural life of the community and its physical environment.

The second aspect is concerned with new models of care, which link hospitals with their communities. Acute care hospitals are complemented by community health infrastructures. In the Stockholm region in Sweden, for example, new mandates for acute care hospitals currently being developed are accompanied by an expansion of community health care.

In this light, getting the maximum benefit from capital investment raises many questions relating to various factors, such as the appropriateness of the services provided, the most appropriate location of health facilities, and the vertical as well as horizontal network of different types of health facilities. This could involve closing down small hospitals located in minor urban centres and their replacement with new health and social care facilities. Will this impoverish those communities, or will the acquisition of new facilities enrich their economic, social and cultural environment?

The changing functions of the hospital do not seem to affect its popular image. This not only applies to major hospitals located in urban centres; even medium-sized or small towns have a historically strong relationship with their hospitals. At the same time, the number of hospitals has declined throughout Europe in recent decades and this trend is expected to continue. In the Tuscany region in Italy, for example, regional planning has reduced the number of hospitals in recent years from 93 to 41. This reconfiguration of hospitals in Italy has two important aspects of relevance to this chapter. First, with few exceptions, the vast majority of the hospitals that have been closed were located in small towns. In some instances, they have been converted into specialized structures, mostly for elderly people. The economic, social and cultural effects of these changes have not yet been sufficiently understood and studied. The second aspect of the reconfiguration was that hospital care had to be integrated with all the other health structures providing what, in Italy, is called "*assistenza territoriale*" (territorially based health and social services). The basic assumption is that good functioning of the hospital is dependent on the good functioning of other structures, given that the hospital is a hub of a network that includes urban, community and rural health services.

In some European countries the process of redefining the network of health services outside hospitals started several decades ago and, everywhere, represents a major transition in the delivery of health services. Northern Ireland and some Italian regions, for example, have developed new models for the configuration of health services, which follow a more integrated approach, as described in the following section.

## Integrated regional systems (Northern Ireland, Tuscany and Veneto)

In Northern Ireland, a review of the NHS led to the decision to focus the strategic capital development programme "not so predominantly on the acute sector but to seek to create an integrated continuum of facilities from the home through primary, community and sub-acute facilities supported by structured networks" (Cole 2007; see also the case study on Northern Ireland in the accompanying volume). Two key policies emerged.

The first policy, and probably the more significant, is the decentralization of less-specialized activities away from the larger acute centres towards community-based facilities. One of the principal objectives here is to facilitate cooperation that is as seamless as possible between the primary, community and acute sectors, with a system designed around the patient's experience, enabling earlier access to diagnosis and any necessary interventions. The second policy has been a movement in the opposite direction (that is, from local general hospitals to acute centres or "Regional Centres of Excellence") of those services that, due to their complexity, require more specialized care and expertise and should not be replicated in every local hospital. There was recognition that there are benefits in terms of improved patient outcomes (including clinical success) and economies of scale for a range of surgical procedures for which local accessibility or travel time is not the dominant factor. This has led to the development of a number of "Protected Elective Centres" to which people would be prepared to travel further in return for shorter waiting times and the assurance of quality in terms of staff, equipment and facilities.

In Tuscany, the new regional strategic plan is organized as a series of interventions with two priorities:

1. creating an efficient management system for the health district which governs community services and monitors the integration between communities and hospital functions;

2. unifying the system of access to health services, improving the quality of health services, and facilitating responsiveness to citizens' requests, while reducing costs.

As elsewhere in Europe, in Tuscany a key development has been the reorganization of hospitals, not only in terms of a reduction of their number and a redefinition of their roles, but especially in the design of new hospitals. These are organized according to integrated patient-focused pathways and differentiated according to intensity of patient needs. In Tuscany, all levels of health care delivery are considered to be part of an overall system and the interactions between different health facilities are essential in the definition of new, integrated regional systems. Ultimately, redefining hospitals is easier than finding an appropriate relationship between community health needs and the structures responding to them. The integration between health services and other community services – such as those related to education, culture and sport – that is being pursued in Northern Ireland and, to some degree, in the Netherlands, seems to be promising in this respect (Cole 2006).

A recent model proposed by the Veneto region focuses on the integration of health and social services, jointly funded by the national and the regional governments. Social services for elderly people, drug (ab)users and other people with special needs are integrated into the health system and supported by home care health services. The Veneto region has based its model of health and social services on "excellence centres", that comprise the two university and hospital centres of Padua and Verona, supported by a provincial general hospital. The horizontal network is composed of "*presidi ospedalieri*" (directly managed acute care and rehabilitation hospitals), which guarantee the necessary emergency care at the local level and provide the first point of contact for health and social services.

## Procurement and local suppliers (Brandenburg)

The German health system already operates in part as a form of public–private partnership. The State supplies the legal framework and contributes to financing of capital; both private profit-making and non-profit-making partners finance health care, particularly at the hospital level. Individuals' health care costs are generally met by statutory insurance funds. Germany's Federal States (*Bundesländer*) are responsible for guaranteeing and accrediting hospital services and for developing guidelines for the structure of regional health care. Any request for public capital funding has to undergo a thorough and fairly lengthy approval process, which includes submission of evidence on patient needs, existing capacity, development of a detailed functional and architectural plan, and consideration of the project within the urban fabric of the region.

The tender process favours large projects (to keep unit costs down) and necessitates, in compliance with EU legislation, the invitation of EU-wide submissions for projects above a certain value. In order to give regional construction and building bidders a better chance of having their bids accepted, the commissioning hospital has to be inventive. The municipal hospital of the city of Brandenburg, for example, has been engaged in a three-phase modernization and rebuilding exercise since 1999. The hospital has 11 medical departments and 520 beds. Its buildings have been developed successively over time, with part of the fabric of the hospital dating as far back as 1901. The *Bundesland* hospital master plan has required the modernization of the central medical functions at a cost of approximately €55 million, a new site for all hospital beds (costing approximately €50 million) and the reconstruction of the old hospital to provide outpatient services. While the federal authorities have provided capital and helped with the planning phases, the construction is commissioned and overseen by the hospital itself. By tailoring the construction phases, the hospital has ensured that regionally based firms supply much of the internal construction and fittings, thus benefiting the local economy (Hoffmann 2006). At the same time, procurement law exists for a reason – to ensure that the contracting authority attains the best deal for its resources – and local bidders should clearly not be used irrespective of quality and costs.

Procurement by health service organizations at the regional or local level has the potential to improve health and develop human capital by stimulating the development of capable local businesses, strengthening their competitiveness in wider markets and supporting achievement of the goals of the renewed Lisbon Strategy. Enabling local businesses to compete for public procurement contracts has other proven benefits to local economies and regional development, including increasing local employment, increasing the skills base in local labour markets, enhancing community well-being and social cohesion, and protecting the environment by decreasing transport miles (Watson et al 2006).

In this way, procurement can be carried out in ways that are both creative and in line with European and national legislation. This is applicable to many examples of health capital investment, where it is possible to subcontract to local construction businesses. It is important to increase understanding of and support for sustainable approaches to procurement by creating processes that benefit health sector organizations and small and medium-sized enterprises at the same time. However, in many European countries, health sector procurement is becoming increasingly centralized in order to promote greater efficiency and manage risks associated with procurement decisions; this may work against local suppliers (Watson et al. 2006).

To overcome the potential pitfalls of this development, there needs to be willingness among purchasers and suppliers to:

- simplify complicated public sector procurement procedures;

- raise awareness of procurement opportunities in the local supply chain;

- identify commodity areas that are easier to open up to local procurement;

- set organizational targets (for example, increase the value of local expenditure by 10%) that would result in monetary gains to local economies and significant efficiency gains to those organizations; and

- work with local business support organizations to ensure small and medium-sized enterprises are able to deal more competitively with e-procurement, e-commerce, e-trading, e-auctions and so on (Watson et al. 2006).

Overall, as in other areas, such as health innovation markets (Watson et al. 2007), there is a need to understand better whether and how local sources of competitive advantage can be transposed to include broader societal considerations (Whitford & Potter 2007).

## Capital investment and urban regeneration (England and Wales)

The LIFT mechanism used in England and Wales is a joint venture between the public and private sectors, with the aim of improving the provision of primary care premises in a particular location. However, LIFT is not just a financial means of acquiring new buildings. It also targets:

- inequalities in facilities between affluent and deprived areas;

- regeneration of poorer localities;

- a shift in care from secondary to primary settings;

- integration of health and social care facilities and services (such as pharmacies or citizens advice offices); and

- flexible, adaptable and sustainable primary care facilities.

Under LIFT, primary care services are provided by a local joint venture partnership, known as a "LIFTCo". This involves a strategic partnering board, local stakeholders (including PCTs and local councils), Partnerships for Health (a national body) and a private sector partner. By the end of 2007, almost 50 LIFT schemes were in operation in England and Wales. The St Helens, Knowsley, Halton and Warrington LIFT scheme is one of the most complex examples, worth approximately €180 million over 20 years. This LIFT project will see the construction of 20 new primary care facilities, including integration with social, community and leisure services, and an emphasis on the regeneration of the most deprived communities. It has been estimated that hundreds of jobs will be created as a result of this partnership, and new space will be provided, not only for health care but also for local businesses and community organizations.

## Discussion: challenges for regional strategic choices

There are a number of factors that can promote or hinder the effectiveness with which health capital investment contributes to sustainable development by improving regional economies and communities. Where regions have been given responsibility for the basic elements of health policy – public health, primary care, rehabilitation services, acute hospitals and mental health services – it is vital that they also have the autonomy to plan, finance and implement the appropriate solutions to health needs, including the capital investment which is integral to the chosen mode of health care delivery. While the EU Cohesion Policy and its national interpretation through NSRFs and (regional) operational programmes have an increased focus on regions and regional leadership, some small Member States are counted as a single regional entity. These are Cyprus, Denmark, Estonia, Latvia, Lithuania, Luxembourg and Slovenia. In other Member States there is a need for capacity building at the regional level with national controls still in place (such as in Hungary), or still strong central control despite considerable investment in regional and local health systems (such as in the constituent countries of the United Kingdom).

Governments have increasingly been looking into sources of finance for health capital investment other than central government funds earmarked for health care, whether this involves the private sector, non-profit-making organizations, or a re-appraisal of how other public funds can be put to use. Regions have to be aware of this shifting ground, and be prepared, using staff with relevant competences, to propose solutions that will benefit their local economies. However, in the context of sustainability, attention needs to be paid to option appraisal, investment choices and contract negotiation that integrate cost-effective outcomes to the benefit of local economies and communities. The experience of PFI and LIFT in the United Kingdom has shown that best value for communities is obtained when local personnel have significant knowledge and experience of the new capital models being used.

Although it is tempting to solve only today's problems (and sometimes only yesterday's), there is widespread recognition that this does not amount to an effective application of health capital investment. Health care buildings should be built, renovated, or reconfigured to meet future needs – as far as this is possible. In particular, and in the interests of sustainability, it should be asked whether it is possible to consider joint capital investment projects with other sectors, in order to reduce the overall capital burden.

Regions with low population density, or with widely dispersed communities, may find ICTs and other health innovation solutions more cost-effective than the traditional hub-and-spoke hospital model.

At a time when the temptation is to commit to new health facilities at the city outskirts, regional authorities should remember that the services for which they are responsible, or at least over which they have influence, need to reflect the needs of local populations. This is especially true in the case of health facilities that have become part of the fabric of a locality, such as municipal hospitals. A clear example here was the decision by the Naples city council to regenerate the Azienda Ospedaliera Cardarelli, rather than pursue the option of a new facility outside of the city.

Master planning (as shown in the Brandenburg example) is increasingly emerging as an instrument for regional development that facilitates an integrated approach to urban regeneration, the stimulation of local economies and the location and functions of hospitals. Master planning can provide a clear vision for sustainability policies and conforms to the first three principles of the EU *Together for Health* Strategy (Principle 1 – a strategy based on share health values; Principle 2 – "health is the greatest wealth"; Principle 3 – health in all policies).

The experience of European regions in dealing with these factors suggests the need for a more structured decision-making process that can bring the wider economic and community benefits of health capital investment into play (Erskine, Dowdeswell & Watson 2006). The lack of measurable economic and social benefits of health capital investment has seriously inhibited assessment of the wider perspective – a perspective for which, for some time, public health professionals and urban planners have argued. What is required is a means of providing:

- the discipline of measuring resource input and usage;

- the basis of relating resources to specific elements of care;

- the means of measuring effectiveness – outcomes against predictions;

- an option appraisal toolkit to assess the effects of changing resource investment patterns;

- the means of handling complex, interrelated service, capital and community connectivities; and

- the basis of comparing "above the line" health-specific resource investment against "below the line" wider economic impact assessment.

Whilst this approach provides a logical system for decision-making, in practice there are obstacles that hinder the implementation of this approach. For example, many public service capital systems are generic in nature and do not fit well within the complexity of health systems. Capital models are often directed by government finance departments, which may be more concerned about whether the model fits in the broader macroeconomic strategy (such as meeting national and/or European debt management principles) than its ease and effectiveness of implementation within the service concerned. In other words, there needs to be consistency between the capital model, the planning system and the outcomes desired. In a similar vein, many governments lack overarching systems or agencies that can span different spending departments, such as health, education, economics, environment or transport. Lack of coherence in planning is a major factor inhibiting the wider view. Many governments have now identified the priority for "joined-up government", but so far results in many countries have proved disappointing in practical terms.

In many instances, capital provision is a provider-led exercise. In this case, there seem to be few regulatory measures or contractual and commissioning priorities that are aimed at stimulating capital investment to create wider economic and community gain. This is not surprising, as the private sector or charitable trust hospitals are primarily concerned with their own bottom line – sustainability and profitability.

What is needed in all these cases is a greater recognition of the mutual dependency of health care, regional economies and communities. If this is to develop, it will require a stronger evidence base that demonstrates the value of capital in more tangible and measurable terms. The outline matrix approach described by Erskine, Dowdeswell and Watson (2006) may create a useful framework for the development of more effective planning and decision-making systems in the future. A starting point for this framework is that the primary purpose of investing in health capital assets is to improve the quality and outcomes of the services provided within them. This may seem obvious, but there is surprisingly little evidence to help policy-makers and managers faced with making investment decisions. For those concerned with health care decision-making at any level, the hierarchy of questions listed here is a useful means of self-examination.

- To what measurable degree will quality be improved by the capital invested?

- To what measurable degree will clinical outcomes improve?

- To what measurable degree will the health status of the population be improved?

For regional authorities, it is useful to add two further questions to those listed above.

- To what measurable degree will the regional economy benefit?

- To what measurable degree will local communities benefit?


## Conclusions

We argue that crucial benefits can emerge if regions and their health systems are able to address the systematic decision-making challenges identified in this chapter. Models of health capital investment should enable health care organizations to stay flexible across time while integrating wider regional factors around sustainability. This will enable health systems to adapt to developments in medicine and to the changing demands on prevention and care that will emerge in future years. In the shorter term, approaches to capital investment by health service organizations have the potential to stimulate the development of capable local businesses and to strengthen their competitiveness in wider markets.

Investment in health care infrastructure can be carried out in ways that help to create dynamic local businesses, boost local employment, widen the skills base, improve population health and strengthen social cohesion. This is the kind of added value that we should expect from public organizations spending public money or money for public benefit.

Innovative and integrated approaches to regional planning exist that focus on the interaction of the different sectors in which the planning activities have been traditionally subdivided (such as finance, education, infrastructure or health). There is also a need for this to be based on a new vision of health as an economic determinant that cuts across the different fields of social and economic development.

# References

Buselich K (2002). *An outline of current thinking on sustainability assessment.* Perth, WA, Murdoch University Institute for Sustainability and Technology Policy (Background paper prepared for the Western Australian State Sustainability Strategy, August).

Cole J (2006). Reshaping the asset portfolio. *EuHPN workshop. Budapest, 19–21 April 2006.*

Cole J (2007). Reconfiguring the Model for Healthcare. *Paper delivered at the Verona II. Conference "Hospital, City and Territory". Verona, 14 September 2007.*

Erskine J, Dowdeswell B, Watson J (2006). *How the health sector can contribute to regional development: the role of capital investment.* Budapest, Health ClusterNET, Report 2 (www. healthclusternet.org, accessed 18 October 2008).

European Commission (2005). *Europe's Regions. Europe in figures: Eurostat yearbook 2006–2007.* Luxembourg, European Commission.

European Commission (2007). *Together for health: a strategic approach for the EU 2008–2013.* Brussels, European Commission Health & Consumer Protection Directorate.

Geddes de Filicaia M (2006). *Gli ospedali 'storici'. Un patrimonio architettonico e una risorsa assistenziale nella realtà urbana delle città europee ['The "storici" hospitals. An architectural patrimony and charitable resource in the urban reality of European cities].* Florence, Edizioni Polistampa.

Glaister S et al. (2000). *The economic impact of the NHS on the regional economy: a report for the NHS Executive.* London, NHS Executive.

Hoffmann U (2006). Capital investment in hospital care in Germany. *Health ClusterNET Health Care Capital Investment Workshop. Krakow, 27–29 April 2006.*

Italian Ministry of Health (2001). Presentation, 21 March. *The Piano Commission – Il decalogo dell'ospedale modello [The decalogue of the hospital model].* Rome, Italian Ministry of Health.

Jenkins B (2003) [Unpublished research paper]. *Regional sustainability strategies.* Perth, Murdoch University.

López-Casasnovas G, Rivera B, Currais L (eds) (2005). *Health and economic growth: funding and policy implications.* London, MIT Press.

Nolte E, McKee M (2004). *Does health care save lives? Avoidable mortality revisited.* London, Nuffield Trust, 2004.

Ollila E et al. (2007). *Health in all policies in the European Union and its Member States.* Copenhagen, WHO Regional Office for Europe (http://gaspp.stakes.fi/NR/rdonlyres/10953639-A2E7-4795-82FB-C67D742D597C/6800/HealthinAllPolicies.pdf, accessed 18 October 2008).

Suhrcke M et al. (2005). *The contribution of health to the economy of the European Union.* Luxembourg, European Commission, Directorate-General Health & Consumer Protection.

SERI (2008) [web site]. Vienna, Sustainable Europe Research Institute (http://www.seri.at/index.php?option=com_content&task=view&id=499&Itemid=142, accessed 1 June 2008).

Watson J (2008) [Unpublished report]. *Health and structural funds in 2007–2013: country and regional assessment.* Unpublished report to DG SANCO (C5), May.

Watson J, Lamprecht R (2002) [Unpublished report]. *NHS spend and the regional economy: scoping study of the contribution of the NHS to the north east regional economy.* Unpublished final report to ONE North East (Regional Development Agency) and Health Development Agency (North East Office), November.

Watson J, Lamprecht R (2004) [Unpublished report]. *How health services in the south east can promote sustainable development and health improvement: a scoping study.* Unpublished final report to the South East Public Health Group, November.

Watson J et al. (2006). *How health sector investment can contribute to regional development: the example of local procurement.* Budapest, Health ClusterNET, (Report 1) (www.healthclusternet. org, accessed 18 October 2008).

Watson J et al. (2007). *How health sector investment can contribute to regional development: the role of health innovation markets.* Budapest, Health ClusterNET, (Report 4) (www.healthclusternet. org, accessed 18 October 2008).

Whitford J, Potter C (2007). Regional economies, open networks and the spatial fragmentation of production. *Socio-Economic Review*, 5(3):497–526.

WHO Regional Office for Europe (2008). Health for All database (HFA-DB) [offline database]. Copenhagen, WHO Regional Office for Europe (July 2008 update).

# Part four:
# Design issues

# Chapter 11

# Translating hospital services into capital asset solutions

*Bernd Rechel, Stephen Wright, Martin McKee*

## Introduction

This chapter explores how capital assets can be used to provide solutions to the challenges facing those delivering hospital services. It reviews some current trends and debates about how hospitals can be designed and organized so as to provide the most appropriate environment to deliver their core business – diagnosing and treating patients. As preceding chapters of this volume have shown, key considerations in the design of health facilities include making them sustainable while creating therapeutic and supportive environments for patients, staff and visitors. This chapter turns to the question of how to integrate facility and service design so as to optimize the process of service delivery while maintaining sufficient flexibility to respond to future changes; or, put more accurately, how to ensure that facility design is for the benefit of service design.

The chapter is focused on a number of concepts exploring the central proposition that hospital care needs to be managed to the maximum degree possible as a "flow" process, avoiding batch treatment of patients. These ideas include:

- 80/20 rules of thumb about, respectively, how much care can be systematized and how much requires individually constructed responses;

- flow should be defined as the number of activities undertaken and not patients treated;

- capacity should be defined as the ability to deliver processes (flows) rather than counting structures (such as beds), and will be constrained by discrete components of critical paths that patients follow through the physical configuration;

- overcapacity is required to handle inevitably variable flows (such as seasonal influenza); space should be as "loose-fit" and standardized as possible; and

- the life of the capital stock should be defined not as a single figure but as an amalgam of components, the working life of which vary substantially.

## What is the function of hospitals?

Before considering how hospitals should be designed in a way that allows them to deliver services optimally, it is helpful to clarify the function of hospitals, asking how they differ from other types of capital developments that are on a similar physical scale. The primary function of hospitals is clearly the delivery of medical care (diagnosis and treatment) to inpatients or outpatients and this can either take the form of elective or emergency care. This means that hospitals should provide an environment "where patients can receive medical treatment and support from doctors, nurses, relatives and friends" (Wagenaar 2006). This is, at first sight, a rather straightforward function and – from a logistical perspective – hospitals are indeed to some degree comparable with railway stations, airports or shopping malls (Crouwel 2006) as facilities where design should facilitate the smooth flow of people along designated pathways linking a series of service points. However, there are several important differences.

First, while diagnosis and treatment are their primary functions, hospitals must also fulfil others, such as teaching and research (following the airport analogy, it has often been argued that many airports confuse their primary function, that of delivering passengers to and from planes, with their secondary one of acting as a retail outlet). Second, compared with most other people-processing facilities, the diversity of people moving through hospitals is extremely complex, with a disproportionate number requiring some form of assistance because of physical or mental difficulties or impairment. In contrast, the number of passengers who require a wheelchair to transit an airport is small and none will actually be unconscious at the time. Third, the pathways that people follow are complex, often involving multiple service delivery points (wards, operating theatres, imaging departments and so on), which may be visited in different sequences, and the flow is often non-linear, with patients looping back on themselves. This contrasts with the fixed pathways in an airport in which passengers invariably move from the plane to immigration, baggage collection and customs.

An important point to note is that the basic pathways followed by airline passengers have changed little since the first airports were constructed in the

1930s. In contrast, the pathways followed by patients in hospitals are changing constantly. Patients that would once have been admitted to a ward to wait for different teams of specialists to visit them are now expected to make their own way around the different departments. Conversely, where in the past they might have had to be taken to other parts of the hospital for imaging or other diagnostic tests, the relevant equipment may now come to their bedside.

A consequence is that the configuration of a hospital often reflects historical institutional demarcations rather than contemporary patient pathways (Wagenaar 2006). This mismatch between structure and function is compounded by the relative permanence of hospitals. As is noted elsewhere in this book, once a hospital is configured, it is difficult to change. This is especially so in particularly large hospitals, which remain common in some countries. Yet the original rationale for the hospital is being challenged, as technological developments have transformed the three key areas – imaging, operating theatres and laboratories – that provided the initial justification for the creation of the modern hospital as a mechanism to concentrate scarce, capital intensive resources. At the time of writing, the services provided in these areas can often be delivered in community settings. However, other factors, and especially the density of interconnections between different specialties, continue to provide momentum for concentration.

As the scale and complexity of facilities increases, so does the time required to design and construct them, with obvious consequences for their ability to respond to innovations in technology and service delivery (Guenther & Vittori 2008). This has led to a situation where, at the time of writing, few hospitals in Europe are purpose-built for today's needs. Instead, they are often "architectural nightmares" (Healy & McKee 2002a) and "hardly ever functional" (Wagenaar 2006).

A fundamental principle in architecture is that form should follow function (Van den Berg & Wagenaar 2006; Wagenaar 2006). This is regarded as one of the critical factors for successful capital investment (Hardy 2004). However, with a hospital an architect is faced with the challenge that functions of hospitals are constantly changing, and what might be a good fit between service and capital asset today may not be so tomorrow. A theme running through the chapters of this volume and the case studies of the accompanying volume is the need for flexibility; an optimal design is therefore one that allows continuous change.

This is recognized in the trend towards a "long-life, loose-fit" strategy, which promotes the development of health facilities that are less specifically "purpose built" (Guenther & Vittori 2008). At the extreme, the "open building approach", health care buildings are designed in much the same way as office buildings and shopping centres (Kendall 2008). In this approach, taking account of the differential lifespan of physical parts and spaces, there is a base building that occupies a defined space envelope and comprises principal circulation paths, a fixed main structure and primary mechanical, electrical and plumbing pathways and equipment. The building can accommodate a variety of functional scenarios (Kendall 2008). This principle has been taken further by the Netherlands Board for Health Care Institutions in their work on the "layered hospital". This concept builds on the prizewinning entry for their European health architecture competition, "Healing and Competition". It questions the convention of a custom-designed hospital and argues that a smaller element of a hospital is clinically specialized than is generally realized. The concept separates facilities that need to be specifically designed and co-located for clinical purposes (the hot floor technologies in operating theatres, central diagnostics and so on) from hotel-type accommodation (such as wards) that can be more generically designed, and from office accommodation which can simply mirror commercial practice. Finally, there are industrial processes including laboratories where the current trends in ICT allow many of these functions to be provided off-site, as with office space. There are examples in the Netherlands of new hospital projects starting to explore this concept, for example, Zutphen – Gelre Ziekenhuizen.

## Responding to changing patterns of care

Before exploring how structures can best fit with functions, it may be helpful to recall the factors that influence the delivery of care and which are changing most rapidly. These were discussed briefly in Chapter 1 and include ageing populations, shorter lengths of stay, an increase in ambulatory surgery and technological advances. The ageing of populations poses particular challenges, although this phenomenon is often misunderstood, as although the number of people living to old ages is increasing, it is apparent that they are retaining greater functional capacity than earlier generations, manifesting what has been termed the "compression of morbidity". They are, however, doing so in part because of the successes of health care, as the diseases afflicting older people are being controlled by long-term medication. This means that hospitals will be faced with changing patterns of disease, with increasing volumes of cancer, fractured hips, strokes, diabetes and dementia. Many of these patients will have multiple disorders, affecting several different body systems. This will require an expansion of geriatric medicine facilities and greater emphasis on access to care for elderly people, including facilities for those with impaired mobility and clearer signposting for those with impaired vision (McKee & Healy 2002a).

Technological advances have a wide-reaching impact on the design of health facilities. As noted earlier, while technology has historically driven the concentration of health care provision in large hospitals, near-patient testing kits, mobile radiology facilities and telemedicine facilitate a further dispersion of services away from hospitals to free-standing ambulatory centres and primary care facilities (Black & Gruen 2005). Integrated hospital information systems, as well as integrated patient records, facilitate the sharing of patient data between hospital and other health care providers, making it easier to coordinate care across interfaces (McKee & Healy 2002a). The rapid pace of change is stimulating increasing efforts to design spaces within health facilities that are responsive to change, such as multifunctional treatment spaces (Glanville & Francis 1996).

Hospitals are changing in other ways, too. Historically, they were a major source of social care, as well as health care, and in many countries of the former Soviet Union they still perform this function (Marx et al. 2007). However, the number of hospital beds is being reduced throughout Europe, so that hospitals can no longer fulfil this function. In some cases, this loss of capacity is being compensated for by the growth of social care facilities outside of hospitals, such as specialized facilities providing nursing care or community-based health and social care services, although this is not taking place everywhere.

Reductions in beds, coupled with changes in the way that care is delivered, are reducing the length of time that patients spend in hospital. However, this means that those who are actually occupying hospital beds receive more intensive treatment. These trends have important implications for the design of hospitals. Fewer beds are required, but more facilities for radiology, endoscopy and surgery (Healy & McKee 2002b). As those in hospital beds are more ill and of higher dependency, the space required around a bed is greater (Glanville & Francis 1996). At the same time, rehabilitation is moving out of hospitals into community facilities (Healy & McKee 2002b; Hensher & Edwards 2002).

Advances in short-acting anaesthesia and new surgical techniques, especially those undertaken endoscopically or using minimally invasive approaches, have driven an increase in ambulatory surgery and one-day admissions, although this varies enormously across Europe (Castoro et al. 2007). This increase in ambulatory care requires an expansion of outpatient clinics, as well as a high ratio of operating theatres to beds (Healy & McKee 2002a; McKee & Healy 2002c). Furthermore, new forms of ambulatory care, including day surgery, can be provided in purpose-built facilities that are separate from hospitals. These ambulatory care centres allow a more integrated management of individuals with common conditions, with an increasing number of streamlined "one-stop" clinics where patients can be examined by a team of specialists within a single visit (Healy & McKee 2002a).

## The potential perversity of performance management

In recent years, policy-makers across Europe have tended to introduce performance management strategies focusing on bed and technology utilization rates, the so-called principle of "sweating the assets". As bed numbers reduced, principally through changes in clinical technologies and models of care (as discussed earlier), these changes were often portrayed as being driven by efficiency improvements. This lulled policy-makers into believing that the downward trend in beds would continue and utilization rates could be driven upwards, generating a double gain in terms of cost-efficiency. The reality has proven to be somewhat different. At some stage the downward trend in bed number requirements will plateau, as a result of the changing dynamics of hospital-centred work. However, the most perverse impact has been an inappropriate focus on utilization rates. This often takes the form of efficiency gain measured by achieving particularly high occupancy or technology usage rates, such as with regard to operating theatres. Such strategies are likely to prove counterproductive by creating bottlenecks for the flow of patients. Departments wishing to achieve their own performance targets often push the problem down the line to someone else. Emergency rooms push patients through to the next stage in the care process, where they recreate a bottleneck, while managers accept high ward utilization rates as a demonstration of performance efficiency, but do not account for the impact on clinical care, such as potential increases in hospital infection rates.

## Ensuring a smooth flow of patients

In the 20th century, medical technology came to dominate the organization of hospitals, with efficiency of care and cure processes becoming the primary consideration (Boluijt 2006). Consequently, hospitals were often designed around specialties and departments rather than patients (Hillman 1999). Since the 1980s, however, the patient's perspective has gained more attention, a development encouraged by recognition of the benefits of shared care for complex conditions. Examples include the management of coronary artery disease by cardiologists and cardiac surgeons; cancer by oncologists, radiotherapists and surgeons; and gastrointestinal haemorrhage by physicians and surgeons.

These factors are leading to the creation of care models that are based on syndromes, flows of patients and care processes (Boluijt 2006). Yet, despite the increasing complexity of care pathways, in many hospitals the flow of patients is inefficient, dislocated and disorganized (Hillman 1999). One of the key challenges is getting processes to flow across organizational boundaries (Institute for Healthcare Improvement 2005).

The complexity of pathways is not, however, the only problem. Another is the nature of work in hospitals. In manufacturing, two broad types of work can be distinguished. The first involves continuous flow processes, characterized by production lines along which products flow in a linear fashion. Henry Ford's success depended on his ability to identify those products that were susceptible to this approach, and to the systematization of processes and components that would make the system flow smoothly. Some health care products will fall into this category, for example, uncomplicated elective surgery for cataracts. In such cases, a quasi-industrial process can be created to ensure the patient flows through the system, as already occurs in stand-alone surgical facilities in some countries. One such case is the Coxa hospital in Finland, described in the accompanying case studies volume. Coxa, in collaboration with the Tampere Region, has designed and implemented a region-wide joint replacement service based on integrated systems flow and facilitated by systematized care pathways, interagency collaboration and a sophisticated ICT platform.

The second approach is where the product is individualized. In manufacturing, this would include the production of unique items of jewellery, fashion or furniture. In health care an example would be the investigation of a fever of unknown origin or the treatment of a cancer that has spread from its origin. Such products are best treated in batches, where a team is engaged in the process of care throughout the patient's journey.

However, while batch processes are clearly necessary in some cases, they have a disadvantage of delaying flows, a phenomenon that is easily observed in metro systems where some stations are accessed via escalators (linear flows) and others by lifts (batch processes). Hence, where possible, they should be avoided.

In reality, batch processes have long pervaded hospitals, although largely by default. The situation is now somewhat improved from that in the 19th century, when the major London teaching hospitals admitted all non-emergency patients on one day each week – Tuesday at St Thomas', Wednesday at Guy's and Thursday at St Bartholomew's – leading to queues of 50–100 patients on each admission day (Rivett 1986). However, even at the time of writing, patients are admitted and discharged in batches, tests are run in batches, operations are undertaken in batches. Patients are treated as though their time were free, so they spend most of their time waiting. Consequently, large areas in hospitals are devoted to waiting rooms.

The situation is exacerbated by inefficient management of these batch processes. Admission and discharge are often inefficiently managed and emergency department crowding is a common problem throughout Europe. This means that when facilities are operating close to full capacity the system easily breaks down. In the United Kingdom, a patient admitted on Friday night may have a length of stay that is 25% longer than a patient admitted on a Tuesday (Government of Scotland 2007). To accommodate this phenomenon, beds and wards in effect become holding areas and have in the past been planned accordingly. Unfortunately, the patient journey from admission to discharge is often only visible to the patients themselves, with no management system in place (Jones & Mitchell 2006). Yet, poor patient flow affects the quality of care, safety, patient and staff satisfaction, and the effective utilization of resources (Government of Scotland 2007).

These considerations point to the need to systematize processes where possible (Institute for Healthcare Improvement 2005). Patient pathways are grounded in the concept of flow across the whole system (Ben-Tovim et al. 2008). They began to emerge in the 1980s, based on the recognition that, in many areas, patients had, at least initially, similar needs. As a rule of thumb, 80% of cases follow standard pathways, while 20% of patients require individualized (batch) management. Examples of the former include the diagnosis of breast lumps or rectal bleeding, or the management of acute chest pain. The latter include those with complications of chronic disease (exemplified by disorders affecting multiple body systems such as diabetes or AIDS), those whose disorders have major social consequences (such as psychiatric disorders or poorly controlled epilepsy), or those with multiple coexisting disorders. Of course, medicine retains the capacity to surprise, so it is important to have escape routes for those patients in the former group who turn out to have complications that require deviation from the pathway they have embarked upon.

Such pathways increasingly extend beyond the walls of the hospital, and it is increasingly being recognized that hospital care is not an isolated event, but often only a short episode in a longer patient journey. Hospitals are located in a wider system of community care, social care, primary care, specialist ambulatory care and tertiary services, and there is an increasing role for primary care in managing chronic disease and some acute conditions. The use of integrated care pathways, which are developed by multidisciplinary teams and plan for pre- and post-hospital care, such as well-organized rehabilitation services, can accelerate hospital admission and discharge (Hensher & Edwards 2002). This has clear implications for the design of health facilities which will need to be integrated with clinical pathways of care. This was the case in the Coxa hospital development, where the briefing for the architects was based on the hospital's compendium of care pathways.

This 80/20 principle has become the basis of the care model pursued by the Orbis medical park in the Netherlands. Orbis has placed the systematization of work processes at the heart of its model. This applies equally to clinical care, ICTs, logistics, financial systems, human resources, architecture and strategic asset planning. Orbis believes that patient outcomes can be improved, average length of stay reduced and staff gain greater professional autonomy. Furthermore, the systematization of work processes aims to create a total chain of care that not only encompasses diagnosis, treatment and rehabilitation, but also links with the primary care sector and other third-party providers of care and services. Systematized care processes can help to ensure transparency of clinical decision-making (transparent to clinicians, managers and patients), allow the hospital management to have a clear view of the degree of financial and clinical variance (and hence risk) associated with medical procedures, and embed the use of medical data in the services that support treatment programmes. Standardization extends to the design of outpatient consultation rooms and inpatient bedrooms. These spaces have the same equipment and the same amount of floor space; they will not be "owned" by any one medical specialty (see the relevant case study in the accompanying volume).

When looked at from the perspective of continuous and batch processes, it is apparent that the assumption that queuing in the health system is due solely to a lack of capacity (in terms of beds, facilities, diagnostics, nurses or doctors) to meet demand, is not justified. In fact, the problem more often lies in the way that the service is configured (Government of Scotland 2007). The seemingly almost random progress of patients may conceal hidden choke points, feedback loops and lines moving at different speeds (Pope, Roberts & Black 1991). This means that investments in "capacity" often fail to increase overall output, because they are not systematically directed at the choke points (Government of Scotland 2007). Instead, it is necessary to examine the work being undertaken and to differentiate those processes that are best undertaken in batches and those that should be continuous flows.

The concept of differentiating production methods has been developed further, distinguishing three theories of production: the transformation model, the value generation model and the flow theory of production. In the transformation model, inputs are transformed into outputs, with production itself being something of a "black box". This model has so far been the dominant method of perceiving health services. In the value generation model, patient and staff experience move to the foreground. In the flow theory of production, production is understood as the flow of materials and information through time between different stakeholders (Tzortzopoulos et al. 2008).

Figure 11.1 asserts the need to move from a transformation-based understanding of health care delivery to one that recognizes flow and value. Appropriate designs will facilitate patient flow and create patient value.

**Fig. 11.1** *Transformation, flow and value generation in health care*

| Health care | Transformation | Flow | Value |
|---|---|---|---|
| **Buildings** | **Buildings house:**<br><br>different, usually isolated functions | **Buildings support:**<br><br>patient pathways<br><br>learning<br><br>visual management | **Buildings promote:**<br><br>patient experience<br><br>staff working conditions |

*Source*: Tzortzopoulos et al. 2008.

Certain management concepts may prove beneficial in promoting these goals. The most important of these is termed "lean management" or "lean thinking". Lean thinking is most commonly associated with Japanese manufacturing and was pioneered by Toyota Motor Corporation from the 1950s onwards (Kim et al. 2006). Lean management principles have been used effectively in manufacturing companies for decades (Institute for Healthcare Improvement 2005).

Lean thinking seeks to provide what the customer wants, quickly and efficiently. It aims to encourage flow and reduce waste (Ben-Tovim et al. 2007). One of the key principles of lean thinking is that each step in production must produce "value" for the customer and that all sources of "waste" should be eliminated. The concept of "waste" is far-reaching and includes unnecessary inventory, waiting, mistakes, or inappropriate procedures or processes (Young et al. 2004; Government of Scotland 2007). It emphasizes reduction of waste and work that does not add value, as opposed to adding technology, buildings and manpower (Institute for Healthcare Improvement 2005). Lean principles promise improved quality, safety and efficiency. Importantly, one of the core tenets of lean management is a no-layoff policy, so that staff are fully engaged in the process. Another is engagement with contractors, so that the adversarial purchaser–supplier contractual relationship evolves towards shared objectives[10] (see also the similar discussion by Dewulf & Wright in Chapter 7 on contingency adaptability in financing contracts and public–private partnerships).

While lean management is not a new concept, it has until recently been applied to health care to only a limited extent (Ben-Tovim et al. 2007). Yet health care

---

[10] This is not to say that Toyota's relationships with its contractors are complacent; the mutual relationship involves information sharing, stakeholding and an attempt to align objectives – but a persistently underperforming contractor will eventually be sacked, probably never to be used again.

does have many features in common with the production of goods. As in health care, manufacturing processes involve concepts of quality, safety, customer satisfaction, staff satisfaction and cost–effectiveness. Hospitals can then be seen as immensely complicated processing plants; thousands of often complex processes are involved with the notable feature that a product failure can cause fatalities (Institute for Healthcare Improvement 2005). In health care, waste, in terms of time, money, supplies and goodwill, is a common problem (Institute for Healthcare Improvement 2005). One major reason for this is that internal "customers" (such as physicians, hospitals, insurers, governments, payers) have often driven processes. In the lean-management approach, it is important that value is defined by the primary, true customer, the patient (Institute for Healthcare Improvement 2005). The application of lean thinking to health care is seen by many commentators as a means to reduce costs and improve patient service and patient safety. A joint study by the National Academy of Engineering and the Institute of Medicine of the United States in 2005 recommended the systematic application of systems engineering approaches for reforming the health care delivery system (Reid et al. 2005).

A similar concept is the theory of constraints, which also aims to improve the efficiency of processes. This concept targets bottlenecks that cause queues. Anything that increases patient throughput by releasing the bottleneck adds value to the system. It is a continuous process as, once one constraint has been identified and relieved, the next bottleneck will inevitably emerge (Young et al. 2004). One of the causes of bottlenecks in hospitals is that semi-autonomous departments aim to optimize their own throughput of patients without considering how this affects the performance of other departments (Tzortzopoulos et al. 2008). Central diagnostic facilities, such as computerized tomography (CT) scanning, commonly form the bottleneck in patient care services (Elkhuizen et al. 2007).

The concept of six sigma (see Box 11.1) was developed by Motorola in the 1970s as a system to assess quality, produce quantifiable results and establish quality goals (Young et al. 2004). It is a data-driven approach to performance improvement and has been advocated as a means to improve care processes, eliminate waste, reduce costs and enhance patient satisfaction (Van den Heuvel et al. 2006). The concept of six sigma entails involvement of health care workers, creation of trained project teams, data analyses and investment in quality improvement (Van den Heuvel et al. 2006). In essence, it identifies variation in processes statistically and seeks to reduce them. One project using six sigma in the Netherlands reduced the length of stay in the delivery room from 11.9 to 3.4 hours (Van den Heuvel et al. 2006). In a case applying the six sigma approach to an obstetrics and gynaecology clinic in the United States,

---

**Box 11.1** *Six sigma methods*

DMAIC

Define process improvement goals.

Measure key aspects of existing process and collect relevant data.

Analyse data to verify cause-and-effect relationships, ensuring that all factors have been considered.

Improve or optimize the process based upon data analysis.

Control to ensure that any deviations from the target are corrected before defects arise.

DMADV

Define process improvement goals.

Measure and identify characteristics that are Critical to Quality (CTQ), product capabilities, production capability and risks.

Analyse and design alternatives.

Design details, optimize the design, plan for design verification.

Verify the design, set up pilots, implement new processes.

---

waiting times for new obstetrical visits decreased from 38 to 8 days (Bush et al. 2007). However, the six sigma approach has also been criticized as stifling creativity where disruptive innovations are required, creating a small industry of poorly trained facilitators, and applying statistical parameters to situations where they are inappropriate. In the health care field it suffers the same problems as all quality control methods based on statistical variation, as – unlike much industrial production – the products (patients) are extremely heterogeneous.

Systems theory also helps to understand patient flow in health systems. Large hospitals are "highly complex systems that are poorly understood, extremely costly, and rife with inefficiency" (Kopach-Konrad et al. 2007). Only a small fraction of the work conducted in hospitals creates value for patients. Numerous disconnections along the continuum of care have a cumulative effect in obstructing patient flow, causing frustration for patients and staff (O'Connell et al. 2008). It is especially important to "know how it works before you fix it" (Holtby 2007), as improving the efficiency of part of the system may not improve overall efficiency. Improvements in the crowding in emergency departments, for example, require strategies that reach far beyond emergency departments (Siegel, Wilson & Sickler 2007). Effective flow is a property of the whole system (Government of Scotland 2007).

There is also an extensive body of literature, much originating in the 1970s, that applies operational research methods to the understanding of health care processes. Paradoxically, as computing power has increased, making such methods easier, they seem to be less extensively used. An example is queuing theory, which explains why queues can most easily be reduced by creating common lines leading to multiple serving points (Cooper & Corcoran 1974).

How can these insights from lean management and systems theory be translated into better-designed health facilities? The first step is to recognize that the initial capital costs of a facility are a small proportion of its running costs. Over the lifetime of a building, the design costs are likely to be only 0.3–0.5% of the whole-life costs, and the capital costs themselves scarcely more than 5%, but both significantly affect – and indeed to a large degree determine – the costs of running the services (CABE 2003). This means that it will often be cost-effective to make changes to the configuration of a facility midway through its life (that is, well before the asset has been depreciated fully in an accounting sense), rather than simply accepting the initial structure.

It is crucial to approach the design and construction industry with a well-prepared strategic brief that outlines what the client wants to achieve with the building project in terms of functional objectives (which may be changing over time) and that defines those attributes that contribute most value. The strategic brief is then translated into a project brief, which is an architectural prescription for how the objectives are met, but should allow sufficient flexibility for future changes. If well done, the facility design will then support, rather than be incidental to, the necessary process redesign. This includes appropriate layouts, departmental adjacencies, more efficient processes and enhanced information systems. However, the core nature of the interactions between health facility design and the health service design has so far not been properly recognized or understood (Tzortzopoulos et al. 2008).

## Grouping according to medical needs and level of dependency

A key consideration in the design of new hospitals is how to ensure a smooth flow of patients, staff and goods. One solution is to separate the different flows, so that they do not interfere with each other. This particularly applies to emergency versus elective care and to outpatient versus inpatient care, but there is also growing recognition of the benefits of grouping patients according to shared medical needs, and of keeping staff and goods away from patient areas.

As already noted, rather than following clinical specialties, increasingly, patients are grouped and treated according to their medical need(s) and level(s) of dependency (Glanville & Francis 1996). The new University College London hospital, which was opened in 2005, includes an Acute Assessment Unit, a Diagnostic and Therapy Unit, a Critical Care Unit, and an Infection Unit (Department of Health 2007). An alternative approach is to base the organization of hospitals on body systems, disease groups or shared expertise (Black & Gruen 2005). In the case of the university hospital in Trondheim, Norway, patients with symptoms and diseases from the same organs are located in the same building, which offers the possibility of innovative organization of activities. For example, one centre includes gastroenterology, gastrointestinal surgery, urology and nephrology – all specialties requiring knowledge of abdominal organs. This offers the possibility of organizing activities as an "abdominal clinic" and as a "kidney and urinary tract clinic", cutting across the specialist divide between medicine and surgery. One of the main aims of this organ-centred organization was to concentrate medical service in smaller blocks around the patient, so as to reduce patient movement and the number of staff involved with an individual patient (see the relevant case study in the accompanying volume). Similarly, in the university hospital in Coventry, United Kingdom, children's facilities are arranged by age group rather than by specialty (Nightingale 2006).

## Outpatients and inpatients

Outpatient clinics of hospitals have long been the least well organized. A report published in *The Lancet* in 1869 describes the outpatient clinic at St Bartholomew's Hospital in London as "a large room seating six hundred people", where patients were seen "at the rate of one every 35 seconds, each with a doubtful dose of physic ordered almost at random as if the main object were to get rid of a set of troublesome customers rather than to cure their ailments" (The Lancet 1869). Even now there is enormous scope for improvements by identifying common conditions and treating them more effectively (Waghorn & McKee 2000). Major gains are achievable by standardizing care, establishing "one-stop" clinics in which teams of different specialists work together, with access to diagnostic and treatment facilities, to enable patients to flow rapidly along clearly defined pathways (Putnis, Merville-Tugg & Atkinson 2004; Agaba et al. 2006; Johnson et al. 2008), while benefits are also achievable by redesigning the system to make the best use of expertise across the whole health system (Black & Gruen 2005; Julian et al. 2007).

Separating the logistical flows within outpatient clinics offers scope for further efficiency gains. In the case of the new university hospital in Coventry, for example, outpatients flow not through the main entrance of the hospital, but through other buildings. There are also separate entrances for children's facilities (Nightingale 2006). In the Martini hospital in Groningen, the Netherlands, the outpatient departments are clustered in such a way as to facilitate "one-stop shopping" (see the relevant case study in the accompanying volume).

## Separating the flows of patients, staff and goods

According to lean thinking, mixing different value streams will cause interference and it is better to enable different value streams to flow according to their own logic and pace, without interference. The focus in this is not on similar clinical conditions, but on similar processes (Jones & Mitchell 2006). The concept of "front" and "back" office services suggests that the separation of processes that deal directly with customers (front office) from supporting processes (back office) encourages the achievement of better environments for patients and efficiency in health care delivery (Tzortzopoulos et al. 2008). Production flow analyses can show which units of the hospital should be placed next to each other. Medical imaging, for example, can be decentralized in order to achieve high-velocity flow (Karvonen et al. 2007).

There are various ways in which the different functions of hospitals can be separated architecturally. The new hospital at the Orbis medical park, in the Netherlands, aims to separate flows of patients, staff and goods. Patients and staff come through different entrances, and staff come to the patient rather than vice versa (see the relevant case study in the accompanying volume). In the university hospital in Trondheim, technical and supply functions are located in the basement; outpatient areas on the first floor; operating theatres and imaging equipment on the second floor; technical support on the third floor; with the fourth floor and above containing inpatient areas. In each block there are offices, research labs and university facilities (see the relevant case study in the accompanying volume). In Rhön Klinikum hospitals in Germany, this separation takes the form of a division between the hot floor technologies and ward accommodation. Technology is housed in accommodation designed to adapt quickly to changes in clinical (interventional and diagnostic) practice, making it possible to manage some of the traditional bottlenecks more effectively (see the relevant case study in the accompanying volume).

## Elective and acute care

There are huge variations in the efficiency of operating theatres, partly related to the limitation of their use to working hours (although calls to use them more intensively often fail to take account of the risks associated with sleep deprivation and shift work among surgical and anaesthetic staff (McKee & Black 1992)). However, there are also often deficiencies in process management and design of facilities (see Chapter 9 by Lennerts). A key to improving patient flow is the smoothing of peaks and troughs in workload (Elkhuizen et al. 2007). Non-random variability is common in elective care, but can easily be removed, for example by spreading surgery evenly among the days of the week (Chaiken

2007). Elective admissions are often a major cause of variation across the hospital system, while the number of emergency patients is generally quite predictable (Government of Scotland 2007).

Accident and emergency departments have the greatest volume of attendances of any department in acute hospitals. In the United Kingdom in the 1990s, approximately 15% of those attending were admitted, comprising about half of an acute hospital's inpatient workload (Glanville & Francis 1996). Those areas providing core functions of the hospital, including operating theatres, diagnostic imaging and intensive care facilities (the "hot floor"), can often be grouped together to improve synergies. In the university hospital in Coventry, a critical care matrix is located on the first floor which accommodates the "hot" departments: accident and emergency, operating theatres, coronary care unit and cardiac care (Nightingale 2006).

In an emergency department in a teaching hospital in Australia, patients were separated into two streams on the basis of complexity rather than acuity, severity or disposition, creating a fast-track patient stream for patients who can be treated and discharged more or less immediately. The new system led to significant improvements in several key performance indicators, such as mean waiting time or mean treatment time (Ieraci et al. 2008). Nurse triage is now common in emergency departments in some countries, for example the United Kingdom, and has been shown to be an accurate method of identifying high-risk patients (Cooke & Jinks 1999). This process is increasingly informed by protocols, some of which are being adopted in other European countries (Van der Wulp, Van Baar & Schrijvers 2008).

The new Martini hospital in Groningen, the Netherlands, has separated its operating theatre capacity into an acute section (high-intensity care) and an elective section (low-intensity care). The high-intensity care area is integrated with the intensive care unit, the coronary care unit and day nursing. This nursing chain, flowing from the high-intensity to the low-intensity care part of the operating block, aims to provide flexible space for functional nursing wards, allowing wards to shrink or expand by using beds from adjacent wards (see the relevant case study in the accompanying volume).

The increase in elective day surgery has given rise to the concept of the patient hotel (Glanville & Francis 1996). Even with reduced lengths of stay, there will be some patients occupying hospital beds whose nursing needs are minimal and who essentially require a hotel function while they recover. Hotel facilities are much less tightly specified than other hospital beds and so have a longer technical lifespan. This is encouraging some hospitals to build (or rent space in) facilities that are essentially hotels, situated adjacent to the hospital.

At the same time, a contrary trend is emerging, in the form of variable acuity beds. Universal rooms or acuity-adaptable single rooms are being adopted in hospitals that are promoting patient-centred care, where family participation is integrated with the patient's healing process. They allow rooms to change relatively seamlessly from intensive care to rehabilitation (Chaudhury, Mahmood & Valente 2006).

## Reconceptualizing hospital capacity

This chapter argues strongly for reconceptualization of how we measure hospital capacity. Traditionally, the number of hospital beds has been used as an indicator of a good health care system, such as under the Soviet Union, which placed great emphasis on a large number of hospital beds and physicians (Healy & McKee 2002b). However, even then the concept of "bed" was problematic, as it was "shorthand for an entire package that includes nurses, supporting staff and, perhaps, advanced monitoring equipment" (McKee & Healy 2002b). The Soviet Union was able to provide the beds but not the support equipment needed to treat the patients in them. Furthermore, beds may only exist on paper or be unoccupied, a common phenomenon in the past in CEE countries, in which budgets were linked to bed numbers (Saltman & Figueras 1997).

Yet, despite growing recognition of the limitations of using "beds" as a measure for hospital capacity, bed numbers are still widely used in both western and eastern Europe for measuring the performance of hospitals and for purposes of capacity and capital investment planning. This continued use of "bed numbers" fails to consider the trade-offs and complementarities from investing in different types of health capital (including IT and diagnostic equipment) (Dechter 2004). It is also rather surprising, given the move away from bed numbers and towards services and outputs that is occurring in the financing of hospital services. Traditionally, inpatient care was the largest physical component of acute hospitals. Much of this care can be increasingly provided in other settings. This trend and the increase in day procedures mean that the number of beds can no longer even be an appropriate shorthand description of acute hospitals (Glanville & Francis 1996).[11]

It is apparent that the measure of bed numbers needs to be complemented or replaced by a measure of services provided. This will ensure that what is measured is important rather than merely being a widely available indicator. However, it is less clear what such indicators could be. DRGs have the advantage of measuring the outputs provided by hospitals and, in various forms, are used

---

[11] However, given the centrality of the bed for rehabilitation care, the metric may for the moment still make sense for these types of hospitals.

in most European countries. However, they are simply a means of categorizing patients according to resource use. They suffer from a fundamental weakness in that they refer to an individual admission, whereas what is important for patients is an episode of care, which may span several admissions and ambulatory care visits (Clarke & McKee 1992).

## Conclusions

There are no magical answers to the question of how to translate health services into capital assets. The fundamental questions include which services should be provided and where they should be located (in hospitals or elsewhere), while allowing for future flexibility. Once this decision has been made, it will be crucial to ensure a smooth flow of patients, staff and goods, and to develop models of care for routine conditions and procedures that can be aligned with facility design.

Management concepts such as lean thinking suggest that a lack of crude capacity is typically not the major issue (although one should not simply assume that it is not a factor) and major gains in efficiency and effectiveness may be possible prior to the design of new facilities and without simply adding additional technology, personnel or infrastructure. For this to succeed, recognition of the value of processes in improving the patient experience will be essential, without forgetting that training future generations of health care workers is also one of the purposes of the health system. Where these ideas can be translated into the design of new facilities, we believe that enormous improvements are possible.

A key message that emerges from this chapter is that hospital design and the delivery of health services need to be planned and implemented in an integrated fashion, internally within hospitals as regards functional flow and externally across the whole trajectory of care, so that the design of hospitals supports the efficient and effective provision of whole systems health care, now and in the future. There is a need for mutual collaboration between all the stakeholders in investment projects to improve the linkages between patient pathways and buildings. Providers of health infrastructure must focus on the performance of health facilities, while those designing care pathways must consider the infrastructure needed to facilitate change. This will improve the patient and staff experience and support operational efficiency and effectiveness.

In summary, what is required is a new way of looking at the hospital, not from the perspective of buildings, beds or specialties, but rather from that of the path taken by the patients who are treated in them and the processes delivered by the health professionals who spend their working lives in them. This will make it possible to identify and overcome the bottlenecks that prevent more efficient use of resources. Indeed, if there is one single dominant issue arising from the analytical work of this book, it is the need for a new understanding of health care flow and health care capacity, along with the consequent meanings and extent of required flexibility and spare capacity in the health care estate.

# References

Agaba A et al. (2006). One-stop rectal bleeding clinic: the Coventry experience. *International Surgery*, 91(5):288–290.

Ben-Tovim D et al. (2007). Lean thinking across a hospital: redesigning care at the Flinders Medical Centre. *Australian Health Review*, 31(1):10-15.

Ben-Tovim D et al. (2008). Patient journeys: the process of clinical redesign. *Medical Journal of Australia*, 17(188):14–17.

Black N, Gruen R (2005). *Understanding health services*. Maidenhead, Open University Press.

Boluijt P (2006). Care models and hospital design in the Netherlands. In: Wagenaar C, ed. *The architecture of hospitals*. Rotterdam, NAi Publishers:396–399.

Bush S et al. (2007). Patient access and clinical efficiency improvement in a resident hospital-based women's medicine center clinic. *American Journal of Managed Care*, 13(12):686–690.

CABE (2003). *Radical improvements in hospital design*. London, Commission for Architecture & the Built Environment.

Castoro C et al. (2007). *Day surgery: making it happen*. Copenhagen, European Observatory on Health Systems and Policies.

Chaiken BP (2007). Patient flow: a powerful tool that transforms care. *Patient Safety & Quality Healthcare*, May/June:6–7.

Chaudhury H, Mahmood A, Valente M (2006). Nurses' perceptions of single-occupancy versus multi-occupancy rooms in acute care environments: an exploratory assessment. *Applied Nursing Research*, 19:118–125.

Clarke A, McKee M (1992). The consultant episode: an unhelpful measure. *British Medical Journal*, 305:1307–1308.

Cooke M, Jinks S (1999). Does the Manchester triage system detect the critically ill? *Journal of Accident & Emergency Medicine*, 16(3):179–181.

Cooper J, Corcoran T (1974). Estimating bed needs by means of queuing theory. *New England Journal of Medicine*, 291(8):404–405.

Crouwel M (2006). Preface. In: Wagenaar C, ed. *The architecture of hospitals*. Rotterdam, NAi Publishers:8–9.

Dechter M (2004). *Health capital planning review. Report*. Toronto, Canadian Council for Public–Private Partnerships.

Department of Health (2007). *Rebuilding the NHS. A new generation of health care facilities*. London, United Kingdom Department of Health.

Elkhuizen S et al. (2007). Applying the variety reduction principle to management of ancillary services. *Health Care Management Review*, 32(1):37–45.

Glanville R, Francis S (1996). *Scanning the spectrum of health care from hospital to home in the UK*. London, South Bank University Medical Architecture Research Unit MARU Viewpoints Seminar Programme 1996.

Government of Scotland (2007). *The planned care improvement programme: patient flow in planned care. Admission, discharge, length of stay and follow-up*. Edinburgh, Government of Scotland.

Guenther R, Vittori G (2008). *Sustainable health care architecture*. Hoboken, John Wiley & Sons.

Hardy PA (2004). Getting a return on investment from spending capital dollars on new beds. *Journal of Healthcare Management*, 49(3):199–205.

Healy J, McKee M (2002a). Improving performance within the hospital. In: McKee M, Healy J. *Hospitals in a changing Europe*. Buckingham, Open University Press:206–225.

Healy J, McKee M (2002b). The role and function of hospitals. In: McKee M, Healy J. *Hospitals in a changing Europe*. Buckingham, Open University Press:59–80.

Hensher M, Edwards N (2002). The hospital and the external environment: experience in the United Kingdom. In: McKee M, Healy J. *Hospitals in a changing Europe*. Buckingham, Open University Press:83–99.

Hillman K (1999). The changing role of acute-care hospitals. *Medical Journal of Australia*, 170:325–328.

Holtby M (2007). Know how it works before you fix it: a data analysis strategy from an inpatient nephrology patient-flow improvement project. *Canadian Association of Nephrology Nurses and Technicians Journal*, 17(1):30–36.

Ieraci S et al. (2008). Streaming by case complexity: evaluation of a model for emergency department fast track. *Emergency Medicine Australasia*, 20(3):241–249.

Institute for Healthcare Improvement (2005). *Going lean in health care*. Cambridge, MA, Institute for Healthcare Improvement.

Johnson S et al. (2008). Fast-track assessment clinic: selection of patients for a one-stop hip assessment clinic. *Annals of the Royal College of Surgeons of England*, 90(3):208–212.

Jones D, Mitchell A (2006). *Lean thinking for the NHS*. London, NHS Confederation.

Julian S et al. (2007). An integrated care pathway for menorrhagia across the primary–secondary interface: patients' experience, clinical outcomes, and service utilization. *Quality and Safety in Health Care*, 16(2):110–115.

Karvonen S et al. (2007). Production flow analysis: a tool for designing a lean hospital. *World Hospital Health Services*, 43(1):28–31.

Kendall S (2008). Open building: health care architecture on the time axis. A new approach. In: Guenther R, Vittori G. *Sustainable health care architecture*. Hoboken, John Wiley & Sons:353–359.

Kim C et al. (2006). Lean health care: what can hospitals learn from a world-class automaker? *Journal of Hospital Medicine*, 1(3):191–199.

Kopach-Konrad R et al. (2007). Applying systems engineering principles in improving health care delivery. *Journal of General Internal Medicine*, 22(Suppl. 3):431–437.

The Lancet (1869). The Lancet commission into the administration of outpatient departments. *Lancet*, ii:553, 577, 613, 677, 774.

Marx F et al. (2007). Reform of tuberculosis control and DOTS within Russian public health systems: an ecological study. *European Journal of Public Health*, 17:98–103.

McKee C, Black N (1992). Does the current use of junior doctors in the United Kingdom affect the quality of medical care? *Social Science and Medicine*, 34:549–558.

McKee M, Healy J (2002a). Pressures for change. In: McKee M, Healy J. *Hospitals in a changing Europe*. Buckingham, Open University Press:36–58.

McKee M, Healy J (2002b). The evolution of hospital systems. In: McKee M, Healy J. *Hospitals in a changing Europe*. Buckingham, Open University Press:14–35.

McKee M, Healy J (2002c). The significance of hospitals: an introduction. In: McKee M, Healy J. *Hospitals in a changing Europe*. Buckingham, Open University Press:3–13.

Nightingale M (2006). University Hospital in Coventry: light and space. *Hospital Development*, 14 November (www.hd.magazine.co.uk/hybrid.asp?typeCode=525&putCode=10, accessed 18 October 2008).

O'Connell T et al. (2008). Health services under siege: the case for clinical process redesign. *Medical Journal of Australia*, 17(6 Suppl.):9–13.

Pope C, Roberts J, Black N (1991). Dissecting a waiting list. *Health Services Management Research*, 4(2):112–119.

Putnis S, Merville-Tugg R, Atkinson S (2004). 'One-stop' inguinal hernia surgery – day-case referral, diagnosis and treatment. *Annals of the Royal College of Surgeons of England*, 86(6):425–427.

Reid PP et al. (eds) (2005). *Building a better delivery system: a new engineering/health care partnership*. Washington, DC, National Academic Press.

Rivett G (1986). *The development of the London hospital system, 1823–1982*. London, King's Fund.

Saltman RB, Figueras J (1997). *European health care reform. Analysis of current strategies*. Copenhagen, WHO Regional Office for Europe.

Siegel B, Wilson M, Sickler D (2007). Enhancing work flow to reduce crowding. *Joint Commission Journal on Quality and Patient Safety*, 33(11 Suppl.):57–67.

Tzortzopoulos P et al. (2008). *Design for operational efficiency – linking building and service design in healthcare environments*. London, HaCIRIC International Symposium, April.

Van den Berg A, Wagenaar C (2006). Healing by architecture. In: Wagenaar C, ed. *The architecture of hospitals*. Rotterdam, NAi Publishers:254–257.

Van den Heuvel J et al. (2006). Implementing six sigma in the Netherlands. *Joint Commission Journal on Quality and Patient Safety*, 32(7):392–399.

Van der Wulp I, Van Baar M, Schrijvers AJP (2008). Reliability and validity of the Manchester triage system in a general emergency department patient population in the Netherlands: results of a simulation study. *Emergency Medicine Journal*, 25(7):431–434.

Wagenaar C (2006). The architecture of hospitals. In: Wagenaar C, ed. *The architecture of hospitals*. Rotterdam, NAi Publishers:10–19.

Waghorn A, McKee M (2000). Why is it so difficult to organize an outpatient clinic? *Journal of Health Services Research and Policy*, 5:140–147.

Young T et al. (2004). Using industrial processes to improve patient care. *British Medical Journal*, 328:162–164.

# Chapter 12

# Sustainable design for health

*Rosemary Glanville, Phil Nedin*

## Introduction: designing for sustainability

This chapter explores how to approach the design of health care facilities in a way that facilitates high-quality and sustainable solutions. It illuminates key decisions that influence the design and operational life of a building. These decisions are made at an early stage in the briefing and design process. At this stage, a project benefits from good communication between client and designers in relation to what characteristics are required. Decisions at the briefing stage lead to specific design responses that aim to satisfy care needs and take account of operational systems.

Sustainability has become a catchphrase used in the design brief of almost all health care facilities around the world. It does, however, have many meanings, depending on the context within which it is used, and can therefore create a lack of clarity. Sustainability has three core elements – social, economic and environmental – which embrace societal needs, affordability, workforce availability, as well as energy utilization and environmental impact (Guenther & Vittori 2008). It is important that providers of health care, that is, the owners or operators and their design teams, adopt this wider view of sustainability. Ideally, a sustainable approach to the design of health care facilities should allow the provision of health care in an efficient and effective manner over the life of the facility.

In health care, a number of essential themes need to be considered when designing a sustainable health care facility (Fig. 12.1). These themes encompass the key decisions to be made: innovative design, creating a therapeutic environment, responding to future change, whole-life cost, and carbon rating. One method of conceptualizing these themes is to view each of them as representing a

**Fig. 12.1** *Key themes to consider when developing sustainable health care facilities*

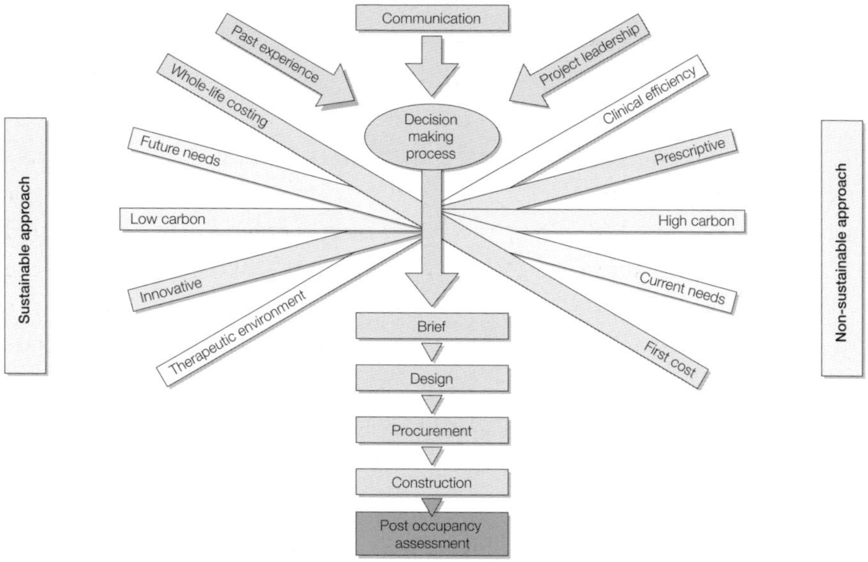

*Source*: Arup Healthcare Design Group, personal communication, 2008.

spectrum of approaches, from sustainable to unsustainable, although it should be stressed that this conceptualization is mainly an analytical and heuristic tool. In particular, clinical efficiency need not be incompatible with provision of a therapeutic environment, especially when the former is defined broadly.

The key decision-making requirement from the briefing stage onwards is to establish from where on each spectrum the client wants to start. This will influence the built environment response. Leadership, knowledge and understanding of these key aspects will depend on the knowledge base of the client and designer, including past experience. This chapter examines current ideas that favour movement to the sustainable end of the spectrum.

## Innovative configuration of hospital services

Given the changing environment in which they operate, if hospitals are to be sustainable in the future, it is unlikely that traditional configurations will continue to be appropriate. This is because a whole systems approach to the provision of health care is leading to innovative ways of organizing patient-centred care. This involves a radical redesign of care pathways to match the patient journey through all levels of health care, from primary to highly specialized care and back. First, however, it is relevant to reflect once again on the nature of the changing environment.

In 2000 the Nuffield Trust and the Royal Institute of British Architects sponsored a study by the Medical Architecture Research Unit (MARU) at London South Bank University. Their report *Building a 2020 vision: future health care environments* (MARU 2001) set out a blueprint for future health facilities. This took account of two agendas: the health agenda, aiming for a better patient experience, better access to care and more emphasis on privacy and dignity; and the built environment agenda, aiming for better public buildings, higher quality of design, and sustainability, including a transport plan that would provide ease of access to the site for patients, visitors and staff. Taking account of the cascade of care out of hospitals to other settings closer to peoples' homes, MARU proposed four settings for future health care: the home, primary and social care, community care and specialist care. This model has been reinforced by a relatively recent United Kingdom White Paper (*Our health, our care, our say*: Department of Health 2006), which proposes that outpatient and diagnostic care should move to community settings.

One driver of these changes is technological advancement. This is driving the provision of care in many different directions. In some cases, such as the introduction of short-acting anaesthetics, minimally invasive surgery and some forms of imaging, such as ultrasound, care can be moved outside the hospital. These services are of course also still required inside the hospital for inpatients because of their complexity, frailty, or for certain other reasons. Within the hospital, some of the most advanced equipment, such as positron emission tomography (PET), acts as a driver of centralization, as a large patient population is required to justify a single machine. Equipment such as this will be used by patients of many different types, all of whom should be assured of easy access (both geographically and in terms of time). At the same time, other equipment is being miniaturized, often coming down in price and requiring less-specialized staff to operate it. Examples include the many diagnostic kits used in near-patient testing, precluding the requirement to send samples to a specialized laboratory. This allows care to be dispersed throughout a whole community as well as across an individual site.

Demographic change, particularly relating to the ageing population, is another driver. Two characteristics of an ageing population are slower recovery from acute episodes and increasing prevalence of multiple chronic diseases. The first requires rehabilitation and the second requires integrated long-term management, ideally in the home environment. Neither care group is now accommodated suitably in an acute care hospital. Acute hospital spaces are becoming increasingly "hotter", as specialist care centres offering high levels of acuity-intensive and critical care procedures with rapid diagnostic and treatment for planned day and inpatient surgical interventions.

As noted earlier, these developments indicate a need to reassess how the work of a hospital is organized. However, there is little consensus about what the optimal approach is, as the following examples illustrate. In each case, the work of the hospital is divided in a different way. It is important to note, however, that there are no rigorous evaluations of the strengths and weaknesses of the different approaches.

The traditional method of dividing workload is according to specialty. However, even here there are new solutions in response to the challenges posed by the growth of particularly large hospitals, which often involve long patient travel distances across the hospital site. Some hospitals in the United Kingdom, Austria and France are reconfiguring their facilities into villages, based on specialties, such as surgery, medicine, obstetrics, or care of the elderly. Each "village" has its own entrance with adjacent supporting services. For example, the surgical village is a cluster of inpatient and day-patient theatres and surgical beds. This has been developed further in the Georges Pompidou Hospital in Paris, where specialist services are brought together in different parts of the hospital but are supplied by means of an integrated and automated transport system, circulating through the basement with vertical access channels. This delivers all supplies, including food, to decentralized user points.

A different organizational concept is represented by the care centre approach. Whereas in the past the hospital organization separated medical and surgical departments, moves to strengthen integrated care are leading to a grouping of services around body systems or disease processes. Examples of the former include cardiology and gastroenterology centres, while the most common example of the latter focuses on cancer. Both the new Edinburgh Royal Infirmary in Scotland, and the new hospital in Trondheim, Norway, have adopted this approach. Relevant diagnostic and treatment services are located adjacent to each care centre.

A third strategy, which is becoming used more widely in the United Kingdom is to divide the hospital organization into planned and emergency patient pathways, creating "hot" and "cold" streams of activity. Sometimes the planned element of consultation, diagnosis and treatment can be dealt with at a separate site, with or without short-stay beds. The rationale is that, in a system with limited capacity, a surge in emergencies can seriously disrupt planned work.

Another approach involves changing the scope of the hospital and how it relates to other parts of the health system. The new Karolinska hospital in Stockholm is to be built on the site of the former hospital, but its new role is to provide only specialized and highly specialized care and to pursue clinical research. There will be 500 beds and a 500-bed patient hotel; specialist services will be networked with other hospitals in the region. The master plan envisages creation of explicit links with the city of Stockholm, with industry (particularly companies based on biosciences), with a new residential zone, and with the airport (to support sparsely populated rural areas).

In the Netherlands, the "core hospital" concept (Netherlands Board for Health Care Institutions 2005) provides a care process approach in a network organization, based on a rigorous appraisal of what has to be in the acute hospital and what can be undertaken elsewhere (see Chapter 8 by Bjørberg & Verweij). Only the particularly acute and high-technology stages of care will be provided in the core hospital. All non-core services will be provided off-site. These include offices in local office blocks, and pathology and other support services in larger centres serving a group of facilities. The new hospital will require only a small area and so can be built on a city centre site. The network organization will include smaller centres in neighbourhoods around the core, for elective outpatient care with some treatment and the management of chronic care. Clearly, developments such as these pose the crucial question, "how does the *hospital* of today fit with the changing *centres of care* required in the future?"

## Creating a therapeutic environment

Environments are considered therapeutic (with healing qualities) when there is direct evidence that a design intervention contributes to improved patient outcomes. The characteristics that make up a therapeutic environment are considered to be the creation of non-threatening facilities through site planning, wayfinding, landscaping, human scale, thermal comfort, fresh air provision, natural daylight, control of the environment, privacy and dignity, reduced risk of infection, acoustic quality, art and colour.

Most of the evidence base for the therapeutic environment to date relates to a single intervention, whereas the real question is how a range of interventions perform when combined. The move from an intuitive design approach to one based on clear evidence is extremely difficult. This is due to the need to accurately repeat the clinical outcomes with varying patient groups and local cultures. It also relies on consistency of the care being delivered by the staff. This is a critical component of any study, as there is evidence to support the view that staff morale is lifted when they move into new well-planned environments, particularly when staff have been engaged in the design process (CABE 2004).

For many years, the key driver influencing the design of the built environment in the health sector has been the need to optimize clinical efficiency, such as patient observation and traffic and the movement of people and goods.

The emphasis today adds the patient's experience of their health care journey to the drivers of design.

This approach to design not only supports the well-being of patients during their stay and may speed recovery (as explored later), but also increases the well-being and motivation of staff (who spend much longer in the facility than any patient). This may bring benefits by attracting and retaining staff and may also in its turn enhance the operational efficiency and increase patient throughput (see Chapter 5 by Rechel, Buchan & McKee). Patient throughput and motivated staff are key requirements for sustainable health care, particularly in countries where patients have a choice of providers and providers are paid according to results. Professional health care designers should manage the compromise of creating clinical efficiency within a therapeutic environment.

Roger Ulrich's classic study (1984) showed that patients recovering from surgery had better outcomes when nursed in rooms overlooking a small stand of trees rather than a brick wall. They required fewer analgesic pharmaceuticals, made fewer demands on nurses and needed shorter lengths of stay. A study in the United Kingdom (Lawson & Phiri 2000), comparing old and new environments for two groups of patients, psychiatric and orthopaedic, found that both patient groups, treated in new or upgraded units, rated the same treatment significantly higher than that in old facilities. Patients in the new facilities reported less pain, as measured by the use of analgesics, and psychiatric patients showed less verbal abuse and threatening behaviour and were discharged earlier. Both groups felt that the environment contributed to their recovery and that colour and decoration influenced their well-being. Key issues of concern to patients included noise and the ability to control the environment, particularly with regard to ventilation and lighting.

These ideas feature in the Planetree approach, developed in the United States and replicated in several other countries. This began as a response by a single patient who sought to personalize, humanize and demystify the health care experience for future patients and their families. The key concept is that care should be patient-centred, focusing on the patient's perspective and empowering patients and families through information and education. The Planetree movement encourages designs that create home-like, barrier-free environments which support patient dignity and encourage family participation in the care process (Gearon 2002).

The Picker Institute (1998) (based both in the United States and Europe) takes these ideas further, and focuses on the patients' actual experience. One study used focus groups in three settings: ambulatory, acute and long-term care. When asked to describe their experience of the building, patients cited parking, lifts, accessibility and barriers to mobility, such as thresholds at entrances. Other studies found that first impressions are the most important, followed by the ability to find one's way. Patients wanted environments that promoted confidentiality and privacy, took account of physical impairments and were close to nature and the outside world.

The value of access to outdoor space is explored in the study by Cooper Marcus & Barnes (1995) for the United States-based Center for Health Design. Patients, visitors and staff all felt that they benefited from access to outdoor space, which provided a contrast to indoor space and provided a sense of getting away.

During a trial of light therapy in the care of depressed patients in Edmonton, Canada, Beauchemin & Hays (1998) observed that those patients in rooms on the sunny side of the building stayed on average 15% less time than those in rooms on the non-sunny side. A similar study took place over four years in a cardiac intensive care unit where four beds faced north and four faced south. A comparison of directly admitted patients with similar diagnoses showed that those in bright rooms stayed 2.3 days on average, while those in dark rooms stayed 2.6 days.

Reviews of evidence-based design have recently been undertaken in the United States (Ulrich & Zimring 2004) and the United Kingdom (Phiri 2006). These identify a number of ways in which environmental design can improve outcomes, such as infections, accidents, medical errors and violence by patients. For example, they find that the use of single rooms facilitates improved infection control and reduces medical errors (see Chapter 5 by Rechel, Buchan & McKee).

The single-patient bedroom is accepted as the norm in some European countries, primarily on grounds of privacy, but in others (such as the United Kingdom) – increasingly on clinical grounds (in relation to infection control) – it must still be justified on a project-by-project basis. The single-patient room, within a narrow plan concept, is often seen as providing the basis for a therapeutic environment.

Noise levels in hospitals have been identified as a concern since the 1950s. Noise has been shown to create stress and affect sleep quality of patients (Van den Berg 2005). In hospitals, noise is largely generated by people and equipment. Where possible, sources should be eliminated by finding noiseless solutions to call systems, pagers and telephones. The spread of noise can be mitigated by acoustic environmental design, particularly when focused on surfaces. However, this illustrates a key challenge in the design of health facilities, the need to make trade-offs. While carpets in corridors and acoustic ceiling treatments absorb sound, neither is easily washable and thus poses problems in relation to infection control. Single rooms may reduce sound transmission, but only if the doors are kept shut.

Ensuring that patients are not harmed whilst they are in a hospital environment must be a key characteristic of the therapeutic environment. Yet, even now, many patients are harmed by their stay in hospital, for example by the acquisition of hospital-acquired infections. It is possible to design hospitals in ways that minimize the risk. Infections are transmitted via five main routes: direct contact, droplet transmission (for example from coughs and sneezes), airborne transmission (for example through ventilation systems), common vehicle transmission (for example equipment not disinfected between patients) and vector-borne infection.

Appropriate design can reduce the risks associated with each of these routes. Ideally, it would take a holistic approach, involving the design, operation and maintenance of all relevant processes, based on an ongoing discussion with the infection control team. Design solutions for infection control are a matter of understanding transmission routes and attempting to eliminate them, taking account of operational and maintenance processes.

Aspects of design may make some solutions possible that would otherwise be unfeasible. Thus, one approach to disinfection is the use of vaporized hydrogen peroxide. Hydrogen peroxide is vaporized using equipment within the patient's room. The vapour is left to dwell in the room at the correct concentration for a defined period. The importance of having single rooms is that they are small enough to have a manageable dwell time. Larger multi-bed rooms will be associated with an increase in dwell time, with a consequent impact on the operational efficiency of the facility.

## Responding to future change

The design of any new hospital will need to incorporate sufficient flexibility to accommodate the many changes in clinical care that are likely to occur over its lifetime. There are two major models that can be considered. These relate to a narrow plan and a deeper plan floor-plate (Fig. 12.2). For a sustainable approach, this flexibility is essential if we are to address the changing needs of providing health care, and to reduce the need for additional construction. Whichever model is in place, although to a much greater degree in the former case, the structural engineering frame will need to accommodate changes in internal partition arrangements and the engineering systems will need to be accessible, with sufficient initially redundant space to accommodate changing clinical needs and new technical equipment, at all times with minimum cost and disruption.

**Fig. 12.2** *Deep plan and narrow plan solutions for design flexibility*

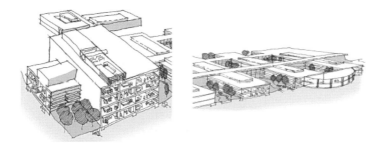

*Source*: Arup Healthcare Design Group, personal communication, 2008.

Changing needs may result in changes in bed numbers, both increases and decreases. In the event of a need to reduce bed numbers, the unused spatial asset should not become a liability. Design solutions should allow a reduction in bed numbers, but make it possible to use the space that is vacated for another income-generating activity. This is particularly important when considering the PFI procurement model in the United Kingdom and elsewhere, where the clients have to pay for the facility irrespective of whether it is used efficiently or not (see Chapter 7 by Dewulf & Wright).

This leads us towards a narrow plan solution, which provides spatial flexibility and reduces the disruptive impact of construction work (such as noise, dust, vibration and problems with accessibility, means of escape and security). However, whilst desirable, this may not always be feasible, especially when the facility is on a spatially constrained site. Particular flexibility is offered, paradoxically, by a return to the pavilion design first used over 150 years ago, where one or more pavilions can be remodelled to allow for change of use. In the deep plan model, any change to the internal layout will create greater disruption and could compromise the security of the rest of the building during the remodelling period. This is because the departmental adjacencies in the deep plan model are far more tightly connected. Although viewed as more efficient in the initial planning and construction, this creates barriers to subsequent ongoing change. Furthermore, there is also evidence that deep plan solutions use more energy.

The need to incorporate flexibility in hospital design has long been recognized, even if rather less often implemented. An early example of the concept of open systems was the 1955 report *Studies in the function and design of hospitals* (Nuffield Provincial Hospitals Trust 1955). Studies led by John Weeks and Richard Llewellyn Davies considered the size and growth of individual hospitals and the effects of change. John Weeks' "Duffle Coat" theories, developed during the construction of the Northwick Park hospital in north-west London, introduced the concept of interdepartmental communications through hospital "streets" for people and channels for pipes and other services. Each department was designed as a relatively independent building with a front door on the internal street and a "free end" for future enlargement. Extensive provision of vertical engineering ducts enabled future connections, and a grid design allowed spaces to be used for a number of different activities.

Subsequent experience with a series of pilot projects informed the construction of an entire hospital site along these lines at Greenwich, in south-east London, with the first phase being completed in 1969. A key element to facilitate future change was the use of long-span structures (structures that span greater open areas) supporting aerated concrete slabs. No internal partitions were structural and there was an interstitial floor for environmental services that allowed flexibility of room layouts and services. Three concepts emerged from this work:

- long-span structures (separating partitions from structure);

- physical communication systems (separating street from activity); and

- engineering installations (provision for new connections and the ability to connect outlets).

The same principles underpinned the Nucleus Hospital programme in the United Kingdom. These hospitals were designed to enable different functions to be provided in standard units built according to templates connected by a street system that included distribution of engineering services. Three strategies were developed for future change: use of standard construction units based on the same template but which could accommodate different facilities; planned "misuse" of space, that is, hard (highly engineered) and soft space (such as administration) in the same or adjacent units to allow for growth; and growth by additional units. There is a stock of 80 Nucleus Hospitals in the United Kingdom. Case studies have shown that most Trusts intend to retain and develop their Nucleus buildings as part of their master planning and estate strategies (Montgomery 2007).

An analogous concept, although on a smaller scale, is the "universal patient care room" or adaptable acuity concept from the United States (Spear 1997). This is a facility that can be adapted to provide all levels of care, from intensive to acute (see Chapter 5).

These concepts imply a need to build a high level of flexibility into all elements of a hospital. Within health care facilities it is useful to differentiate four types of space: high-technology diagnosis and intervention (operating theatres and imaging facilities), patient fostering (wards), public and social space, and factory spaces, such as sterilization units. New technologies are most likely to impact most on spaces used for diagnostics and interventions. Patient fostering space may need more space around beds for equipment and more engineering connections, but as equipment becomes smaller this is likely to pose fewer challenges. Factory space, if designed with long spans and partitioning separated from structure, can easily be remodelled to a new process.

In France, for example, the high-technology areas for diagnostics and treatment of the hospital are typically co-located in a *"plateau technique"* (technical platform), with other functions placed around this core. The core can be constructed in a way that facilitates future change.

An open building concept has been developed in the Zentrum für Intensivbehandlung, Notfall und Operation (INO; Centre for Intensive Care, Emergencies and Surgery) in Berne, Switzerland (Kendall 2004). This separates components of different life expectancies into primary, secondary and tertiary systems, with 50–100 years, 15–50 years and 5–15 years of life expectancy, respectively. Primary systems are the supporting structure, building envelope and site development. The secondary system includes the inner walls, ceilings, floors, fixed installations, and internal logistics with a discipline of component coordination and separation, allowing replacement of individual components. The tertiary system is most easily changeable, comprising devices, architecturally significant equipment and furniture.

In the United Kingdom, a typical PFI acute hospital contains some 4000 rooms, of which only 10% are considered "special" for the integration of "architecturally significant equipment", while 85% are common rooms with no more than 15 repetitive types (Buckle 2006). Reducing the range of room sizes can allow for more future interchangeability and enable more varied use. The basic health care activities can be divided into "talk", "talk and examine" and "treat". Except in the most specialized areas, these demand only three basic room sizes. Within these categories, rooms can be changed on three different time scales to reflect changes in the activities undertaken within them. First, they can have sufficient flexibility built in to allow changes of use timetabled over a single week, for example to allow their use by different specialties. Second, over a longer period they can have furniture and equipment refits (for example, changing a gynaecology consulting room into one for ophthalmology). Third, over a period of years they can be remodelled, with new partitioning and engineering services arrangements to allow for a complete change of activity.

An added dimension facilitating flexibility is the off-site construction in factory conditions of complex spatial and engineered spaces, such as bathroom pods. However, to be useful, there must be systems in place for extracting and replacing such units.

## Whole-life costing

Organizational and design options should be selected with economic rigour. A sustainable approach requires that selections be based on a whole life-cycle cost model. The principles have already been described in detail in Chapter 8, so what follows are only examples of the method in use. It may, however, be helpful to recap briefly. Initial capital costs and running costs have traditionally been accounted for in separate budgets and the capital cost of a building was the main criterion for design choices. Gradually, it has been understood that, over the lifetime of a building, the operating and maintenance costs of the building are far greater, in net worth terms, than the initial capital expenditure (Kishk et al. 2003). The operating costs of a hospital often consume the equivalent of the capital cost every 2–3 years (BSRIA 2008). Life-cycle costing takes account of the initial cost to build, together with the costs arising over the whole life of the building, including energy, equipment maintenance or replacement, staff training and finally the disposal cost at the end of the life of the building. Whole-life costs can then be related to benefits to assess "value for money", so that "the optimum combination of whole-life cost and quality (fitness for purpose) to meet requirements" (Government of Scotland 2008) is achieved.

Figure 12.3 illustrates three different footprints enclosing the same clinical departments. The whole-life cost model makes it possible to compare a narrow plan (Option 1), an intermediate plan (Option 2) and a deep plan facility (Option 3). Design changes can be evaluated on the basis of whole life-cycle costs, and an optimum solution can then be developed on a firm financial basis. The fundamental elements of this approach involve comparing different construction solutions, beginning with a first cost model (a single cost for construction) and then evaluating the solutions through a whole-life cost model (the cost of the building over its lifespan, typically taken to be 60 years). Two historic indicators of building efficiency are normally used to justify a first cost model. The net-to-gross ratio is the area-based relationship between "usable" departmental space and "non-usable" communication and engineering system space. Although originally developed from private sector commercial and retail facilities, the relationship is now used in almost all construction sectors. The second is the relationship between the wall area and the floor area. Where more floor is contained within the least amount of wall, the space is deemed to be used most efficiently. Maximum efficiency relies on the introduction of mechanical ventilation systems and reduces the connection between the occupants and the external environment.

The whole-life cost model approach includes, in addition, an evaluation of the running costs of the building, including cleaning, maintenance, plant replacement, energy and, if possible, a cost for carbon. Ideally, it should

**Fig. 12.3** *Simple example of whole-life cost appraisal: using inflated costs over a cumulative 10-year period*

**Option 1 – narrow plan**
Capital cost = £31 447 315 (€39 263 500)
Running cost at year 10 = £3 115 815 (€3 890 246)
Accumulated running cost after 10 years = £29 015 574 (€36 227 353)

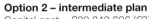

**Option 2 – intermediate plan**
Capital cost = £30 243 696 (€37 760 723)
Running cost at year 10 = £3 776 903 (€4 715 647)
Accumulated running cost after 10 years = £30 716 021 (€38 350 444)

**Option 3 – deep plan**
Capital cost = £28 128 205 (€35 119 430)
Running cost at year 10 = £3 463 526 (€4 324 380)
Accumulated running cost after 10 years = £31 936 837 (€39 872 195)

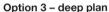

*Source*: Arup Healthcare Design Group, personal communication, 2008.

also include an estimate of the costs of providing health care. Once costs are calculated for the first year of operation, the total is then projected forward and all necessary increases applied on an annual basis to ascertain the likely running costs over the life of the building. To complete the exercise, the financial results across the life of the building are compared with the first cost for the respective building configurations, and decisions can then be made with all the appropriate information to hand.

The example in Fig. 12.3 shows three configurations housing the same departments. The deep plan option, when compared with the narrow plan option, costs £3 319 110 (€4 142 249) less and so is more economic from a first-cost perspective. However, after 10 years of operation and applying a whole-life cost model, there is a saving in the narrow plan compared with the deep plan of £2 919 263 (€3 643 240) on accumulated running costs. This saving increases on a cumulative basis over the life of the building and does not take into account the value of increased flexibility in the narrow plan arrangement for future remodelling, nor the benefits to staff and patients of having greater connection to the external environment. However, it does assume that the narrow plan is predominately naturally ventilated and that the deep plan is predominately mechanically cooled. The model assumes a 3% increase in the cost of energy, operation and maintenance, life-cycle and carbon per annum. The 3% increase per annum applied to the energy cost is optimistic, given the rapidly rising cost of energy between 2007 and 2008.

Another example of a life-cycle approach is in the selection of a system for removal of used laundry and waste in an acute facility. The selection of such a system will add extra capital costs, as well as having an impact on the internal space planning and engineering design. However, there are several benefits to be considered. First, there is an immediate removal of potential reservoirs of infection from the ward area, which has the added advantage of eliminating the need to carry the dirty material through other wards on porters' trolleys, so reducing the risk of spreading infection. There is also a reduction in the damage done by trolleys to internal walls and doors and the reduction in the numbers of porters needed to operate the automated system. The savings are therefore in staff numbers, facility management operating costs and risk of spreading infection. All these benefits can only be realized through a whole life-cycle approach.

## The carbon agenda

The use of energy in any sector is important in terms of depletion of hydrocarbons, the increasing cost of energy, the security of fuel supply and the impact on the environment in the form of global warming. The latter, in particular, has focused widespread attention on the need to reduce the use of carbon. The health care sector, which has historically been a major user of energy, is understandably coming under increasing pressure to reduce its energy use and hence its carbon emissions.

It is important when embarking on a low carbon strategy to develop an auditable approach, to facilitate the right decisions at the right stage of the process (Fig. 12.4).

**Fig. 12.4** *An audit trail representing key activities in achieving low carbon building solutions*

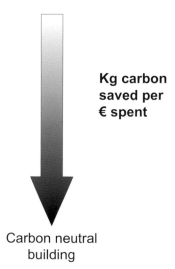

- **Building form and orientation**
- **Passive ventilation strategy**
- **Lighting controls**
- **Reduced air leakage**
- **Exposed mass**
- **Glazing specification**
- **Increased shading**
- **Increased insulation**
- **Biomass boilers**
- **Solar hot water generators**
- **Ground source heat pump**
- **Wind turbines**
- **Small-scale hydroelectricity**
- **Fuel cells**

**Kg carbon saved per € spent**

Carbon neutral building

*Source*: Arup Healthcare Design Group, personal communication, 2008.

The use of higher thermal insulation standards, heat recovery techniques, lighting control, natural ventilation and so on represent only a few of the matters to be considered. Of particular interest is the use of mixed mode systems, where, because of the climate, it is not possible to utilize natural ventilation all year round. In this situation, it is easy but unimaginative to default to a mechanical cooling system and to seal the building, that is, have no opening windows. This decision, made in the earliest stages of the design, eliminates any chance of the facility ever utilizing the benefits of natural ventilation. It is far better to recognize that all climates allow some degree of natural ventilation and design with that in mind. In many countries the design codes preclude opening windows being part of the design solution. These countries will need to review their codes in order to maximize the potential of health care facilities to respond to the low carbon agenda.

As shown in Fig. 12.4, once ventilation has been addressed it is necessary to focus on renewable sources of energy, that is, technologies developed to provide energy, but without using fuels that emit high levels of carbon. It is also possible to add these alternative energy sources at a later stage, if they were not part of the initial investment.

Of particular importance when considering the energy and carbon emissions from health care facilities is an appreciation of the role of the facility. Much of the energy used in the acute hospital setting is not required to create thermally comfortable environments, but flows from clinical and safety requirements. Whilst paying due regard to all energy and carbon legislative frameworks, it is also important to ensure that the technical guidance for that facility within its geographic region is fully understood and that technical standards are maintained.

## Achieving a sustainable approach through a design model

The benefits of employing a sustainable approach in the design process of a large health care facility are clear: decisions are made for the long-term benefits of the facility and the facility underpins the ongoing effectiveness of the business. Furthermore, if a sustainable model is used, then the stakeholder group normally engaged in the decision-making process will find the process more inclusive, as there will be an auditable trail and decisions will be more logical and consistent.

The model shown in Fig. 12.5 illustrates an approach to making decisions during the design process. Options are considered through quadrants, representing the environment and natural resources, as well as economic and societal factors. Options can be evaluated by posing a number of agreed questions that test the

**Fig. 12.5** *The Sustainable Project Appraisal Routine (SPeAR) developed by Arup*

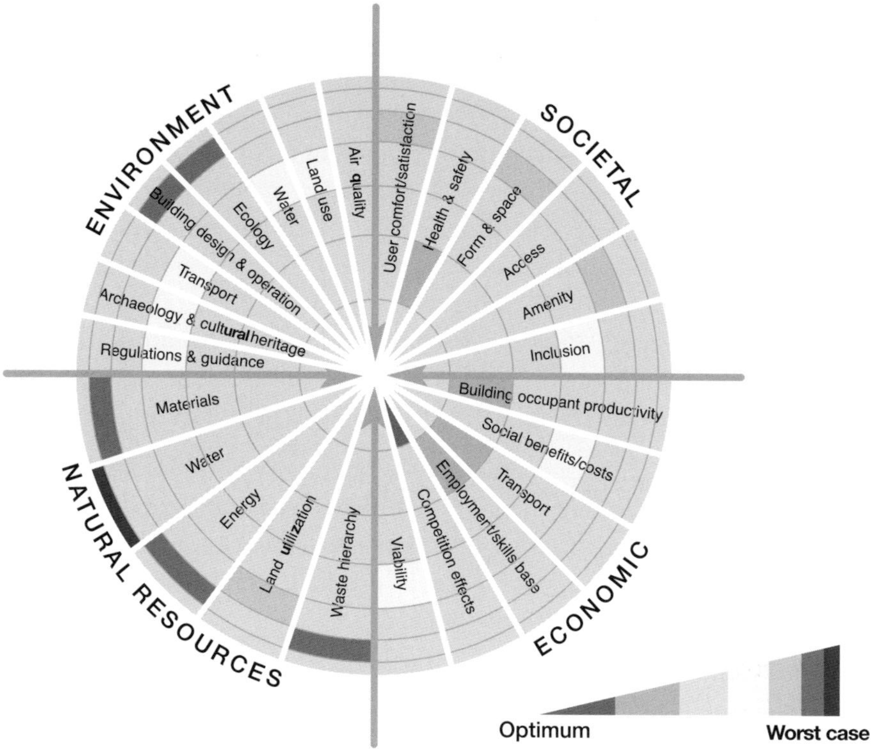

*Source*: Arup Healthcare Design Group, personal communication, 2008.

brief and – by working the issues through with the client and the design teams – develop, compare and contrast solutions.

## The economic argument for creating sustainable facilities

There appears to be little doubt that there will be an increase in the initial capital cost of a project when developing it as a sustainable model. However, these additional costs can be offset over the life of the facility. Achieving a sustainable design can typically add 6–12% to overall capital costs (BRE Trust & Sweett 2005), depending on the size of the facility, how realistic the initial budget is, client expectations, site constraints, the commitment and inventiveness of the team engaged in the process, and the ability of the procurement route to support a whole-life cost approach. What is clear from the modelling that we have carried out is that, by adopting a holistic approach to the design and evaluation process, solutions become mutually supportive across a number of aspects of sustainability. The whole then becomes greater than the sum of the parts in terms of the savings generated over time, as well as the less easily identifiable clinical, carbon, staff and societal benefits.

## Conclusions

A sustainable approach to the design of health care facilities is essential to maximize the business effectiveness for the whole life of the facility. In developing a sustainable design solution, a range of factors must be considered. While each can be assessed initially in isolation, ultimately they must be considered together.

Understanding of the process of delivering care in different settings will then point the way to the appropriate building shape and level of environmental technology. The goal must be to create a sustainable facility that is capable of being adapted to changing circumstances and which provides a healing or therapeutic environment, with decisions based on an understanding of costs over the whole life of the facility and not just the construction phase. This is inevitably challenging, as the future is intrinsically unpredictable. The task is further complicated by the scarcity of appropriate research-based evidence. The first step is to develop a holistic approach to design which takes account of all the factors involved.

## References

Beauchemin KM, Hays P (1998). Seeing ward design in a new light. *Hospital Development*, 6 (http://findarticles.com/p/articles/mi_qa3873/is_199810/ai_n8825087/pg_2, accessed 18 October 2008).

BRE Trust, Sweett C (2005). *Putting a price on sustainability*. Watford, BRE Centre for Sustainable Construction.

BSRIA (2008). *What is whole life cost analysis?* Bracknell, BSRIA Ltd (The Building Services Research and Information Association) (http://www.bsria.co.uk/news/1886/, accessed 18 October 2008).

Buckle M (2006). *Powerpoint presentation to MSc Planning Buildings for Health*. London, London South Bank University.

CABE (2004). *The role of hospital design in the recruitment, retention and performance of NHS nurses in England*. London, Commission for Architecture & the Built Environment.

Cooper Marcus C, Barnes M (1995). *Gardens in health care facilities: uses, therapeutic benefits, and design recommendations*. Concord, The Center for Health Design.

Department of Health (2006). *White paper: our health, our care, our say*. London, United Kingdom Department of Health.

Gearon CJ (2002). Planetree (25 years older). *Hospitals & Health Networks*, 76(10):40–43.

Government of Scotland (2008). *Whole-life costing*. Edinburgh, Government of Scotland (http://www.eprocurementscotland.com/toolkit/Documents/Whole%20Life%20Costing%203.pdf, accessed 5 February 2008).

Guenther R, Vittori G (2008). *Sustainable health care architecture*. Hoboken, John Wiley & Sons.

Kendall S (2004). Open building: a new paradigm in hospital architecture. *AIA Academy Journal*, 31(1):89–99.

Kishk M et al. (2003). *Whole-life costing in construction. A state of the art review*. London, RICS (Royal Institution of Chartered Surveyors) Foundation (www.rics.org, accessed January 2008).

Lawson B, Phiri M (2000). Hospital design. Room for improvement. *Health Service Journal*, 110(5688):24–26.

MARU (2001). *Building a 2020 vision: future health care environments*. London, Nuffield Trust & Royal Institute of British Architects.

Montgomery R (2007). *Nucleus hospitals – do they have a future?* [MSc Dissertation]. London, London South Bank University Medical Architecture Research Unit.

Netherlands Board for Health Care Institutions (2005). *Future hospitals, competitive and healing. Competition report*. Utrecht, Netherlands Board for Health Care Institutions.

Nuffield Provincial Hospitals Trust (1955). *Studies in the function and design of hospitals*. London, Nuffield Provincial Hospitals Trust.

Phiri M (2006). *Does the physical environment affect staff and patient outcomes: a review of studies and articles 1965–2005*. London, United Kingdom Department of Health.

The Picker Institute (1998). *Working paper: Consumer perceptions of the health care environment: an investigation to determine what matters*. Concord, Center for Health Design.

Spear M (1997). Current issues: Designing the universal patient care room. *Journal of Health Care Design*, 9:81–83.

Van den Berg A (2005). *Health impacts of healing environments. Foundation 200 years*. Groningen, University Hospital Groningen.

Ulrich R (1984). View through a window may influence recovery from surgery. *Science*, 224 (4647):420–421.

Ulrich R, Zimring C (2004). *The role of the physical environment in the hospital of the 21ˢᵗ century: a once-in-a-lifetime opportunity*. Concord, Center for Health Design.

# Part five:
# Conclusions

# Chapter 13

# Conclusions and critical success factors

*Bernd Rechel, Stephen Wright, Nigel Edwards,*
*Barrie Dowdeswell, Martin McKee*

## How to improve the effectiveness of capital investment

This concluding chapter seeks to identify the critical success factors that increase the chances that capital projects will achieve successful outcomes. One of the key tasks of the health system is to translate health needs into services and to translate these services into appropriate facilities. However, this is not easy. The context within which capital investment takes place is complex and constantly changing. The rapid pace of change means that health facilities must be able to respond rapidly to changing expectations and needs and to new opportunities offered by innovations in technology and configurations of care. In practice, although service and capital development plans and initiatives may be concurrent, capital support on the ground will inevitably lag behind service initiatives and often dictates the pace with which service change can be achieved. This adds impetus to the need to rethink capital asset strategies. An added problem is that of path dependency; only some aspects of capital investment are susceptible to rapid change, while others are constrained by history, undergoing only evolutionary change.

While this chapter strives to identify a number of factors for improving capital investment, it is important to recognize the hugely different contexts in which hospitals in Europe operate. National health systems differ greatly in terms of funding, organization and governance, a diversity that reflects different histories, cultures and political trajectories. Hospital systems have different levels of resources and different institutional and cultural legacies. Levels of investment in developing professional competences also differ greatly, in some cases leading to off-the-shelf solutions that rarely meet expectations. Furthermore, while some general trends are clear, each country faces specific opportunities and constraints. When making decisions on capital investment, the specific context in which it is taking place will have to be borne in mind, to identify those success factors that will have the highest impact.

## Making the best use of policy levers

The scope for policy-makers to improve capital investment is a function of the ownership, funding and regulatory mechanisms of hospitals. It is possible to identify the following main policy levers:

- planning
- regulation
- capital financing
- capital management
- service financing
- service (re)design.

### Planning

There seems to be a consensus in most European countries that, whilst market mechanisms have a role in determining some aspects of health systems and can increase the efficiency and responsiveness of providers, on their own they do not necessarily produce optimal patterns of provision. The reasons for market failure in health care have long been recognized, but are especially relevant in relation to capital investment. As a result, no developed country – not even the United States – leaves decisions on hospital provision purely to the market. Particular problems include the presence of crucial interdependencies between services, particularly high costs of market entry, and areas where patient choice does not operate effectively, such as major trauma. Market mechanisms are being harnessed increasingly – but only once the broad pattern of provision has been decided by policy-makers; to draw on an analogy used widely in health policy, markets are, in a sense, used for rowing but not for steering.

The most common way of overcoming these problems is to establish effective systems for capacity planning. It is, however, essential to be aware of the risk that planning decisions will become subject to political processes (and in some countries corruption), leading to compromises that can delay the process and lead to decisions that are sub-optimal. In all but the smallest countries, planning is likely to take place at different levels. Central governments are best placed to establish the context, by virtue of their overall governance of the health system, but regional governments are more likely to have sufficient understanding of the local context. It must be recognized, however, that there is a shortage of skills in planning hospital services, affecting almost all countries, and this is exacerbated because few people working in regional authorities will ever be responsible for building more than one hospital. Consequently, there has been a significant growth in the market for bought-in external expertise. This support is rarely custom-designed and is more likely to draw on the databases that the major players have compiled from their various projects. However, as most of these will be largely historic and reliant on the common currency of bed numbers, recourse to this approach to planning is more likely to sediment services than inspire new initiatives and innovations.

## Regulation

In all European countries, the government plays a regulatory role in the health sector, covering both purchasers and providers of health services. Initially focused on the processes required to ensure that the system functions, such as the establishment of payment systems and minimum standards of provision, in many countries there is a shift towards using regulation as a tool to achieve the goals of the health system and, in particular, health gain and responsiveness to expectations. Quality assurance mechanisms, such as the licensing or accreditation of health care providers, can have an immediate impact on the hospital landscape and encourage or discourage new capital projects. In the CEE countries, for example, many governments have encouraged the creation of private practices and clinics, slowly departing from the still largely public provision of secondary and tertiary care. The accreditation of health care providers was used by some countries as an instrument to reduce the overprovision of hospital care characteristic of the communist period (and a similar approach was used a decade earlier in Belgium to close many small hospitals). Accreditation has also been used to focus private investment, such as with the stimulation of new treatment centres to deal with high demand and excessive waiting times. Regulation in these circumstances also gives rise to new financing instruments in the banking sector. Effective regulation, like planning, requires a high degree of skill. Too often, regulatory systems are misaligned with the goals being pursued or send out contradictory messages, leaving those who must manage the system confused and frustrated.

## Capital financing

Access to capital is one of the main external levers shaping capital investment in the health sector. In most European countries, the public sector continues to be involved heavily in financing capital investment projects, but there is an increasing use of public–private partnerships, in which the private sector is contracted by the public sector to provide certain services, particularly accommodation, by building, managing and maintaining health facilities. This is not solely focused on the health sector, but represents a broader view on the part of many governments and the EU that this model of funding stimulates competition within the public sector and accelerates access to capital. However, it is important to realize that public–private partnerships do not generate new financial resources for the health sector. They are simply another way of raising debt finance and ultimately the debt will need to be repaid. Where governments have separate revenue and capital streams, this also shifts provision of capital to the revenue stream and invariably transfers risk down to the operational level, such as the hospital management. This is of benefit to those governments that need to ensure fiscal debt targets are met. In the most common variants, such as the United Kingdom PFI, money will be paid in the future, with contract payment periods now reaching 40 years, transferring the cost to future generations. The total sums involved may be greater than under the traditional system, and there is now increasing concern that this intergenerational transfer of responsibility, which coincides with policies having a similar effect in areas such as pensions, could have profound unintended consequences in the future.

A key challenge facing public–private partnerships is how to achieve efficient and effective contracting. Contracts are designed to reduce uncertainty and opportunism, but involve high transaction costs and often legally binding rigidity. Long-term contracts also tend to be incomplete due to information shortcomings. They often fail to pay attention to future problems, conflicts and contingencies. A crucial question is how to ensure that investment value continues beyond the initial purchase, in order to enable the hospital to adapt to changing circumstances. Ideally, contracts should make it possible to adapt to contingencies in order to ensure asset flexibility, although this has been difficult to achieve. One of the major questions is who bears the risk of capital investments. Experience shows that private partners have been particularly reluctant to take on significant risks in capital projects, and evidently never unfunded ones. This tends to focus the concerns of private partners on building durability as opposed to building flexibility – flexibility carries a cost premium which is difficult to predict and even more difficult to incorporate into contract frameworks. On the other hand, the contractual nature of the arrangement usually reveals risks which always exist in projects, but in other circumstances (when, for example, entirely within the public sector) are internalized, and opaque or completely invisible.

## Capital management

In many health systems, the cost, risks and value of capital are ignored, as investment and revenue costs come from different streams, with hospital managers having very little control over the former or interest in the latter. This removes any incentive for those managers to manage assets efficiently. However, this traditional split is gradually eroding in many European countries as hospitals are increasingly becoming responsible for their capital assets. In the Netherlands, for example, the risks of capital investments have now been shifted entirely to hospital trusts, and similar trends can be observed in other countries in Europe. While it is too early to gauge the final consequences of this development, it has the beneficial effect of focusing managerial attention on the need to use assets more efficiently. Although there is some evidence of new thinking about the valuation and depreciation of assets, this is still in its infancy and the future does not look bright when it comes to the renewal of the present health care infrastructure, which is still dominated by the traditional capital allocation model based on grants that has been the hallmark of capital financing in Europe for almost 50 years.

## Service financing

The mechanisms for paying for health services can impact powerfully on capital investment. Under the Semashko system, in place throughout CEE during the Soviet period, the allocation of budgetary funds to hospitals was based on bed capacity, regardless of what those beds were being used for, and this created an incentive for the inefficient use of resources. Throughout Europe, similar perverse incentives continue to exist, such as incentives not to treat patients in the public sector where health care workers work within private and public services in parallel, as for example in Malta and Greece.

Throughout Europe, there is a trend away from hospital funding based on historical budgets towards funding based on activity levels. This will tend to encourage capital investment that is flexible and more efficient. In the Netherlands, for example, the introduction of competitive DRGs (with tariffs negotiated between hospital organizations and insurers) was an important driver of hospital change. However, it is critical to keep such payment systems under constant review, as they contain many possible pitfalls. These include incentives for gaming (DRG "drift", either by changing patterns of care to maximize revenue even though this may diminish the quality of care, or by changing how data are recorded, typically by increasing reporting on minor co-morbidities), or failure to recognize centres providing genuinely more complex care, such as highly specialized orthopaedic or paediatric centres. What is also worrying here is the naïveté over methodologies – if they exist at all in some countries – to incorporate the capital dimension in service tariffs. One of the key conclusions that can be drawn from the contributions to this volume is that a dynamic service strategy depends on a dynamic capital model. The danger is that commissioners, when driving hard bargains over contract prices, will fail to recognize the need for a sufficient margin to service debt and for reserves for reinvestment when needed, and that providers will fail to account sufficiently for reinvestment need. This further emphasizes the need for new concepts in depreciating assets.

## Service (re)design

The "hospital" is a major capital (and labour) asset, used to produce services. The ultimate concept lying behind the way that the institution works is the model of care. This is a multi-layered concept capable of being expressed at national, regional, local, network or institutional levels. Such a slippery notion runs the danger of being all things to all people. To whatever degree this is the case, it remains true that the hospital is generating processes of services, and is doing this using capital and other resources. The nature of the processes being delivered, which inevitably is changing with demography, epidemiology and technology, means that the capital stock needs to be configured correctly for those services to start with. And it needs to be capable of flexing over time, to accommodate these changes over time. The model of care adopted within any one institution is then both a reflection of the drivers mentioned and a separate decision about the most efficient process (in terms of cost or clinical outcomes). Capital must be designed as a facilitating element in investment strategy, rather than one that has, as undoubtedly in the past, had a propensity towards sedimenting services.

# Designing better hospital systems

## Restructuring hospitals

Hospital services should be designed to meet the legitimate expectations of patients and to improve clinical outcomes. It is clear that there is a need for a strategic rethink of the way care is delivered, leading potentially to fundamental changes in hospital systems. These may include a redefinition of the principles underlying the provision of care, including placing more value on patients' time and increased emphasis on a smooth flow of patients through the system, with minimal waiting times. Hospitals will also need to provide more one-stop services and extend opening hours beyond the traditional working week.

## Incorporating flexibility

One of the key lessons emerging from the contributions to this volume is the importance of flexibility. Too often, hospitals reflect outdated patterns of care. They continue to be used beyond their functional lifespan and are caught in a straightjacket of inflexible financing mechanisms and capital reimbursement. Flexibility must encompass all aspects of the hospital system, including scale and scope of facilities (with possibilities to upsize or downsize), architectural design, supporting infrastructure (including transport links), definition of services to be provided on- and off-site, relationships with the rest of the health care system, revenue financing and sources of capital investment.

Paradoxically, in a few countries policy is moving in the opposite direction. The best known example is PFI in the United Kingdom, a model introduced in part to overcome accounting rules that limited government borrowing. The reluctance of private providers to accept risks means that contracts are specified in enormous detail covering the usual 30 years of the project, with very little scope for change. In Australia, which has also used this approach, the public sector has had to buy out many of the projects at substantial cost. These capital models place an emphasis on minimizing the risk of future changes to one party – the private sector – rather than necessarily on long-term effectiveness and adaptability to the benefit of both parties.

It is important to recognize that the flexibility of different areas of hospitals differs. Those areas providing core functions of the hospital, including operating theatres, diagnostic imaging, and intensive care facilities (the "hot floor"), are particularly expensive to build and they tend to have a comparatively short technical lifespan. The hotel function, especially where it involves low-intensity nursing, is less specific and has a longer technical lifespan (although this is changing, with the introduction of variable-acuity beds). The most flexible parts of a hospital are its office facilities, including administration, staff departments and outpatient units. Effective long-term management of facilities can benefit from an understanding of these functional distinctions, which are increasingly recognized by sustainable design.

As the functional lifespan of hospital buildings is far shorter than their technical lifespan, there is a need for adaptable buildings that allow for changes in layout, function and volume. One way of approaching this need for flexibility is to include easily removable inner walls and partitions. The inclusion of "soft space" next to complex areas and the provision of other architectural expansion possibilities make it possible to adapt the hospital building to changing needs, although it will also be necessary to consider clinical adjacencies. Another option is to standardize hospital space and facilities as far as possible and to separate logistical flows, as well as elective from acute care. A standardized hospital room may not only be cheaper to produce, but could also be usable for non-health purposes. These approaches create what has been termed "agile space". Agile space facilitates the effective long-term management of changes in demand (elasticity), changes in need (functionality) and sustainability (delivering capital value over the lifetime of the building). Yet, even where such possibilities are envisaged at the design stage, it is important to recognize that even the most flexible of buildings will experience disruption when changes are made. This can be minimized by providing services in discrete blocks.

Another, similar concept is acuity-adaptable rooms, which are configured in such a way that different intensities of care can be delivered from the same space. Achieving this flexibility requires, however, a capital and potentially labour cost trade-off, and the optimum choice of technology intensity in a patient room will probably remain a case-by-case decision, in particular as acuity-adaptable rooms engender more complex mechanical systems and potentially higher energy usage for many people who do not require that level of infrastructure.

In this discussion, determination of the desired degree of "flexibility" requires determination of the desired "capacity". Historically, this has been proxied by numbers of beds, but it is becoming increasingly obvious that this is an inadequate metric. True capacity must be understood in terms of the processes being delivered, recognizing that a single item or area of activity may act as a critical bottleneck for the entire system. To release this capacity constraint, it will be necessary to focus on such choke points that stop the institution from processing more patients.

## Ensuring access and availability

As noted earlier, most governments in Europe have some control over major capital investments in hospitals through regional and national planning mechanisms, even when they are not the owners. In general, governments have accepted the responsibility of ensuring that health services are available, accessible, affordable, equitable and of good quality. To achieve these goals, government bodies at central, regional and/or local levels engage in health capacity planning, determining the geographical configuration of service providers and the distribution of services within them (for example, access to emergency care as well as highly specialized care such as organ transplantation), on the basis of population health needs and available resources. Their focus is often on hospitals, where approval is frequently required for new developments, the restructuring of facilities, and investments in expensive equipment and technology. These planning processes need to take account of travel times to hospitals and the opportunity to take services normally provided in the hospital to other settings where they are more accessible.

In practice, however, capacity planning in the health sector often fails to move beyond hospitals and does not take account of the overall health needs of the population and the entire spectrum of health services required to meet those needs. Furthermore, as mentioned earlier, bed capacity is still the most commonly used unit for determining future capacity, even though a growing amount of the work of a hospital does not involve beds, such as day surgery. It is also biased towards historic utilization patterns. This – still widespread – use of bed numbers is surprising, given the trend for hospital financing mechanisms to focus more on patient throughput rather than bed numbers, for example through measures such as DRGs. There is a clear need to shift the currency in which hospitals are measured from bed numbers to services delivered.

## Taking a whole systems perspective

Hospitals cannot be considered in isolation from the rest of the health system. The hospital treatment episode often forms only part of a much longer care pathway for the patient. The role of hospitals has significantly changed in recent decades, with hospital capacity in much of Europe being reduced, while other areas have expanded. Much care previously provided in hospitals has been shifted to other settings and the potential for substitution by primary, social and free-standing ambulatory care is increasingly being recognized. This is creating increasing interest in planning on a system-wide basis and has found expression in terms such as "territorial health care", "continuity of care", "integrated care pathways" and "care networks". For many common conditions, it is possible to standardize processes across service providers and to establish new networks of care that are not confined to hospitals. An example of a hospital linked closely with community services is the Alzira II "model", from Valencia, Spain, which is described in the accompanying volume of case studies. However, while definition of common care pathways may be able to bring considerable benefits for patients and providers, it is essential to incorporate sufficient flexibility to meet the needs of patients with specific medical requirements and, in particular, the many who have multiple coexisting disorders.

The need for thinking in systematized care terms is increasingly reinforced by looking at hospitals (and health care generally) as places of process activity. Like in other complex process areas, something like an 80/20 rule applies, where 80% of activity can be readily standardized and subjected to cost-minimization protocols. This point has implications for capacity planning, since spare capacity needs to be built into the system for two reasons: to cope with the 20% of care which is non-standard, and to allow for inevitable surges of demand from the population.

Contributing to local development

Throughout Europe, the health sector is one of the most important sectors, often constituting one of the largest "industries" as a percentage of gross regional (or municipal) product. It is increasingly being recognized that health projects can contribute significantly to regional development, both in economic and social terms. They can help local businesses, boost local employment, widen the local skills base, improve population health and strengthen social cohesion. Capital investment projects can also contribute to urban regeneration or renewal.

It is therefore crucial to consider the community and not just the hospital when making decisions on capital investments. To be sensitive to local contexts, many decisions should be made locally, drawing on intersectoral collaboration. Ideally, health capital projects should be part of a coherent single vision for the future development of an entire area. Of course, this needs to be achieved while taking into account other, equally binding strategic considerations, such as the fact that local procurement preferences can be both inefficient and illegal under EU law.

## Designing hospitals

Improving hospital design

It is increasingly recognized that hospitals should provide a therapeutic environment, in which the overall design of the building contributes to the process of healing and reduces the risk of hospital-acquired infections, rather than simply being a place where healing takes place. There is a growing body of evidence on how this can be achieved, which identifies issues such as daylight, noise reduction, privacy, safety, opportunities for family participation, ease of finding one's way around the hospital, and imaginative use of nature and arts.

The design of hospitals must meet the needs of staff, who spend much more time in them than patients. Good working conditions can in part ameliorate the pressure on staff faced with high-intensity workload(s), as well as the growing challenges of recruitment and retention in many countries. Good design can also contribute significantly to reducing the risk to staff of injuries and occupational diseases and is essential if maximum value is to be extracted from investments in expensive equipment.

Standardization

The role of health facilities is to enable the delivery of high-quality health care and to enable health workers to achieve optimal results. This requires the integration of facility design with clinical pathways of care. Clinical pathways began to emerge in the 1980s and involved standardization of procedures, based on the recognition that, in many areas, patients had – at least initially – similar needs. Examples include the diagnosis of breast lumps or rectal bleeding, or the management of acute chest pain. However, almost always, a significant number of patients will need to depart from the care pathway. Instead of trying to fit capital planning to large numbers of different pathways, a more fruitful approach may then be the standardization of the processes that are shared between pathways.

## Taking a life-cycle perspective

In most western European countries, health assets have thus far been virtually free for health care providers, as they were financed by government budgets, with little or no risk to providers. Due to this relative ease of capital availability there is often little awareness of the real costs of capital assets, so concepts such as life-cycle economics are underdeveloped. When taking a life-cycle perspective, it becomes apparent that it is not so much the initial investment that counts, as the costs of the building over its life-cycle, from the early design phase to planning, construction, use and demolition (the latter is an aspect that is often ignored). Although often substantial in simple cash terms, the initial building costs are comparatively small in comparison to the operational costs during the life-cycle. It is thus important to recognize that a considerable, but often inadequately recognized part, of hospital costs are not related to core, "primary" medical processes, but to ancillary, "secondary" services, such as facility management. Hospital design that takes full account of facility management costs is likely to result in significant efficiency gains – work reported in this volume indicates that 20% cost gains are readily achievable by benchmarking.

As the costs and risks of capital investment are increasingly shifted to health care providers, it will be essential to increase awareness of the life-cycle costs of capital investment. One result of this shift will be that the long-term market value of health assets will become more important, especially where the building can be put to other uses if no longer required. This could include the use of parts of hospital buildings for nonmedical purposes, such as hotels.

## Ensuring quality at entry

What happens at the beginning of hospital projects is often critical for their later success or failure. Yet, too often there is no comprehensive analysis of needs and projects are not related sufficiently to the ultimate objective of health facilities – to improve population health. Furthermore, most projects tend to suffer from a rush to certainty, the need for planners and politicians to feel the security of being able to offer precise and measurable definitions with which to describe the project. This inhibits concept development, particularly where the links between capital input and health outcomes remain somewhat elusive. The challenge is to keep the concept open as long as possible to allow these links to emerge. The priority has invariably been to keep capital projects within budget and on time, with insufficient attention being paid to long-term functionality and efficiency, again a result of the rush to certainty which crowds out strategic objectives. This emphasis on tactical versus strategic performance has often undermined the relevance, effectiveness and sustainability of health facilities. In order to ensure that capital investment projects align their objectives with needs and priorities, achieve their intended outcomes and sustain benefits, it is essential to ensure quality at the initial phase of projects. This will necessitate policy-makers allocating sufficient financial resources, human resources, and time from the start to make sure that health facilities are fit for purpose and that they enact appropriate regulatory instruments for quality-at-entry controls. A major challenge will be to operationalize quality in a way that can keep pace with changing expectations.

## Ensuring value for money

A key criterion of successful capital investment in the health sector is value for money. But how is the value being achieved to be defined? Is it an economic return on investment, or are broader issues involved that may be much more difficult to measure because of the specific nature of the health sector and the complexity of health services? The fundamental aim of health services is to improve the health status of the population, to be achieved by making health services available, accessible, affordable, equitable and of good quality. This means that capital investments in the health sector have to enable core clinical services that are appropriate to the health needs of the population. Other issues, however, are also at play. Capital investments can contribute to the local economy and environment, to the training of new staff, to medical research, and they are also a source of civic pride and political legitimacy. To optimize capital investments in the health sector, it is crucial to address the question of what it is that we want to achieve and to do so in a transparent, inclusive and intersectoral way.

## Making capital investment sustainable

Sustainable development meets the needs of the present without compromising the needs of future generations. Sustainability has economic, social and environmental aspects. In the face of climate change, the ecological sustainability of capital investment is particularly pressing. Hospitals are in fact quite energy intensive, and increasingly so (energy consumption in volume terms rising by perhaps 5% per annum). One of the main products of most hospitals is thus carbon dioxide, in part through the number of journeys they create, in particular where hospitals are located at the outskirts of towns. The better use of new communication technologies and the dissemination of services into community settings could improve the ecological sustainability of health services. Modern design and construction trends offer the possibility of achieving a decreased carbon footprint, including altering the balance between deep plan and narrow plan structures, which also has implications for the quality of the environment perceived by both staff and patients. Moreover, five overall success factors have to be fulfilled: efficiency, effectiveness, relevance, impact and sustainability. These imply that projects should have no major negative effects, their objectives should be consistent with societal needs and priorities, and they should produce not only short-term efficiency, but also long-term benefits. These are requirements that go far beyond the issues that are usually covered by health planners and decision-makers.

## Investing in people

Health care workers are central to health systems and any attempt to improve capital investment in the health sector will need to take account of the implications for their productivity, safety and well-being. In many cases, poor design of facilities and work processes place them at risk. Well-designed and sustainable hospitals and other health care facilities can, however, improve the health and well-being of health professionals, resulting in improved staff recruitment, retention and performance. Better equipment can reduce the risk of injuries and minimize the hazards to which health care workers are exposed, and facilities should ideally be located near to where staff live, provide sufficient daylight and ventilation, and minimize walking distances within them. This is not only beneficial to health care workers, but also improves patient outcomes by reducing medical errors and hospital-acquired infections.

Although this book concentrates on capital investment, it has repeatedly stressed that this should be undertaken within a whole system approach. Thus, it is important to consider how to coordinate investment in capital with investment in people. In Europe, there are few convincing models of effective workforce planning and there are major difficulties in ensuring that health systems have the right numbers of qualified staff, with the right skill mix and appropriately distributed. The ageing of European populations means that an increasing health care workforce will be required at a time when the pool of health care workers is shrinking and the migratory movements facilitated by European integration can undermine national workforce plans. Just as is the case with hospital design, it is essential to ensure the flexibility of human resources to meet changing needs and roles. It is important to have systems of lifelong learning that will allow staff to acquire new skills and competences. Again, in an analogy with hospital design, where adjacencies and interlinkages between departments are important, it is necessary to find ways of strengthening multi-professional teamwork to meet the challenge of increased complexity of care. The design of health care buildings can facilitate or hinder these processes.

The need to invest in people, however, extends beyond health professionals. The ability to envision and implement major capital projects is often lacking among those responsible for bringing about such accomplishments. Often, partners to a new development have no experience of undertaking a major capital investment and few people will work on more than one in their entire working lives. This lack of competence is one of the major barriers to successful capital investment projects and needs to be urgently addressed by policy-makers.

Finally, hospitals are important settings for teaching and research. Although there are some innovative approaches in primary care, the bulk of teaching of medical and nursing students continues to rely on hospitals as training locations and sources of patients. When making decisions on capital investments in the health sector, it is essential to take account of the role hospitals play in teaching and research. Another important issue relates to the rise of medical subspecialties, which has been a major determinant of capital allocation.

## Planning process

### Involving patients and staff

In many European countries, there is an increasing awareness and recognition of patient rights. This is creating an expectation that patients' views will be considered in new capital projects. It is particularly important to consider the views and experiences of those with reduced mobility, hearing or vision, those with allergies and those suffering from chronic conditions such as asthma or obesity. It is equally important to involve health care workers in the design of new facilities. They are often most aware of the practical obstacles in existing facilities and have frequently identified possible solutions. Consultations with these and other stakeholders, such as the public, will need to be managed effectively and sensitively, not to fall victim to idiosyncrasies or outdated styles of working.

## Managing change

Improving capital investment in the health sector will require fundamental changes in widely held assumptions and practices. Changes include taking life-cycle and systems perspectives and putting patients and staff first. They also include seeing health spending as an investment, rather than simply an expenditure.

Changing hospitals will involve a culture change. Hospital managers are faced with the task of anticipating future trends and their potential impact on the work, skills, motivation and well-being of employees. Managers will need to develop programmes that provide support to health care staff as they go through the process of adapting to change. This has long been recognized in industrial facilities, but the management of change has so far received insufficient attention in major hospital projects and there is much scope for sharing experiences on how to facilitate change without endangering achievement of hospitals' core objectives.

## Expanding the evidence base

Research on capital investment in the health sector has so far been sparse, although this must be seen in the context of the weak evidence for many other assumptions that have underpinned health reforms in recent years. Too often, these assumptions reflect ideology rather than empirical evidence, as illustrated by the view – common in some countries – that competition increases efficiency and that private providers offer more efficient services than those in the public sector.

Research on major capital investment is intrinsically difficult. There are few opportunities for unbiased comparisons, as would be the case if randomized controlled trials were used. The implementation of investment is typically highly dependent on context and thus it may not be possible to generalize lessons learned. In many cases, the basic data are unavailable to researchers. This may be a deliberate policy decision, as with PFI in the United Kingdom, where contracts are deemed to be commercially confidential, even though they involve large sums of public money. More often it is because data systems are simply inadequate for the task. Even when hospitals have data on the direct costs of treating patients, data on the use of secondary services, such as facility management, are often scarce.

There is also the challenge of forecasting future demand and supply. Too often, expectations about future changes in population and morbidity are not made explicit, nor are they supported by evidence, while the modelling of future scenarios for health services, such as the implications of new models of care or new technologies, remains underdeveloped. Finally, there are few attempts to document the experience of capital investment, perhaps because there is such a sense of relief that the project was actually completed that no one wants to look back to see what lessons can be learned. The few examples where this has been carried out have involved major failures. Post-occupancy planning is – but should not be – a luxury.

This book and the accompanying volume containing case studies from across Europe are only the first step in making this knowledge more readily available. In order to facilitate the learning of lessons and make future capital investment more effective and sustainable, evaluations should become integral to major hospital changes, so that "best practices" can be identified. These evaluations will need to make their analytical framework explicit, making it clear whether they analyse the strategic or tactical performance of hospital projects. The editors hope that these two volumes will provoke a debate on the main issues pertaining to health capital investment, to the benefit of good hospital planning, design and implementation in Europe and beyond.

# Index